Insane Therapy

Portrait of a Psychotherapy Cult

Insane Therapy
Portrait of a Psychotherapy Cult

Marybeth F. Ayella

Temple University Press
Philadelphia

Temple University Press, Philadelphia 19122
Copyright © 1998 by Temple University
All rights reserved
Published 1998
Printed in the United States of America

Text design by Eliz. Anne O'Donnell

♾   The paper used in this publication meets the requirements
of the American National Standard for Information Sciences—Permanence
of Paper for Printed Library Materials, ANSI Z39.48–1984

Library of Congress Cataloging-in-Publication Data
Ayella, Marybeth F.
    Insane therapy : portrait of a psychotherapy cult / Marybeth F.
Ayella.
        p.   cm.
    Includes bibliographical references and index.
    ISBN 1-56639-600-X (alk. paper).—ISBN 1-56639-601-8 (pbk. :
alk. paper)
    1. Center for Feeling Therapy.   2. Psychotherapy patients—Abuse
of—Case studies.   3. Feeling therapy.   4. Therapeutic communities—
Case studies.   5. Cults—Psychological aspects.   6. Control
(Psychology)   7. Social control.   I.   Title.
RC489.F42A97   1998
616.89' 14—dc21   97-38146

Contents

Acknowledgments

Many people have helped me in many ways during the researching and writing of this book. I am grateful to the persons I interviewed who generously shared with me, a stranger, very painful details of their lives. William Carter, the deputy attorney general of California who handled the case against the Feeling Therapists, carefully explained its legal history during our interview. John Hochman, M.D., also spoke with me and helped me find people to talk with.

Professional colleagues have been extremely gracious in sharing ideas and reference materials. I thank above all Richard Ofshe, of the University of California at Berkeley, and Margaret Singer, Arlie Hochschild, and Charles Sweeney, all of UC Berkeley, for their assistance. I am grateful to John B. Williamson of Boston College for having been my mentor since my undergraduate years at that school.

Michael Ames has been a wonderful editor, and his comments have greatly improved this book. The anonymous reviewer's critique aided me in rewriting. Others who have read parts of the manuscript and greatly helped with comments include Claire Renzetti, George Dowdall, Dan Curran, Judi Chapman, Alison Williams Lewin, and Rick Malloy, all colleagues at St. Joseph's University. Judith Lasker of Lehigh University and Vicki Smith of the University of California at Davis also provided valuable insights on several chapters.

Beth Tarrant provided research assistance par excellence, as well as child care on occasion. Donna Tozer and Marny Reardon also helped with research. Denise Shaw and Joanne Devlin aided in various ways with preparing the manuscript, and provided moral support.

Two other individuals made it possible for me to work by taking wonderful care of my children. I thank Sharon Naughton Russell and Priscilla Baxter.

I am also grateful to friends who have stuck with me through thick and thin: Julie McDonald, Ricky Jacobs, Jacki Reich (who helped with the subtitle for the book), Jan Singer, Evy Bogen, Jerry Himmelstein, Liz Symonds, Linda Wardlaw, Patty Ratliff, and Yigal Arens.

Finally, my family has enabled me to complete this book. My mother, Agnes Ayella, has offered various kinds of support at all stages of the project. My husband, Larry Silver, has as usual been a constant source of encouragement and support. Michael and Rachel, my children, have inspired me with their enthusiasm, curiosity, and energy.

Insane Therapy

Portrait of a Psychotherapy Cult

One
Introduction

My interest in "cults" began with a chance encounter with a "Moonie" in Sproul Plaza, Berkeley, in August 1975. In response to what I thought was a pick-up attempt by a man standing behind me at a sandwich vendor, I began a conversation with a man about my age. We wound up sitting and talking as I ate my lunch. He described a wonderful communal group he lived in, in which there was never any conflict. This intrigued me—no fights over who does dishes? over who hogs the bathroom? He invited me to come and see for myself; in fact, I could come home with him that night, since they were having a special Friday night dinner.

I was twenty-three years old, just beginning a doctoral program at the University of California at Berkeley. Since I knew no one in town I did not have dinner plans, so I accepted the invitation. Jack was taking public transportation home, and I felt safe in accompanying him. Before going, I asked if the group he belonged to was religious, since I was not interested in religious communes. He said no.

Jack and I arrived at the Oakland house, located next to a Roman Catholic church, together with a second group member, a woman we had met on the bus. We all took off our shoes at the entrance, and I was invited into the kitchen to meet others who were making dinner. This was the first thing that favorably impressed me—the members preparing dinner were all men, yet they seemed to know just what to do. I had known several male housemates and plenty of male friends who were unable to prepare anything but frozen foods (according to directions); these men were not only washing and chopping vegetables but doing so happily. I joined in, and everyone was very friendly and warm to me. The apparently changed gender roles fit my feminist orientation.

Everyone seemed to be about my age, and I was curious as to how they earned their living. I had just arrived from Boston, and one of the members came over to talk when he heard that. He had just dropped out of the University of Massachusetts at Amherst, only a year before graduation. I asked why. He said that since he had met the group, he felt like he wanted to stay and give communal living a try. I asked what he did to support himself, and he said he worked in a group-owned business. This made no sense to me—why not finish up his last year, come back to the group, and earn a living in journalism, as he'd planned? His explanation that he had quit because he had never met such a great collection of people made no more sense. I was mystified; others in the house told similar stories of being in college, meeting the group, and deciding to drop out to work in businesses with group members. What was it about this group that would lead a person to decide to change career and life plans so abruptly, all for a "great" group of people?

Dinnertime came, and it was obvious that I was not the only guest. Our hosts and hostesses were clearly solicitous of our comfort from the moment we walked in. Before we started dinner, a man sitting at the head of the long table began a lengthy grace. At this I turned to Jack and asked why say a grace if the group was not religious? He replied that some of the members were religious, and whoever led the dinner could begin with grace if she or he wanted.

Later, we went into the living room to hear more in a lecture. It was very vague, describing the group's interest in such things as living in peace and harmony, first on a small-group scale, then nationally and internationally. I did not find myself disagreeing with anything that was said, but I had no idea how the ideals were put into practice. After the lecture, we saw color slides of the group at their Boonville farm, north of San Francisco. It looked like summer camp, with a large number of people clowning around with each other, mugging for the camera.

We had dessert afterwards. We sat around on the floor, in small groups, getting to know each other. As the conversation was winding down, we were all invited to come for a weekend seminar in "group living" for twelve dollars. I was intrigued, and I said I would like to go.

It seemed as though the bulk of the guests were also deciding to go. Group members brought out consent forms for us to sign, in the event we were hurt. I asked what kind of injury they anticipated, and I was told "sprained ankles," because the farm's terrain was hilly and rocky. That didn't seem too bad, so I signed. One other thing had aroused my curiosity—the letterhead said Unification Church. I asked whether the group was a church; I was told no and given some answer about simply using their letterhead paper, but not being connected in any way. The impression I got was that they were cheap, using the excess letterhead paper of some church.

I was told I could drive up with Jack and some other members in one of the group's cars that night. We stopped at my apartment so that I could pack a suitcase, then we got on the road about 11:30 P.M. When we got into the car, I suddenly realized I was traveling alone with three men, and I had a momentary qualm as I remembered my mother's warnings about not talking to, let alone traveling with, "strange men." I wondered what I was doing in a car with three men, at midnight, going to a farm outside a town I had never heard of until that day.

Shortly after we turned onto the northbound highway my companions produced songbooks and suggested we sing. I refused; it seemed too corny and reminded me of those musicals where people going about routine activities burst into song. Further into the trip, when I noticed Jack, the driver, dozing off, it was I who suggested we sing, fearful we would be in a car crash. I also suggested we get coffee and something to eat. We stopped at a roadside restaurant, and I was the first in line to order. I was also the only one to order—suddenly the others were not hungry, and they didn't want coffee, not even Jack. Thinking they had no money, I offered to buy them food, but they refused, insisting they were just fine. On our way out, we came across another carload of people also headed to Boonville. I began to wonder how many of them there were.

We at last reached Boonville, which appeared to me to be a one-street town in the middle of nowhere, and we turned off the main street down a winding road, with steep inclines at various spots. Jack was still nodding off, and I was seated within elbow's reach. I jogged his arm every time his head dipped forward, and I sang or asked questions the rest of the ride. I was really scared for the last half hour or so, because the road was so dimly lit, winding, and especially precipitous around curves. Jack had refused all my offers to drive, so I sat with my heart in my throat.

When we finally arrived at the farm, we approached a gate topped with barbed wire and a barbed-wire fence, with what appeared to be a guard at the gate. When I asked about the barbed wire, Jack told me people were always trying to sneak in. Soon after we arrived and parked, a car full of women from the restaurant pulled in; Jack asked one of them to help me find a sleeping bag and get settled. Sleeping quarters were segregated. We entered a mobile trailer that was wall-to-wall bodies in sleeping bags. As I crawled into the bag I was given to use, I had an acute anxiety attack: what am I doing here? what kind of people are they? what if they're like Charles Manson's Family? are they into drugs? violence?

I didn't sleep that night. The last time I looked at my watch it was 7:00 A.M., and people had been coming in all night. An hour or so later, I was awakened by people playing guitars and singing "when the red red robin comes bob-bob-bobbin' along." At this novel wake-up call, everyone seemed to wake up, jump up, and roll up their sleeping bags, except me. I had decided I was too tired and would prefer to miss the morning seminar. Of course, after being asked repeatedly to get up so as not to miss any of the day's exciting activities I finally realized I was wide awake and not likely to fall back to sleep. So I got up.

Wandering out after dressing and washing, I stood on the sidelines observing the group exercises. Again, I was repeatedly asked to take part, and I finally gave in to "This guy is so shy, and you're so friendly and outgoing, would you be his exercise partner?" During my stay, I frequently wished I had asked more questions in my methods class in college, as I confronted a myriad of situations in which I did not know how to act. Key was how much to participate. Get up or sleep in? exercise or watch? were just the first of many choices I had to make.

When we were put into small groups after the exercises, Noah, the head lecturer for the weekend, instructed us on how to behave in order to "get the most out of the weekend." Should I do exactly what Noah said, for example by not talking to other newcomers? I did not feel constrained to go along with group directives completely, because I felt I could not get a full picture of the persons involved: how could I find out why these others were thinking of living communally with this group if I did not ask? But I wanted to fit in, I did not want to stick out like a sore thumb, and to have members act normally, I did not want always to point up my research interests.

I ate breakfast with the small group I had been assigned to. Introductions were made, and we began to eat. Abruptly I realized that none of the people I identified as members of the group (including Jack) ate any food—suddenly thinking that the food was poisoned, I stopped eating, and decided to eat only what they ate. I had to wait until lunch to eat, and I carefully observed the members' choices.

The remainder of that day was a comedy of misperception on my part. My definition of the situation—that I was participating in a "weekend seminar in communal living"—was rudely shattered during the first lecture, which dealt with Adam and Eve's fall from grace. There I realized the definition of the situation on their part—conversion. This was obviously a religious group (something I had repeatedly been told it was not). Anger at having been lied to was the first feeling I shared with my small group after the lecture. We were asked, "What do you think of the lecture?" I said, "You lied, this *is* a religious group." The response was, "Would you have come if we said it was a religious group?" When I replied no, I was told that was precisely why they lied, to get people who otherwise would not have come to come, so that they could appreciate the organization's obvious merit.

My uncertainty, always a part of field research, increased because I did not know what kind of a religious group this was. I did not know how to act,

I had been lied to about what I considered a major thing, and so I wondered what if anything I could believe. As I learned over time, this was one example of "Heavenly Deception," which was explained to me as justifying various instances of deceptiveness that I saw members engage in during different aspects of recruitment.

I had been clear about my identity from the start. I felt betrayed by the group, my naïve trust was destroyed, but I still felt compelled to be truthful with them in answering questions about my reaction to the group and my research interests. How much to be revealed of self, and where, were two key questions I had. How open to be in lectures and groups (public settings) as compared to casual talks with members and other prospects (some of which were private settings)? I later found out that I had also misperceived the nature of public and private settings. I discovered this when I learned that information I had confided to only one other person was suddenly revealed by someone else and that this information was being used to persuade me to stay.

Other occasions caused me to question how much to participate: Afternoon dodge-ball game—watch or play, cheer while playing or not? Composing a skit about life in the "family" for Saturday night, telling how one came to group—how to express my research interests as all around me members told dramatic before-and-after stories. During lectures, deciding how much to participate was difficult—I kept questioning the lecturer, because he asked for questions and the lecture seemed so flawed, so one-sided. "Not everyone," I might say, "would agree that Richard Nixon was on the side of good/God and feminists are on the side of bad/Satan." I couldn't help but try to get answers, since I was really curious, and more so after getting the impression that this group really believed we were in the "last days." Moreover, many "questions" other participants offered were in the form of comments praising the group— "I really loved that lecture, everything is so clear now." Soon, the lecturer began to ignore my raised hand, even when there were no other hands raised.

I learned when I went to the bathroom before returning to the lecture that a woman I had been introduced to in my small group, who sat next to me at breakfast and at the first lecture, was intent on sticking to me like glue. When she accompanied me the short distance to the bathroom, and came into the two-stall building, I did not know what to make of her. Overly friendly? lesbian? weird? That caused me to see how everyone who was new seemed to have the same kind of "buddy." It soon became clear that I was expected to confide all my reactions to this buddy. My problem was that I just did not like this woman, so I kept trying to change our conversations around to elicit information on why she had joined the group.

Early on Sunday members began questioning us newcomers about whether we wanted to stay for the "advanced" set of lectures. My choice as I saw it was to stay and study a millenarian religious group or leave. I still did not know the organization was the Unification Church (UC), but at that time the name would not have meant much to me. The chief attraction of staying was the chance to study a group dramatically different from what I was familiar with, churchgoing Roman Catholicism. I was sure someone would want to publish an analysis of the community because it seemed so interesting in its strangeness. I was puzzled at how people who seemed similar to me could want to become or remain members. Some of my students can not understand this initial decision: "Why not get out when the going's good? They're a bunch of crackpots! You must have been crazy to stay, with a bunch of strangers, of religious fanatics, in an isolated location." Looking back at the twenty-three-year-old, I too wonder at her staying, but not at her interest.

When I made the choice to remain for the next set of lectures, I felt fairly certain that the group was not violent and did not use drugs, my two biggest fears. Their beliefs seemed opposed to both. I was intensely curious, I had time on my hands before the school semester began, and I had dreams of glory (my master's thesis had just been accepted for publication).

Weighing against these pros were the cons: twinges of anxiety aroused by certain things, such as that no one knew where I was and the one public pay phone bore an out-of-order sign. I wondered how much I could trust my new acquaintances. I questioned whether they were as they appeared to be, a peaceful group; if so, why the barbed wire? What happened to the guy from my group, the one other person seeming to have doubts, who disappeared Saturday night? Why didn't Jack and the others eat at first, either at the roadside diner or at Saturday breakfast?

I was heavily pressured by various members to stay, and I agreed to do so on the one condition that I be allowed to write about them. The members agreed, and even introduced me to a woman who they said had also come to study the organization and who had remained.[1] This only increased my anxiety: I did not want to become like her, I did not want to lead this kind of life.

I filled the requirements for what the Moonies were looking for then in a convert—young, unattached, idealistic. I did not know this at first, but very few of the members or prospects I encountered were older than their late twenties or early thirties. This made it more difficult for me to be objective. Members seemed to be very similar to me, and one of my initial questions was why they were taking such a different path. I could not believe anyone would decide to join such an organization virtually overnight, with dropping out of school and not returning to one's home state or native country (the United Kingdom and Australia, for the people I met) being among the consequences.

But, the people in my group seemed to have made this choice. So one thing that differentiated "us" was impulsiveness—no listing of pros and cons, no talking to people to weigh options (a major reason being that we were on the farm and couldn't contact anyone).

After the weekend I was given a phone number and an address, and I included the number in a letter to friends. Later, I learned that those who tried to call me were told "no one lives here with that name." This was not necessarily a case of malicious withholding by the UC; it seemed, rather, to be a result of not knowing where all prospects were at all times. However, my friends did wonder where I was, and I wondered why no one wrote or called me during my three-week stay. Thus, I was effectively isolated from all but members and prospects during my participant observation.[2]

My account differs from Barker's (1984) in that she well knew what the UC was when she finally went to the northern California farm. Older than I, with a family, and an established sociologist of religion, she was approached by the UC to do research (intended by the church to counter other, negative reports). Barker made her visit with the realization that this was the organization's most effective, and most deceptive, branch. This deceptiveness may have contributed to the effectiveness of the northern California branch of the UC. For example, it was only on the tenth day of my stay that I learned the church was headed by the Reverend Sun Myung Moon. Accordingly, the view I present is more or less similar to that of the ordinary newcomer to the UC.

Thus began three of the most interesting weeks of my life. This participant observation resulted in two graduate-school papers on Moonie conversion attempts and left me with an abiding interest in "cults."

When I was writing my two papers, very little scholarly analysis of conversion attempts had been published. Much of what appeared in the media assumed that people who became Moonies (or Hare Krishnas, etc.) had been "brainwashed."[3] This seemed too simplistic to me. My analysis of the Moonie attempts at conversion I had observed persuaded me that interaction between members and prospects was key to prospects' staying. The information presented on the group seemed secondary in making initial decisions to remain. What was it about the interaction that was most effective? "Love bombing" seemed essential, with prospects being bombarded with loving attention at all times.[4] This style of interaction helped to develop strong personal ties between members of the group and prospective members.

My analysis of Moonie conversion attempts also emphasized that the prospective convert was not a passive recipient throughout the process. Rather, I pointed to ways in which individuals participated in acquiring the belief system and becoming a committed member. I concluded:

In sum, it is not a matter of an individual being assaulted by information and losing "self" in a one-sided process of conversion, but a far more complicated process in which interaction figures most prominently, wherein the individual gradually "chooses," for various reasons, the new belief system. (Ayella, 1981:4)

Normality, Influence, and Deviance

A dissatisfaction with popular explanations available at the time of my meeting the Moonies in 1975, implying that these were essentially "crackpots" who were involved in cults, has remained with me. In the past ten years of discussing my research with college students, their chief question has been, "What kind of people are they?" The students insist that "they must be nuts," and thus dramatically unlike "us." Such thinking reflects the "kind of person" explanation of deviant behavior, which emphasizes that "deviants" can be clearly differentiated from "normals."

Similarly, the psychologist Margaret Singer (Singer with Lalich, 1995:15–16) mentions the "not me" attitude she believes the general public has about who joins cults. Yet, much of the by now burgeoning research on persons who enter cults has emphasized the essential normality of such people. In Lofland's (1966) early work on the Moonies, the clearly incompetent could not last in the group because they could not make a commitment; Barker's (1984) later research shows that participants are normal. Levine's (1984) main conclusion after looking in depth at individuals who joined a variety of cults is that they show no serious psychopathology and are "normal" adolescents. Singer's more recent book, based on more than three thousand interviews with current and former members of cults, indicates that the "majority of adolescents and adults in cults come from middle-class backgrounds, are fairly well educated, and are not seriously disturbed prior to joining" (Singer with Lalich, 1995:17).

This does not mean that behavioral and attitudinal changes, a "before" and "after," do not occur in individuals, but rather that both can be accounted for by reference to social processes and interaction, rather than by a "they're crazy" psychopathological explanation.

Although the Unification Church, with its seemingly "overnight" transformations of young, middle-class kids into "Moonies,"was the subject of some noteworthy media stories (e.g., mass marriages performed in Madison Square Garden), it was the 1978 mass suicide-homicide of 912 persons in Jonestown, Guyana, that was most important in bringing "cults" to national awareness. Investigation of how the People's Temple could have come to this terrible end revealed many strange practices within the group, among them extreme disciplinary methods and the regulation of sexual and affectional matters so as to promote allegiance to Jim Jones alone (Coser and Coser, 1979; Hall, 1979, 1987; Reiterman and Jacobs, 1982; Richardson, 1982).

Not long after, we read about the "Synanon Horrors" (Anson, 1978), which included the forced shaving of heads (of members and nonmembers), sterilization of all males within the group (except the leader, Chuck Dederich), coerced abortions, forced breakups of marriages and other relationships, beatings and other attacks, and harassment of past members and nonmembers. Perhaps best known was the rattlesnake attack on Paul Morantz (the snake was put in his mailbox, minus its rattles), a lawyer who had just won a judgment against Synanon. Before information about the "horrors" emerged, Synanon had received great acclaim as an unprecedentedly effective drug-rehabilitation group, generating many imitators (Ofshe, 1980).

Two other groups labeled as cults that got lots of media attention were the Hare Krishnas and Scientology. The full title of a book about the former, *Monkey on a Stick: Murder, Madness, and the Hare Krishnas* (Hubner and Gruson, 1988), gives a hint of the deviant practices (arms buying, drug running, child abuse, murder) within parts of the movement; these attracted great negative coverage of the group in the 1980s and 1990s.

Scientology has been controversial since its founding in the 1950s (Cooper, 1972; Wallis, 1977b). It achieved more notoriety through a series of 1990 *Los Angeles Times* articles and with the publication of the journalist Richard Behar's highly critical article "The Thriving Cult of Greed and Power" (*Time*, May 6, 1991). Behar described the cost of "enlightenment," estimated at $200,000 to $400,000 for the average person; deceptive attempts to attract mainstream members through an array of "front groups and financial scams"; the commission of federal crimes; and harassment of critics, especially through litigation (paying "an estimated $20 million annually to more than 100 lawyers," according to Behar). This harassment extended to Behar himself, who said that "for the *Time* story, at least 10 attorneys and six private detectives were unleashed by Scientology and its followers in an effort to threaten, harass and discredit me."

Many others have also discovered that being critical of cults can bring various forms of retribution. A whole chapter of Singer and Lalich's *Cults in Our Midst* (1995), "The Threat of Intimidation," details a multitude of instances of cults' harassment of their critics. Singer herself uses assumed names because of cult scrutiny. Among many other things, her office has been broken into, video and audio interviews of erstwhile cult members have been stolen, a woman from a cult posed as a student and "helped" in her office, her trash has been repeatedly stolen, and two dozen large brown rats were put into her home through a duct to the attic (Singer with Lalich, 1995:239–42).

Some later newsworthy examples of cults include David Koresh's Branch Davidians in Waco, Texas, which group met a fiery end on April 19, 1993, killing Koresh and seventy-seven followers (CQ Researcher, 1993:396). In October 1994, fifty-three members of the Order of the Solar Temple died in Canada and Switzerland "of various combinations of bullets, fire, stabbings, plastic bags over their heads, and injected drugs" (Singer and Lalich, 1995:339). Members of this group were affluent people, who retained their jobs while following Luc Jouret, a "forty-six-year-old Belgian homeopathic doctor," who was one of the dead (ibid.).

In 1995 a Japanese cult, Aum Shinrikyo (Supreme Truth), got great media attention when it used homemade nerve gas to poison subway riders in Tokyo. And last, the March 28, 1997, suicide of thirty-nine members of the group Heaven's Gate called to mind the 1978 Jonestown suicides (see Hoffmann and Burke [1997] book for more on this group). In addition, the revelation of the castration of some adherents recalled the sterilization of men belonging to Synanon.

There are many other stories of persons interested in change or self-improvement joining cultlike groups. And today we are more aware of a proliferation of cults. Margaret Singer (Singer with Lalich, 1995:5) estimates that there are from three to five thousand cults in our society and that "between two and five million Americans are involved in cults at any one time" (12). Singer describes as the fastest growing "cultic groups" the ones "centered around New Age thinking and certain personal improvement training, lifestyles, or prosperity programs" (13). As we approach the millennium, she estimates that there are "more than 1,100 end-of-time groups" (quoted in McCullough, 1997).

All kinds of strange happenings in cults have become known to us through the news media. To many, these experiences may seem so bizarre that we cannot imagine people like ourselves being involved. But in fact we are all vulnerable to influence, and it is only through influence that we change, for good or for ill. This book is concerned with the power of social influence, with authority and groups influencing individuals. In particular, I will focus on the story of one group where the abuse of influence and authority damaged many lives.

The Center for Feeling Therapy

In 1981, the Los Angeles Times reported the story of the disintegration of the Center for Feeling Therapy. Nineteen former members filed a $95 million suit against their onetime therapists in June of that year. They charged that they had "been defrauded of their money, brainwashed, and abused physically and emotionally." These patients were described as "mostly college educated men and women in their 20s and 30s" (Horowitz, 1981; Morain, 1981; Oliver, 1981; and Timnick, 1981). In addition, the Los Angeles affiliate of CBS broadcast a five-part investigative series, "The Cult of Cruelty." These media accounts whetted my interest in looking behind the scenes of this group.

The accusations against the therapists claimed that patients were "broken down" during three weeks of intensive psychotherapy, that they were forced to have abortions and to give up children, that they were forced to strip physically and emotionally before the group, that they were assigned sexual partners and told how often to have sex, that they were beaten up, that they were forced to donate money to the group, and that they were economically exploited while working in businesses affiliated with the Center.

The Center for Feeling Therapy was an offshoot of the Primal Scream Therapy of Arthur Janov. It began in 1971 when nine people left Janov's Los Angeles institute to set up their own therapy program.[5] Both of these therapies, having developed from the countercultural human-potential movement, were at the margins of the traditional therapy community.

The Center lasted about ten years, collapsing suddenly during three days in November 1980. It then had a stable population of about three hundred individuals living communally in a "therapeutic community," with another six hundred outpatients in a separate clinic.

Like Primal Scream, Feeling Therapy's initial emphasis centered on one's very early relationship with one's parents. It emphasized intense reexperiencing of childhood traumas, considering "feeling" more important than understanding or insight. As Feeling Therapists saw it, in the course of socialization individuals developed "defenses" to cope; the undesirable effect was that these defenses prevented them from fully feeling what they experienced. It thus followed that one needed to get rid of the defenses. To achieve this end, aggressive, confrontative therapists hammered away at patients from the very first therapy session.

The Center as presented in media accounts interested me because of the large number of people involved, because of the middle-class composition of the group, and because the allegations against the therapists implied extreme control of the patients. The organization sounded very similar to Synanon, the drug-rehabilitation group in California. Synanon, too, employed a very aggressive, confrontative therapy, and it spawned a host of similar programs (Ofshe, 1980, 1981). I was interested in what I saw as a paradox in both Synanon and Feeling Therapy—their claim that a truly autonomous individual emerges from a very restrictive environment, variously described by critics as fascistic, totalist, or infantilizing.

In contrast to the People's Temple, the bulk of whose members were poor and black, the center for Feeling Therapy was composed mainly of middle-class whites. The group sounded crazy. How could licensed therapists be involved in a situation so like a cult? If the group was as terrible as people claimed at the collapse, why did they stay, some for as long as nine years?

A large number of former patients filed complaints with the California Board of Medical Quality Assurance. Investigation of their complaints led the State of California to proceed with license-revocation hearings against thirteen therapists who headed the Center for Feeling Therapy. On September 29, 1987, the state revoked the licenses of the two pre-eminent psychologists at the Center, bringing to a total of twelve the number of therapists associated with the Center who had lost or surrendered licenses since its demise in 1980. Administrative law judge Robert A. Neher, after a hearing that lasted ninety-four days, found four of the psychologists guilty of acts of gross negligence, incompetence, patient abuse, aiding and abetting the unlicensed practice of psychology, and false advertising. (A fifth psychologist, the thirteenth therapist, was also accused, but he had died early in 1987 and charges against him had been dismissed.) Of the five psychologists who appeared before Judge Neher, only this last therapist had admitted to the accusations against him (Neher, 1987).

The license-revocation proceeding, which had gone on for six years, was the "longest, costliest, and most complex psychotherapy malpractice case in California history" (Timnick, 1987). Judge Neher found that the "respondents developed and enjoyed the seat of power in a cult; that it was a psychological cult or cult of personality rather than a religious one is certain, but by any definition it was a cult" (Neher, 1987:18).

Looking Behind the Scenes

My Moonie experience served as an entree to researching the Center for Feeling Therapy, helping me to appreciate two basic points. "Intelligence" does not always protect one from making "stupid" decisions. Former patients were not necessarily "psychological basket cases" or "brainwashed automatons" for having been involved with such a group. In consequence, I was biased toward not feeling I would be interviewing "dumb dodoes" and toward the notion that their experience, and the Center for Feeling Therapy, had both good and bad aspects.

My requests of the therapists to be interviewed to give their perspective on the Center and the civil and administrative hearings were not successful. Accordingly, I have allowed the therapists' written work to speak for them. The narrative I present here is often from the "bottom up," an analysis derived largely from the patients' perspective.

Finding past members, let alone finding a representative sample and persuading them to be interviewed, were two major difficulties in my research. I spoke with twenty-one former members in depth; most of these interviews lasted about two and a half hours, with the shortest running an hour and a half. Although our conversations were open-ended, I had a list of questions I asked each person. In addition, I probed when the interviewees seemed confused (or when I was confused), or when they had a lot to say, beyond what the question asked for.

Eleven of the twenty-one people I spoke with are women, ten are men. Thirteen interviewees were involved with lawsuits or license-revocation hearings or were involved in prior lawsuits. Of the eight who were not involved in lawsuits, two reported good experiences at the Center for Feeling Therapy. One of them reported being unaware of much of the "dark side" of Feeling Therapy. The other, although giving a positive analysis of his experience there, described the Center in a way that corroborates the stories of the former patients who felt that their experience was harmful.

Two persons reported being involved for about the duration of the Center, almost ten years. Two others were Feeling Therapy patients for only a year, although they had earlier ties to the Center. The remainder spent from two to eight years at the Center.

Ages at entry into Feeling Therapy ranged from twenty to thirty-eight. About half of my interviewees were in their early to mid-twenties when they began, with the other half being in their late twenties and early thirties. All those interviewed were Caucasian, except for one Asian. Nineteen persons came from middle-class backgrounds, with two others coming from the upper class. Sixteen had completed at least college before entering Feeling Therapy, and three had graduate degrees.[6]

When interviewees asked how I had become interested in "cults," I told them of my experience with the Moonies and of subsequent discussions with past members of other groups. This seemed to reassure them that I would not immediately label them as "crazy." This seemed to be a major issue for the people I interviewed, a concern with being believed, with being seen as respectable, "normal" persons.

In this book, I am concerned with a psychotherapy group that, soon after its collapse, was labeled a cult by the news media. Its insularity, its radical goals, and its controversial treatment methods all generated concern. As I heard the allegations against therapists made by onetime patients, the question of why anyone would willingly endure such abusive treatment was prominent in my mind.[7] This book considers that general question, examining the Center for Feeling Therapy as a case study of therapy abuse and comparing it to other situations, looking for common contributors to extreme influence situations.

Although I will be exploring in detail one particular psychotherapy group, my interest is much broader. I see the Center as an extreme case, but one that reflects problems in mainstream therapy. These problems cluster around the largely unrecognized role of social influence in the therapy process. Michael Yapko's 1994 book, *Suggestions of Abuse*, comments on present-day therapeutic resistance to recognizing the influence of therapists:

> Their desire to avoid influencing their clients was entirely unrealistic given that clients come in for help and answers—in other words, *expecting* to be influenced in *positive ways*. Influence in therapy is inevitable, but many therapists still don't recognize their ability to influence their clients, and so avoid feeling responsible for the direction the therapy moves in. They actively deceive themselves and believe their own self-deception. (203)

In addition, I see the center for Feeling Therapy as only one of many such organizations, ranging from religious to political to therapeutic to commercial, which promise identity, meaning, intimacy, and community to individual participants. These extreme groups are part of a social process that sociologists term "deviance defining." By this they mean that such groups, with their (in many ways) deviant beliefs and practices cause us as individuals and as a society to grapple with the question of where to draw the line between "normal" and "deviant" behavior among individuals and groups. These organizations also illustrate the role of social influence in shaping individuals' decisions to join, remain, and leave groups.

Two
The Center for Feeling Therapy

A forty-year-old patient became pregnant after trying to have a baby for seventeen years. She wanted the child very much. She was required to have an abortion as part of her "feeling therapy." When she strenuously protested, her therapist "personally guaranteed" that she would be able to become pregnant again "even in her fifties." She had the abortion.

> "Jewishness" was loosely defined as cultural negativity, and was a term that could be used to describe anyone who was "negative." As part of a group therapy exercise, a therapist had the patients surround one patient, point their hands and fists at him while shouting "Jew, Jew, Jew" for several minutes.

> A therapist required members of his therapy group to physically beat one member because he admitted to having thoughts that the head therapist was a "Nazi-type leader."

> A therapist convinced a female patient to divorce her husband as part of her therapy. He then convinced her to abandon her infant because "kids are basically a suck." She did so. When she expressed a desire four years later to be reunited with her child, she was told she "was not nearly ready," and that she was "empty" in her life.

> A female patient was told by her therapist that she was too fat. She was forced to crawl around on the floor imitating a cow.

> A therapist forced a female patient to stand in a "stress position," while being yelled at, until she fainted. She was later forced to undress before her therapist and another therapist and told to "do a strip-tease." She was forbidden to have any contact with her parents without permission and only in the presence of a member of the Center. She was regularly ridiculed by her therapist for being "cold, hard, and hateful."

These examples come from people who were involved in one form or another with the therapeutic program of the Center for Feeling Therapy. The Center was registered as a psychological corporation in 1971. The "Intensive" therapy program offered cost $2,500 then (compared to $6,000 for Primal Therapy).

In an interview in *Personal Growth* (1974), three of the founders list four reasons that led to their gradual dissatisfaction with Arthur Janov's approach to therapy. They noticed that time passed and they personally did not experience "cures"; although people *were* primaling (regressing to infantile and childhood traumas), not everyone was showing the primal changes of lowered body temperature, pulse rate, blood pressure, and EEG frequency; persons who did show these physiological changes might not show psychological change; and although patients they were working with were having [primals], these patients were not changing their lives.

As they increasingly questioned Primal Therapy's results and practices, they "became suspect as not being true believers." And so they left to set up their own institute, which would incorporate their broader perspective on what produces change. They credit Janov with "one significant discovery and one important rediscovery." The discovery was the intensive three-week format, which they saw as significant because it allowed momentum to build during the process of "breaking through" defenses. The rediscovery was Janov's emphasis on primaling, which they saw as a return to the abreactive, or cathartic, process initially used by Freud in his development of psychoanalytic therapy.

In the 1974 article, the three founders most strongly disagree with Janov's pairing of the results of primaling with the notion of "cure." What most bothers them about his idea of cure is that it implies that an end to suffering is possible. This end is achieved by dredging one's finite pool of pain, by returning to a limited number of primal scenes. At this point, one is cured. In place of a notion of "cure," the founders substitute the notion of patients

> making progress: feeling better, feeling more, making choices from inside themselves, from their own needs and wishes, rather than choices based on somebody else's demands and expectations. (*Personal Growth*, 5)

In place of a few really big traumas, they substitute the notion of "disordering—an ongoing daily deprivation." Joe Hart, one of the founders interviewed, defines "disordering" thus: "Everyday lack of contact, everyday dishonest contact—that's disordering, and that's what most people come to us with" (6). They claim not to struggle to achieve some "perfect end-state" in their therapy; they do assert, however, that "as we feel more and more of ourselves, our lives become better and better."

Rather than follow Janov in his sole emphasis on returning to early primal scenes and replaying them, the founders of Feeling Therapy assert the importance of dealing with the present, by living from feelings in the present and by making changes in the present. Getting patients to do these things appears to have been difficult, at least initially. As the founders describe it, patients came to them with specific expectations of what they wanted and how they were going to attain these goals: through primaling. Hart explains the difficulty:

> Wanting desperately to primal. That's the first thing we have to take away from them. Trying to primal will keep them from their feelings forever, because when they find they can't do it, they'll either give up or they'll begin imitating primals that they've read about or seen.(*Personal Growth*, 7)

As the founders see it, they put the primal in its correct place in their therapeutic program: unless patients attend to that which is primary (in their eyes), which is attending to feelings and making changes in the present, primals will "only" be repetitive. If patients follow the Feeling Therapy program, however, they will achieve more fundamental results.

Their discussion of patient expectations of what therapy should be hints at a demand for a particular kind of experience, that of Primal Therapy. They seem to be appealing to these same kinds of potential clients, even as they are trying to differentiate their therapy from Primal Therapy.

What did they think they were offering in place of Primal Therapy? They mention many things they are *not* offering: a cure, a simple tension release, something as easy as feeling something in the past, a ritual, or something "symbolic." Central to what they are offering is "community." Because there is no end to "disordering" and pain in life, people will need continuous help. Thus, they offer a "therapeutic community" to fill these needs. They claim that after nine months or so of therapy, they trained patients to be co-therapists, or therapists for each other. Therapists and clients also lived, worked, and played together. Central to their theorizing on the function of therapeutic community is their belief that therapists too need continuing therapy, and that living in a therapeutic community allows both therapists and patients to realize continuous benefit. It helps the patient because, according to Dominic Cirincione, the second founder interviewed,

> [i]f you have a therapeutic community, you first of all break your dependency on a therapist, and second, you break your dependency on a totally neurotic environment. I think this is a major contribution of our therapy. (11)

It also benefits the therapist, says Hart, for

> [i]f you accept the premise that everyone is basically crazy, disordered, that means that any therapist is going to be in his disordered state every now and then. Unless he gets help, that's going to affect how he does therapy. And you don't always want help when you're crazy. So then you need

someone around you to say "Hey, what's going on?" You may need more than one other person. (10)

They differentiate their approach from every major therapy in its successfully avoiding the limitations imposed by a single founder. Hart claims that in every major therapy he knows about the founder "limits the practices and ideas, and because the founder doesn't get the therapy for himself, the therapy becomes organized around his neurosis." In contrast, the Center for Feeling Therapy would avoid both the premature stunting of theoretical and technical development and the institutionalization of a single founder's neurosis, because a community of therapists founded it. Hart says that

> [a]s far as I know, there's never been a therapy developed by a community of therapists, and that's what we're about. That kind of activity allows us to have a continuing evolution in our ideas and practices. Most of the spinoffs from founders of therapeutic systems occur right at the point where one set of projections conflicts with another. But we can sift out a person's projections and not let them get organized into the system. That's the value of community. (11)

They do not seem able to conceive of the possibility of a community of therapists institutionalizing a collective "neurosis." And the self-description of nine therapists leaving Janov's institute and starting their own center may imply a diversity in the large number of therapists that is more apparent than real.

What they have retained from Primal Therapy is an emphasis on "direct" as compared to "symbolic" ways of acting. They scorn the "symbolic" and express this disdain in many ways. One is their criticism of "ritual" in therapy. Richard Corriere, the third founder interviewed, in commenting on patients' desires to have something happen to them by doing something (in therapy) the right way, speaks of how easy it is for a therapist to gratify this hope.

> I could take anybody I know and put them through a Gestalt ritual, a bioenergetic ritual, or a primal ritual—those aren't hard to do. But if I put myself through a ritual, I've done myself a disservice, and if I put someone else through a ritual, I've done him a disservice, too. But patients love to be put through rituals. They love it. Because everything that happens is controlled—even if it's a primal. (8)

Corriere's remarks seem to reflect his change from being a Primal Therapist to being a Feeling Therapist. Even though he saw the limits of Primal Therapy, he cannot yet see the limits of Feeling Therapy. All that occurs in Primal Therapy is disdainfully seen and termed as a "ritual"; all that occurs in Feeling Therapy is elevated to ultimate reality, and no part of it can be seen as "game" like, implying less than complete involvement in the process.

What is the alternative to therapeutic ritual? Dominic Cirincione, in criticizing encounter and sensory-awakening groups, explains their shared problem as one of trying "to ritualize something instead of continuing to be in contact, and it didn't work" (9). Feeling Therapists' ways of promoting continuous "contact" are obviously not in the category of ritual.

And what do they mean by being symbolic? Several comments express their understanding. These remarks illustrate as well their attempts to differentiate themselves from the "cultic milieu" of alternative therapies. (See Wallis [1977b] for discussion of Scientology's early attempts to differentiate itself similarly.)

> We feel [says Corriere] that a lot of mysticism and transpersonal psychology is basically horseshit. It's cosmic crap. Instead of a little kid asking for a piece of candy directly, it's a little kid wanting a substitute—something symbolic. (Personal Growth, 9)

> To get your direction from a symbol is to reject yourself and opt for something grandiose, like God [says Cirincione]. Or maybe something a bit less grandiose, like being the most gestaltized or bioenergeticized or Rolfed person in the world. That's symbolic, too. (10)

> It's an attempt to integrate your life around being a Gestalt patient, or being a bioenergetic patient, or being a primal patient, or a feeling patient rather than just feeling yourself and exactly where you are [says Corriere]. (10)

Clearly, they see themselves as offering something that transcends the limitations of "ritual" and "symbolism." All their works exhibit this same attitude toward their therapy: it alone is authentic and worthwhile.

Later observers can see the founders' claims for what they offer from a very different standpoint. Certain kinds of organizations have traditionally prohibited open dissent, most especially religious and political groups, but also psychotherapy schools. The history of the discipline from Freud onward is rife with schisms after which new schools of therapy coalesce around dissenters. Janov's Primal Institute, in asserting its brand of therapy as the cure for neurosis and psychosis, seems a likely candidate for generating splinter groups. Such was the case with the founders of Feeling Therapy; Rosen (1979:175) mentions another group.

A second factor seems important in examining the claims of Feeling Therapy's founders: the concept of an established market for psychotherapy. A product introduced into an established market needs to differentiate itself, and it usually does so by claiming to be new and better than comparable products. It needs to answer the question of how it is new and better, and then it needs to advertise that answer, to lure consumers away from its competitors. Feeling Therapy made its appeal to persons who were attracted to Primal Therapy and who had some knowledge of it through Janov's books. Once it attracted them, however, it had to differentiate itself from Primal Therapy and argue that it was new and better. It made these claims by rejecting the notion of cure and by adopting the idea of therapeutic community. With these two elements, it argued implicitly and explicitly for its ability to bring about more fundamental and more "realistic" change in individuals. It then advertised its claims in pamphlets, workshops, and a series of how-to books. The latter included *Going Sane* in 1975, *The Dream Makers* in 1977, and *Psychological Fitness* in 1979. A fourth book, *Dreaming and Waking*, described as being serious in contrast to the earlier, "popular" books, was published in 1980.

The Founders

Two people seem crucial in the development of the Center for Feeling Therapy. Foremost is Joe Hart, who was then a psychology professor at the University of California Irvine (UCI). He attracted a following of undergraduate and graduate students, especially through his "Psychology of Awareness" class. One of the undergraduates, who became Hart's teaching assistant, was Richard "Riggs" Corriere. Their relationship was fateful for both; Hart became known as the foremost theoretician, and Corriere as the leading exemplar, of the new therapy. Werner Karle, another of Hart's students, organized and ran his UCI laboratory. Dominic Cirincione, a high school teacher of Corriere's, obtained a temporary teaching position in the psychology department through Hart.[1]

Hart, Corriere, Karle, and Cirincione all entered Primal Therapy, where they met the rest of the persons initially identified as founding therapists. Lee Woldenberg, M.D., was medical director of the Primal Institute, and Jerry Binder and Steve Gold were certified Primal therapists (as well as each other's close friends). Linda Binder, Jerry's wife, was training to be a Primal Therapist. Carole Suydam, the other female founder, was a licensed social worker who also came from the Primal Institute.

The journalist Carol Lynn Mithers (1994:65) estimates that between twenty and thirty students from UCI entered therapy at the Center from the early to mid-1970s. Joe Hart resigned at the end of the 1976 school year under allegations that he was exploiting his students by having them go into the Center. When the founders left the Primal Institute in 1971— either in rebellion against

Janov (their account) or before being kicked out of training (Janov's account)—about twenty-five patients went with them, including Dominic Cirincione's girlfriend, who would eventually become Corriere's girlfriend and then his wife (58).

Initially, only four founders offered Intensive therapy: Jerry Binder and Steve Gold, the certified Primal Therapists, Joe Hart, and Linda Binder (who had almost completed Primal training). The others were training to do Intensive therapy. Eventually Binder and Gold (who both had master's degrees at the start of their Feeling Therapy association) entered and completed the doctoral program at UCI, working under Hart, who chaired their committees.

Hart and Corriere emerged over time as the primary theoreticians, co-authoring four books about the Center (Binder also co-authored the first book, *Going Sane*). At the time the Center broke up, Corriere was acknowledged by the other therapists and patients to be the most powerful member; Hart had left eight months before the end. Apparently he was convinced the group had become a cult, having requested and read articles by the psychiatrist L. J. West about "brainwashing."

Corriere is credited with several crucial innovations in the evolution of the Center. He originated its therapeutic emphasis on the present rather than the past (he created the first "Reality Group," which was seen as a success and extended to include everyone at the Center); "sluggo therapy" (if someone was not getting it or resisting, you slugged the person to make your point) developed within his group; he helped to push the idea of living in a community, and of living more openly within it (e.g., tearing down walls between bathroom and bedroom); his early interest in dreams, the subject of his dissertation, became a Center interest and a means of reaching out to the public; he led in supporting the idea of the community buying a retirement property, which led to the purchase of the Doll Baby Ranch in Arizona; he originated and the Center's extreme emphasis on looking good and being materially successful.

At the end, Corriere headed the most prestigious therapy group, Group 1; his former roommate and close friend Werner Karle headed Group 2; Lee Woldenberg headed Group 4; and Dominic Cirincione headed Group 3. These were the four most prestigious groups, composed of the older, most successful patients. The therapists heading them were closer to Corriere than were other founding therapists.

Three of the therapists who first provided the Intensive therapy, and thus were initially among the most prestigious, had been "demoted." Binder stopped running Intensives and did not get a group in the reorganization; earlier, although a co-author of *Going Sane*, he was not a big part of the lecture/talk appearances promoting the book. Group 5, the "Tombstone Group"—for those

who were "losers," patients not making progress, and thus not a plum assignment for a therapist—was given to Steve Gold. Linda Binder no longer did
therapy (except co-therapy, as did other patients); Carole Suydam, the other
female founder, had been demoted as well. In later written accounts, neither
woman is any longer referred to as a founding therapist, which explains the
depiction of only seven founders (as compared to earlier mentions of nine).
One woman (who acted as a therapist) did rise to become the most powerful
female member of the Center: Corriere's girlfriend, later his wife.

Development of Programs: Emphases Change

The three books written for a broad public seem to represent three stages
in the Center's development. The first, *Going Sane* (1975), presents the founders'
early descriptions of themselves and the work at the therapeutic community.
Their key innovation, the idea of organizing themselves as a therapeutic community, places them in a secure position of superiority, in their eyes.

Their second book, *The Dream Makers* (1977), supposedly increases the
emphasis on dreamwork in how they conduct their personal relationships and
in how they handle therapeutic relationships. It describes incorporating their
discovery of "breakthru dreams" into the Center.[2] Reading between the lines
of the book, however, seems to suggest the process of change from a structure emphasizing participatory democracy to one emphasizing hierarchy,
with Corriere at the top.

The third book, *Psychological Fitness* (1979), expresses an imperialist tendency of the institute. It reaches beyond the confines of a therapeutic community to the average person, to those desirous of "transformation" but not
desirous of living in a highly structured community setting. Believing their
discoveries and work impressive, Corriere and Hart wanted to reach a far
larger audience. They coined the phrase "psychological fitness" to encompass
a process of psychological growth comparable to physical growth. They also
seemed to be caught up in the burgeoning interest in physical fitness in America. In this third stage the Center's emphasis turned outward, moving beyond
its earlier concern with relationships and work within the therapeutic community.

What is most noteworthy is the incestuousness of this therapeutic
community. The therapist-founders and clients worked, lived, and played together. They spent all their time with people associated in some way with the
Center. They developed and tested their theories together, using Center patients for their samples and themselves as "patients" for their own research.
Combining the roles of clinician and researcher, they found dramatic changes

occurring. But they were oblivious to the role of influence in what they observed clinically and experimentally. This conflation of roles, however, is never made explicit in their articles; one assumes the researcher is not the theorist and the therapist as well.[3] What Bainbridge (1978) describes in his analysis of the evolution of a psychotherapy group into a religious cult as "implosion" seems to have occurred here.

Practices and concepts were incorporated into the group only as they fit the founders' changing schema. The founders intended to bring this schema to bear on the world at large. They believed that they provided a new theory of psychopathology, the disorder theory, and an unprecedentedly effective new therapy. They thought both would change the contours of theory and therapy relatively rapidly, and they propagated this notion wholeheartedly.

The appendixes to the founding therapists' books seem to indicate a continuous change in interests, programs offered, and ways of participating in Feeling Therapy. What is implied is that this continuous change is positive and reflects progressive elaboration and refinement of theory and practice. My research indicates that, to the contrary, most of this description was part of a public relations strategy. Phoenix Associates was set up sometime in 1975 to handle publicity for the Center, after Going Sane's relative lack of exposure. An increasingly impressive image of the Center and the Center Foundation was presented, accompanied by an even more impressive display that seems to have been designed to attract people by implying impressive growth in programs and research emphases.

In these appendixes, the authors also warn against those who wrongly call themselves Feeling Therapists. They suggest that individuals contact the Center for a list of persons they have trained to practice Feeling Therapy; in 1975, they described three training programs that would train individuals as practitioners. The authors of Going Sane attribute the problem of "fake" Feeling Therapists to the increased popularity of and the increased professional recognition given to Feeling Therapy.[4]

The Dream Makers

Riggs Corriere and Joe Hart coauthored The Dream Makers, which was published in 1977. The inside jacket describes the authors and their work in glowing terms:

> Experts in their field, Drs. Corriere and Hart blended their therapeutic, writing, and research skills in what is the life-style of the future. Their other major work, Going Sane: An Introduction to Feeling Therapy, was hailed by professionals as marking a "supersonic dimension of feeling compared to which the feeling in other therapies is pallid."

In addition to an appendix concerning the Center for Feeling Therapy and the Center Foundation, this book has a second appendix with information about "Dream Maker Programs," which presumably reflects the increased importance the authors were giving to dreams in their theory, practice, and research.

Also, Feeling Therapy is placed for the first time within the Functional school of psychotherapy. In the authors' view

> Functional therapies blend together both of the major historical trends within modern clinical psychology: the Analytic-Experiential and the Behavior-Modification. For more information about the Functional Orientation as it relates to dreams consult The Transformation of Dreams or write for a listing of articles from the Center Foundation. (Corriere and Hart, 1977:192)

Again, the clinic is portrayed as only doing long-term therapy, but it is also described as having two additional programs

> of both short-term intensive therapy (one month) for patients who will continue their therapy elsewhere and long-term intensive therapy (twelve plus months) for patients who can stay in the Los Angeles area. (192)

Psychological Fitness

Corriere and Hart collaborated again on Psychological Fitness, published in 1979. The book jacket here records an even more impressive list of their achievements than that of The Dream Makers. The coauthors are described as

> founding therapists of the Center for Feeling Therapy and the Clinic for Functional Counseling and Psychotherapy in Los Angeles. They are the authors of Going Sane: An Introduction to Feeling Therapy and The Dream Makers: Discovering Your Breakthrough Dreams. Both men have published many research articles in such journals as Psychophysiology, Psychotherapy, Science, Nature, [and] The Journal of Educational Psychology, and have lectured widely and given many workshops at numerous universities and public forums throughout the United States and Canada, as well as appearing on many radio and television shows. The ideas in Psychological Fitness, the result of over ten years of clinical work and research, have helped thousands of people and are changing the way other psychological and mental health professionals look at mental health.

In this book's appendix one learns that there are now two kinds of "Fitness Training Programs" offered through the Center Foundation.

A third program, the "Associate Program," consists of "guided-at-home fitness training with written and phone follow-ups from a fitness counselor." This looks like their most ambitious program to date, as they describe the history of psychological fitness:

> The programs and ideas of psychological fitness are derived from a specific therapy, Feeling Therapy, and a general orientation to psychotherapy and counseling called the Functional Approach. Feeling Therapy is an intensive, long-term, community-based psychotherapy which is offered only at the Center for Feeling Therapy in Los Angeles. The Functional Approach to Counseling and Psychotherapy combines features of Humanistic Psychotherapy, Analytic Psychotherapy, and Behavior Therapy into an integrated theory and method for feeling better and functioning better. The Training Center for Functional Psychotherapy and Counseling is located in Los Angeles, with branches in other major cities.(Corriere and Hart, 1979:236)

Psychological Fitness is described in a vein similar to their previous claims for a theory and practice that will revolutionize the treatment of psychopathology.

> Although Psychological Fitness Training originally developed from a psychotherapeutic context, the direction of influence is now two-way. We believe that the ideas and methods of psychological fitness are so powerful and effective that they will eventually replace the medical model of psychological treatment. We also believe that the fitness emphasis in psychology, psychotherapy, and counseling is much more desirable and more widely effective than the traditional mental health and mental hygiene emphasis.(236)

In the description of the Center Foundation, otherwise similar to that in the first two books, they add a passage emphasizing the worldwide scope of their work: "and service organization based in Los Angeles with affiliated Psychological Fitness Training Centers located in various parts of the United States and the world" (235).

In short, as the Center developed, its goals became more grandiose. From its inception in 1971, its founders were convinced of its novelty and superiority of organization. They remained sure of the value of their theory and practice, and they wanted to share their discoveries much more widely. Over time, the founders became increasingly interested in expanding—first locally, then nationally, and then throughout the world.

The founding therapists made many public-speaking appearances, touting Feeling Therapy and the Center, to accomplish their goal of expansion. For example, after *Going Sane* was published in 1975, Joe Hart and Riggs Corriere were on about thirty Los Angeles and San Francisco radio programs. By the end of 1975, they had been on almost a dozen Los Angeles and Bay Area television shows (Mithers, 1994:136–37). By gaining such media coverage, they were able to present to patients in the therapeutic community "proof" of their success. That is, in giving them access to the viewing and listening public to share their message, the outside world was acknowledging their therapeutic effectiveness. This extensive media access, gained through publishing books and articles and by making radio and television appearances, further buttressed their authority in the eyes of patients. Not only were they psychological experts, they had become minicelebrities.

Demographics of the Center for Feeling Therapy

After the first couple of years, the Center's population seemed to stabilize at between 250 and 300 persons. A community roster dated June 8, 1977, listed 250 individuals, including the therapists. In their last account of the Center, in *Dreaming and Waking*, published in 1980, Corriere, Karle, Woldenberg, and Hart describe their community as numbering "more than three hundred people" (123); newspaper accounts of the collapse give a figure of about 350 (see Horowitz [1981] and Morain [1981]).

This community, however, was distinct from the Clinic for Functional Counseling and Psychotherapy. Founded in 1978, it provided outpatient therapy; at the time of the Center's downfall, it supposedly had 600 clients. The Clinic was staffed mainly by the "junior" therapists, that is, those persons who had been trained to do Feeling Therapy by the "founding" therapists, and who had also earned outside degrees permitting them to do therapy. (Some of the therapists came to the Center with degrees in psychology or counseling.) According to my interviews, the therapists who staffed the Clinic worked very hard and had high patient loads. I am not certain whether unlicensed individuals also worked at the Clinic.

The therapy provided at the Clinic resembled mainstream therapy more than it did the therapy at the Center. There was very little of the "busting"—harshly confronting a person with her or his failure to live up to Center norms—that occurred in the therapeutic community. The Clinic did, however, incorporate concepts developed during the later years of the Center, like psychological fitness. As I will point out later, therapists here were pressured to persuade clients (some, not all, it seems) to consider entering the Intensive.

At the Center, the patient/therapist ratio was high. All told, there were about twenty-five "founding" and "second generation" therapists.[5] Perhaps thirteen of them did Intensives; the others did everything but: they headed groups in the Intensive, and (along with the other thirteen) they headed regular groups after the Intensive.

Given this small number of practitioners, the co-therapy program was very important. Through this program, I hypothesize, the therapists were able to monitor and control the behavior of a large group of people. "Co-therapy" seems to have had two meanings. One did co-therapy routinely on members of one's group after a time, emulating therapist behavior. The second sense refers to a more organized program, where people received "training" to do therapy on "younger" patients. This program seemed to involve a method of selecting individuals to become co-therapists that was at once organized yet also haphazard. Not every individual eventually became a co-therapist, despite what Going Sane seemed to suggest. One person I interviewed estimated that about a third of the patients were co-therapists when the Center fell apart.

As with the Moonies, where recruits were assigned to partners who went through the conversion process with them, anxiously monitoring each recruit's behavior and demeanor (Ayella, 1981), co-therapists made it possible for relatively few therapists to control a large group. They provided, in many instances, the "therapy" that therapists did not provide: they saw people individually or in small groups, they saw them regularly, and they checked out how they were doing in general. Again like the case of the Moonies, this was a position to aspire to within the Center hierarchy. Some co-therapists sound very good—"good" in the sense of providing some support and helpful suggestions, even an understanding ear. They sounded like they could be supportive, able to "help" people. Less busting seems to have characterized these relationships, although it certainly was present. In other words, it seems there was more room for leeway, less demand for busting, in relationships involving co-therapists than in those involving therapists. Yet, the system also served to pass along information on individuals to the therapists that they could not readily acquire, given the smallness of their number.

Most of the Feeling Therapy community lived within blocks of each other at the foot of the Hollywood Hills. The centering of the community here seems to have begun in 1974, when the therapists moved to this location; patients followed soon after. The size of these households ranged from four to ten individuals. Household composition was unstable. All of my interviewees reported moving between houses frequently. For example, a couple might ask to move in together and be granted permission to do so.

Households might be broken up if they got along too well. Some that I heard of seemed to get along in ways I would consider good: they were fairly harmonious, with infrequent busting, and they afforded some privacy to individuals. Nevertheless, such houses were often termed "dead" and then were broken up. The norm for Center houses was that they be "stimulating" at all times, to "raise" individuals' "feeling levels." Houses where a lot of busting occurred, where persons for the most part strongly adhered to Center norms and demanded that adherence from each other, might be termed "righteous."

Friendships and romances developed, yet many were not "authentic," those that would have come about "naturally." Even many naturally developing relationships were interrupted, however, ostensibly in the name of the higher good, one's greater potential, but in ways designed to maintain total commitment of each individual to the Center and to its therapists. In the early years of the Center, many entering couples were broken up. This was not necessarily a direct breakup of the relationship by therapists, although in some examples related to me this did seem to be the case. Parent-child relationships were also disrupted, as individuals were persuaded that they were bad parents and should give up their children. No children were born to women at the Center during its ten-year life. Several interviewees told me of their abortions or of those of other women.[6]

On the other hand, "artificial" relationships and friendships were developed. Individuals might be "assigned" to be involved with a person, or to become friends with another member. For example, one women I interviewed was told to select a person to become her best friend, and to tell that friend everything. She selected a woman who was cold and distant toward her; no doubt, she was not that woman's choice for best friend. This relationship consumed much of my interviewee's time, as she sought to win the aloof woman's friendship. Another interviewee, homosexual at entry and seeking help on that account, was encouraged to do the same thing with a man in his group whom he "loved." Although he did not intend a sexual relationship with this man, because he knew of and accepted the Center's complete rejection of homosexuality, he followed the suggestion. Each man was told he had much to gain from this friendship; again, although my interviewee tried very hard, he could not achieve a reciprocal friendship.

And last, all these relationships developed within the confines of the Center. Individuals, for the most part, spent all their time not devoted to work with Center people. The "outside" world came to look "insane" and thus frightening to Center patients. Furthermore, they were repeatedly told they would not be able to make it in the arena of society.

The Center for Feeling Therapy fell apart in November 1980. The collapse began when the acknowledged head therapist stayed in the Center in Los Angeles while the other therapists went to their ranch in Arizona. There, after discussing their similar resentments of the head therapist, they decided Corriere needed to be "busted." Returning to the Center, they allowed patients, as part of an attempt to even out the power imbalance, to express their dissatisfactions with the therapy. Unexpressed resentments poured out, particularly from the "older" patients, those who had been there for the duration or a large part of the Center's existence. In the end, all the therapists were engulfed in waves of recriminations from these longtime patients. Horowitz (1981) and Morain (1981) provide two newspaper accounts of the Center's downfall. I discuss the collapse in greater detail in Chapters 6 and 7.

Three
The Production of Feeling People

Two ideas are central to understanding Feeling Therapy's theory of personality, theory of society, and the therapeutic techniques supposedly derived from them: "transformation" and "community." Feeling Therapists promised individual transformation through community.

The term "Feeling Therapy" succinctly expresses the therapists' major theoretical assumption: "feelings" are crucial in the process of remedying social psychopathology. Individuals are born with an innate drive to "complete" their feelings. Such feelings are known as "integral" feelings. Young children naturally express integral feelings until they learn from parents and other members of society to "disorder" their feelings. This process of disordering results in "reasonably insane" individuals, no longer aware of their innate drive, and so unhappy and unfulfilled.

The therapists hypothesize three components of feelings: sensations, meanings, and expressions. Thus, "a feeling is the expression of a sensation with a meaning." Sensations are the "impulses of our sensorium. . . . There are literally thousands of sensations that people are capable of feeling each day." A meaning "is the cerebral interpretation of a sensation. Expression is any gesture or action which shows feeling" (Hart, Corriere, and Binder, 1975:69). All three components must be correctly matched for "emotional ordering" to occur. Most often, "emotional disordering" is what happens. Such disordering occurs repeatedly, day in and day out, from early childhood. In this theory, there are no large traumas (necessarily, although there may be), but there are innumerable small and unnoticed disorderings occurring in parent-child interactions throughout society.

The difference between "feeling," that is, experiencing integral feelings, and "non-feeling" is purportedly so great that once a person experiences real feeling he or she has an internal reference point from which to discriminate between the two states of being.

> We are certain that every person who completes even one cycle of feeling
> knows himself inside out; he has a lifelong reference for what it is to feel in the

past, feel in the present, and untangle past from present. He can never again completely forget himself. During periods of retrogression, as a person begins to close down and live from defenses, he is denying everything he knows from the innermost center of himself—but that feeling center can never be obliterated. Weeks or months or even years later he will move back toward the feeling life he is denying. (Hart, Corriere, and Binder, 1975:392)

This internal reference point, however, must be continually nurtured by a community of feeling people. The community teaches the individual how to live from integral feelings, while it protects against the "reasonable insanity" of the larger world. The persons of the community, living from feeling, are only "life-enhancing." Thus, the theory does not allow the possibility of feeling people doing harmful or wrong actions.

In this conception of the individual, waking and sleeping states are parallel. Disordered individuals live disordered lives and dream disordered dreams. "Symbolism" taints both states. As disorder diminishes, "symbolism" recedes, leaving in its place "direct" ways of being and dreaming.

The therapists' understanding of society incorporates many of the criticisms made by mass-society theorists: we live in a "media," rather than a "contact," culture, which isolates persons, thus separating them from their very humanity; a striving for material rewards rather than for spiritual or nonmaterial rewards (here, that of feeling) drives people to act; and individuals are externally rather than internally motivated. The result of all this is that the bulk of society is "reasonably insane." While they offer this as their social critique, the therapists do not offer suggestions for change on a society-wide scale. They focus, rather, on changing individuals into feeling people; on the level above individuals, they suggest the desirability of small communities of persons living in a contact culture. They seem to assume that such communities will act as a stimulus and a demonstration (of an alternative) to the larger world, and in this way create an ever widening circle of change.

In conceptualizing what they offer as the chance to "go sane," the therapists reverse the usual therapeutic characterization of individual and society. Feeling Therapy rejects the goal of a return to normative conduct, of individuals adapting to the existing social reality. Instead, they disdain that social reality and suggest a new one in the form of a therapeutic community. Such a group is essential if the newly "sane" member is not to be contaminated by the larger "neurotic" society.

Thus, they generalize that their aim is to produce "feeling" people and to sustain them. Going Sane, written just four years after the Center for Feeling Therapy was established in 1971, is the most explicit description of their theory and their therapy, and this chapter will draw heavily from it. The therapists' later books describe the increased importance given to dreams in their therapeutic practice, and offer a popularized version of the "intensive" therapy they present in Going Sane, which they term "psychological fitness."

At the outset, note that the theory was derived from their practice. They stumbled upon their "discoveries" after a ramble down various byways of the human-potential movement: "Client-Centered Therapy, Gestalt Therapy, Encounter Therapy, Bioenergetic Therapy, and Primal Therapy" (Hart, Corriere, and Binder, 1975:4). They describe these discoveries as painful, accepted only after long struggle individually and as a group. This quest into the unknown was largely successful, and it forms the basis for the Feeling Therapists' superiority to other therapists: they have been there. They subject their clients only to what they themselves experienced. What is it that they were subjected to? The major thing was confronting with their own "insanity." They forced themselves and each other to face their "insanity" and to go beyond it to "sanity." This claim for what the therapists' superiority rests on, their experience of their own insanity, is also the basis for what they describe as the patient's essential right in therapy:

> It is the patient's right to not be asked to do or to live anything which the therapist has not done. In essence, the patient's right is to see the therapist as a person, whose limitations are the end point of the therapy. (405)

The patient also has the right to know explicitly what a therapy offers. In addition, the therapist, too, has rights:

> A therapist has the right to have a person come to him who is seriously interested in what he has to offer. Does he want Gestalt or Bioenergetics? Does he want meditation? He has the right to a patient who is not in a smorgasbord line. He has the right to a patient who is willing to live out the therapy as he practices it, a patient who wants to take responsibility for himself. (406)

What do they mean by "insanity"? It is not what is usually thought of as "insanity," the behavior exhibited by psychotics. Rather, the therapists say that the

> performances in mental hospitals are outlandish displays and not insanity. Psychotic displays are merely nonfunctional social behaviors. They are no more or less psychotic than the behavior of the top level executive who works seventy-five hours a week and drops dead from a heart attack at forty-five. Psychotics are pretending. However, they get trapped in their pretenses, just as the young executive or average housewife gets trapped. . . .
>
> . . . Insanity is not a stable, recognizable type of bizarre behavior. It is an experience. Insanity is experienced only when there is an awakening from the pretense of life: when the businessman stops one day and says, "This kind

> of life isn't for me, I've got to change"; when the housewife turns off her
> dishwasher and cries about the futility of her life; when the psychotic
> realizes his crazy behavior is crazy. (401, 402)

Feeling Therapists, knowing what is intra-and inter-psychically possible
(which is far more than most experts and lay people), thus have a huge potential market for their therapy: everyone is insane. They claim that R. D.
Laing's Anti-Psychiatry is most similar in style and thought to their therapy.
Laing, however, neglected "going sane," which these therapists stress.

In spite of their self-proclaimed distance from other therapies, including those they had experienced, the Primal Therapy of Arthur Janov holds
pride of place in their theoretical structure. For this reason, I will analyze Primal Therapy in the next section, before mentioning a few other therapies and
then going on to a discussion of how Feeling Therapy translates into therapeutic practice.

Primal Scream

Arthur Janov, a Los Angeles psychotherapist, announced the therapeutic approach he had been working on since the late 1960s in his first book,
The Primal Scream (Rosen, 1979:154).[1] Published in the spring of 1971, it proclaimed a cure for all neurosis.

Janov's treatment program consisted of three weeks of intensive individual therapy with a Primal therapist, followed by several months of twice-
weekly group sessions. The object was to discover one's Deep Pain by "Primaling," or regressing to infantile and childhood traumas, and to get rid of
the Primal Pool of Pain by reliving these traumatic events. This would enable
one to throw off the unreal, neurotic self. The real, un-neurotic self that
emerged would be far more flexible and better able to learn from new situations. Primal therapists set the stage for a "natural" unfolding of the "real" self
by acting as taskmasters, forcing an individual to stick to the difficult task of
self-confrontation.

A "hydraulic" model of intrapsychic energy underlies Janov's therapeutic program. The driving force is "need," which has been channeled into
numerous unsatisfying outlets. Janov's predominant emphasis is on the unfulfilled "child" buried within his adult clients. The entire therapeutic situation revolves around an approach to this "child." Indeed, the "child's" point
of view triumphs.

Understanding Janov's dichotomy of "real" and "unreal" selves is crucial to comprehending this approach. Children are born "real," with a variety

of "needs" they require their parents, especially, to fulfill if they are to be happy. But the usual fate of the child, in Janov's account, is consistent frustration of all these needs; one day, the frustration crystallizes into a complete understanding of estrangement from parents. This is the most shattering moment of childhood, what Janov terms the "major Primal Scene." The child finds this realization so painful that henceforth it must be concealed from the self. She or he constructs an "unreal" self "over" this "real" self with its fatal knowledge.[2] The self is now bifurcated, and it will remain so until this early traumatic event is remembered and resolved. Recovery depends upon returning to the "actual" event.[3]

Janov speaks as though this Primal Pain is actually "back" there in one's "deepest" self, in pristine form, as intense as the day it occurred. If we can figure out a way to reach "back" to it, we can assuredly handle it. And this is indeed what Janov says he can do.

While the deep, "real" self remains always aware of the Pain, the superficial, "unreal" self is completely unaware of the cause of its constant misery. Janov's notion of self thus combines total knowing, of the "real" self, with total unawareness, of the "unreal" self. This "unreal" self, our most familiar sense of ourselves, pursues a variety of satisfactions to compensate, unknowingly, for its Pain. It strives to get ahead, to impress others, to acquire tangible signs of success, to eat and drink well, to have good relationships, to feel loved by parents—all to no avail. Janov terms these strivings "neurotic" needs, and posits that their defining feature is that they cannot be fulfilled. They do, however, prevent the Pain from arising and overwhelming one.

Janov structures his whole therapeutic regime on aiding and abetting this Pain in its struggle to emerge. Accordingly, he first must prevent "neurotic" needs from being fulfilled. Individuals beginning Primal treatment must not take "refuge" in their usual "hiding" places. What this means practically is that they must not drink, smoke, watch television, listen to music, read, or talk to others: they must be "alone" with themselves for twenty-four hours before they begin treatment. Sometimes they may be told to stay up all night. In this fashion, they begin treatment "closer" to the self they unwittingly "hide" most of the time. Janov sees this as increasing the individual's state of tension, which he believes to be quite necessary. When the tension gets great enough, the Pain is likely to emerge almost "automatically." To create this state of great tension, Janov exhorts his patients not to "piss away" their feelings. He means this literally. The metaphor is that of energy which must be forced back into one location, until it becomes so great that it "explodes" to release the pressure.

Janov will not tolerate anything but the "real" self in his sessions with patients. He begins his approach to this "real" self almost immediately. He can "see" it, and he will not accept the "unreal" self. Patients report on this claim of Janov's with increasing awe. Initial outrage gives way to amazement, and then to acceptance of all Janov's comments as being insightful.

Neurotic "tension" is an important concept to Janov. The neurotic "unreal" self does not "feel," but experiences "tension" instead. "Pain," he says, "is always there; only it is spread out in the body in a generalized tense state" (Janov, 1970:40).

> In Primal terms, there is no neurosis without tension. By this I mean unnatural tension, which has no place in the psychologically normal human, not natural tension, which each of us needs to move about. Unnatural tension is chronic and is the pressure of denied or unresolved feelings and needs. Whenever I discuss tension, I am referring to neurotic tension. What the neurotic feels in place of real feelings are degrees of tension. Less tension usually feels good; more tension feels bad. What the neurotic tries to do with his behavior is feel better. (47)

The only means of relieving this chronic neurotic tension is by connection. What does connection involve? Most basically, feeling the original Pain and connecting that feeling to one's present living. When this happens, one's tension, as expressed in "defenses," will no longer be necessary—one will then live with a very low level of tension and without defenses, and one will then "feel."

Janov's understanding of how the individual psyche relates to the social world is seriously deficient. His theory implies that there is a way of experiencing the world that is not mediated by concepts or "symbols." This unmediated way is vastly preferable. It is what people will experience when they become "real" selves. Janov juxtaposes "symbolic" and "unsymbolic" ways of being. Neurotics who have "unreal" selves are primarily "symbolic" beings; "normals" with "real" selves are "unsymbolic" beings. When "real" selves emerge, "symbolic" behavior disappears in waking and sleeping states. This understanding places a very great emphasis on the possibility of directly reproducing "outer" social life within "internal" psychic life. The psychic life of a Post-Primal individual will be comparable to a videotape that exactly reproduces everything that happens to that individual. In this view, there is no "redefining" of the past from one's present situation.

Children are born with a set of needs, and if parents do not interfere, but fulfill these needs, individuals will develop by a "natural" process. In the actual process of early childhood development, however, Janov implies that only imposition occurs. Parents have clear, well-formed, and rigid ideas of what they want, and they demand that children conform to these. Children have no "say" in their own behavior, yet they too have clear needs that demand only one resolution (which may vary depending on every individual's "innate" needs, but which include general needs to be held and to be loved). Janov thus depicts a conflict between two clear and well-formed lines of development, with the parents' line winning out time and again. And so, his account lacks any notion of complexity of motivation and interaction. He fails to consider, for example, a concept like "ambivalence"; here, one can conceive of parents feeling both strong love and strong hate for what parenting involves, resulting in varying and conflicting responses to their offspring. Children, similarly, can experience both intense love and hate for their parents, emotions not necessarily based on "realistic" needs. In plain contrast to the early parent-child relationship, which he characterized as almost solely one of parental domination, Janov can recognize no aspect of imposition, no influence occurring in his therapeutic practice.[4] What Janov sees is a situation in which the therapist sets the stage for a natural unfolding of the real self. Yet he or she is essential to this process in the role of taskmaster, forcing an individual to stick to the difficult task of self-confrontation. And it is precisely this paradox that most undermines Janov's theorizing about his practice. He arrogates an incredible omniscience to his therapists, and very little to his clients' selves, even their "real" selves, until they have completed their Primal Therapy. Janov's therapists can tell precisely what is "unreal" and what is "real" in the patients they treat, and they can do so very quickly. This extreme assertion places the capabilities of these therapists beyond those of most of their colleagues, who would make much more modest claims for what their knowledge consists of and how they use it.[5]

Again and again, Janov implies or directly states that therapists must take a very directive and active role with the patient, yet he explicitly denies that these terms apply to the therapeutic role. He seems to have an inordinately strong belief in the power of words, especially as he uses them: if he does not *name* something so, it is not so, regardless of how other observers would see it.

What Janov sees are individuals all reaching to the "deepest" part of self and emerging as "real" selves from this voyage. Therapists are necessary, but ultimately auxiliary, to what emerges. There is little interaction of any kind, and no modeling of individual behavior based on therapists' or patients' behavior occurs. They do not influence or persuade each other. The new, "real" self can be easily maintained because it is "natural," and "natural" processes have greater resiliency than unnatural ones. These "new" people do not need others to maintain their "real" selves; they effortlessly make the right choices on their own.

Patients bring their personal history into therapy in only one situation—that where they Primal, where they "relive" their past Pain "psychophysiologically," or fully. They do not bring any of their past, in the form of perceptions or beliefs about themselves and other people, to interactions with either therapists or other patients. The concepts of "transference" and "countertransference" thus disappear from the theoretical scheme. Janov, of course, assumes that if he says these do not exist, they do not exist.

One can construct a very different reading of what happens in Primal Therapy. Central to this interpretation, in contrast to Janov's central emphasis on the individual's autonomy, is deference to authority and small-group dynamics. The small group has certain characteristic group properties of influence that "automatically" occur.[6] Accordingly, a picture emerges of a group of individuals engaged in intensive interaction with all members of the group, including therapists and other patients. In this picture the therapist is essential and not incidental to the outcome of the process. Primal therapists reinforce positive changes and discourage negative changes in patients—that is, they reward what they determine to be healthy behavior and punish what they determine to be unhealthy, or neurotic, behavior. They further shape behavior by acting as models. For example, they illustrate the correct terminology to use when describing one's self and one's past and present experience; they display appropriate behavior by modeling expressions and gestures, as well as other bodily actions like breathing, standing straight, and appearing to be calm around people who are "fully" feeling; and in group discussions they provide an interpretation, a cognitive framework, of all that the members are experiencing, and they help them to apply this to their individual lives.[7] From this alternative standpoint, patients play a major role both in their own transformations and in those of other patients. They act as a reference group to whom individuals compare themselves and their behavior. In this way, patients influence each other greatly in the performance each of them presents. They offer embodied examples of the norms of "really" getting into one's feelings. When individual therapy ends after three weeks, one is placed within a group to enhance further one's ability to Primal. Here the person conforms to the desired norms for "reaching down" to the "real" self and then for being a Post-Primal person, and in the process transforms the self.

Rather than being a matter of individuals looking for anything that will help and simply discovering their Primal Pain because this is the truth, the reality, to be found when one seeks, individuals are motivated from the start to accept uncritically what they will hear. All their expectation for relief of psychic suffering is mobilized to an acceptance that amounts to complete trust in Janov and his therapists, and in what they say and do as being therapeutic.

Frank (1974:315) sees this initial state, when one is seeking psychotherapy, as one of heightened suggestibility.

Contrary to Janov's notion of a straightforward unfolding of "natural" processes that requires little active participation by either therapists or patients, I argue that both parties are engaged in intense participation in defined roles. Primal therapists are actively eliciting particular behaviors that they consider beneficial to their patients, and patients are actively acquiring these to make "progress" in therapy. Patients learn a new ideology, complete with a language for interpreting bodily sensations in a new way—for example, the physical sensation of needing to urinate comes to be interpreted as a psychological desire to "piss away" one's feelings, rather than face them and their associated pain.

What Frank (1974:424–25) describes as healing cults more closely resembles what I think occurs in Primal Therapy than does Janov's description. Frank says:

> The cult leader glories in his claimed healing powers, *exerts them without self-doubt, and his ministrations are supported by a group of believers in his powers.* These healing approaches prize emotion above intellect, subjective certainty above objective analysis, and seek to foster belief and dependence rather than insight and autonomy. Those based on a religious doctrine add another powerful ingredient to the therapeutic brew by claiming to bring supernatural healing forces to the sufferers' aid. For persons who can abandon skepticism, these cults obviously mobilize strong psychological forces for the production and maintenance of therapeutic change. (emphasis added)

In Primal Therapy, the notion of a "true" self following an innate developmental sequence resembles greatly the notion of a religious doctrine. What Janov in a sense provides one with is not what he might wish. By reading between the lines of his book, one can make a strong argument for the potency of social mythology in affecting bodily states. What a person believes influences what a person feels, even to the point of generating physiological changes.[8] But Janov attributes the bodily changes that occur to only one thing: the actual reliving of past trauma so that energy "escapes," so that one's Primal Pool of Pain is emptied (leaving, presumably, only a Birdbath).

Janov's problem here is his assumption that what is essentially a metaphor for understanding psychic life nonetheless corresponds to real entities within an individual. That is, he implies that there is a real Pool of Pain and that one needs to drain it. He thus misattributes what results he achieves to the efficacy of his therapeutic procedures, and he then takes these "successes" to be unquestionable "proof" of this efficacy. What this perspective loses is a properly nuanced understanding of the relationship between an individual's body and mind.

I suggest instead that the claimed changes are the product of a state of intense social influence, in which the patient is a willing and active participant. In other words, Primaling may produce changes, but not for the reasons Janov claims. This leaves unexamined the question of whether the changes are long-lasting or transient. Janov, arguing from his initial premise, concludes that they must be permanent. If they are not, he thinks this would cast doubt on his initial premise.

Even assuming the changes to be permanent, do they persist for the reasons Janov offers, or for other reasons that a social influence perspective might suggest? For example, to maintain any kind of change in oneself, one needs continuing motivation until the change becomes a habitual part of the self (Wheelis, 1973:101). In addition, high morale helps one persist in the face of obstacles. Can the Primal Therapy framework help maintain motivation and morale? Insofar as it instills hope of success, much about Primal Therapy can do so. The concept of a strong, resilient "natural" self inspires hope. The cognitive framework also provides a sense of mastery, which alleviates anxiety, enabling one to try new behaviors and to remain hopeful. But most important, if one surrounds oneself with others who have experienced the same things, a group of "believers," then one has a new community to reinforce daily and continuously this changed sense of self. Without such a community, I think the changes are far less likely to become habitual; even with it, permanence is not a sure thing. Janov obliquely acknowledges the formation of a "community" by his comments that Post-Primal individuals find it very difficult to relate to their former associates, whom they now think of as too "unreal" for them. As he sees it, "Post-Primal patients cannot put up with unreal behavior, and so they avoid many old friends. They tend to see a good deal of one another, and marriages within the group are common. The friendships are nonpossessive; they are relaxed" (Janov, 1970:167). Janov describes this community without recognizing it for what it is, a collection of persons who can offer support for a changed sense of self.

Feeling Therapy and Other Therapies

Two essential notions guide Feeling Therapists' understanding of what they do: (1) that there is such a thing as "complete" feelings and that one person can help another to reach them; and (2) that there is a way, a lifestyle, to live from them. With these notions they justify an entire therapeutic regime whose sole ostensible purpose is to arrive at complete feelings by any means. They situate this regime within a larger structure, a "therapeutic community." Throughout their first book, *Going Sane*, they compare their approach to other therapies and continually find them lacking, usually because they do not measure up to what Feeling Therapy holds to be the major therapeutic factors. In comparison with other therapists who also deal with feelings in some fashion, they do something very different:

> All of these therapeutic endeavors can yield helpful results, but they are limited in one essential way—*patients do not acquire a sense of what complete feelings are or how to live from them.*
>
> Yet despite these commonalities, we believe there are no other transformative therapeutic systems, although there are very likely some therapists who go beyond the conceptual, structural, and technical limits of a particular orientation to make transformation possible for their patients. . . .
>
> So, when we refer to parts of our therapy which resemble other therapies, remember that a part of a therapy is much less than a part of a puzzle. An incomplete puzzle does no harm, but an incomplete therapy will foster incomplete lives. Our opinion is that none of the major insight and behavior therapies offer more than parts of the whole. The effects of partial abreaction, partial counteraction, and partial proaction will be partial integration. . . .
>
> Real therapy is the transmutation from nonfeeling into feeling. Therapy is not possible in most cases because the therapist has little or no contact with his own insanity. What most therapists know is academic. They lack self-experience. . . .
>
> At lectures and seminars we are often asked questions like, "But what do you do that is different from what every other therapy does?" or "Isn't responding from feeling just what a good friend does?" Our answers to these questions are, "There is no one thing that we do that is different. There isn't a Feeling Therapy technique or process that is totally unique. It is everything we do that is the difference." (Hart, Corriere, and Binder, 1975:386, 387, 402–3, 403)

In spite of what might seem to be insistence on Feeling Therapy as the only worthwhile therapy, the founders claim that their approach is not for everyone and that they favor "therapeutic multiplicity" (385). Their idea of what these other therapies should be, however, seems modeled on what they think Feeling Therapy is, for

> [w]e believe that a desirable model for psychotherapies is the tribal model. Tribes influence one another but each retains its independence and special characteristics. Scientific and medical efforts tend toward eclecticism and generalism, but these tendencies are incompatible with the commitment to a lived-in reality that must be at the center of transformative therapy. (385)

The other therapies that they find to be "incomplete" or not transformative (which is every other therapy they examine) do have some value, however.

They "may still fulfill a valuable helping function. Adjustment therapies have an important place in society because they provide help of various kinds to many people in need of it" (385).

Not only do Feeling Therapists disdain most individuals' ways of living as mere "answers", they assert that neither they themselves nor their claims nor their practices offer and answer:

> Not only do people speak an unintelligible language, they are also foreign to themselves. This is not a problem which they can somehow solve. The answer in Feeling Therapy is that there is no "answer." For when there are no longer answers, people can begin to feel life as it is and not as it should or could be. Young children do not have answers—they feel. (11–12)

What happens once a person discovers integral feelings? This is the crucial next step. Thinking of the discovery of integral feelings as similar to the concept of insight, the question becomes how to incorporate the integral feelings, the insight, into one's life. Feeling Therapists answer "Go sane!" Although "solving problems is an important function for a therapy, it must remain secondary to the task of opening the individual to a sane life" (13). Therapies that fail to do this are thus "incomplete." One goes sane within a therapeutic community. As they say:

> To move a therapy from a partial therapy to a complete therapy requires that partial feelings be tested in a life setting. To be tested means that a person lives from what he feels with others who are willing to test the completeness and truth of his feelings. . . . Many people never want to test their feelings. They believe that their partial feelings are all the truth they can ever have or need to have. A test of feelings does not have right or wrong answers. It is a moment of trial in which the person confronted and the person challenging move toward complete truth.
>
> There can be no test of feelings without the context of community. This is another point of serious difference in philosophy and practice between Feeling Therapy and other therapies. We know that to have more than partial feelings requires the support of a therapeutic community in which the context and consequences of feelings can be lived fully. The feeling community is necessary because when the consequences of partial feelings are felt, there must be a structure available which will support the collapse of an individual's personality. (14–15; emphasis added)

These quotations illustrate Feeling Therapists' beliefs in a complete truth and the positive effects of disintegration of personality. These beliefs separate them from much of psychotherapy.

"Transformation" is the word Feeling Therapists use to describe what happens to one of their patients over time. Supposedly the word does not signify some dramatic change, but refers to a very "basic" kind of change that comes from "inside" rather than "outside" a person.

> A patient in Feeling Therapy actually transforms himself and his life. Transformation is metamorphosis; the person who transforms his life emerges from a cocoon of nonfeeling and partial feeling. We apply the word transformation only when a person shifts from one way of living in the world to another based upon the way he feels inside himself. Transformation is not synonymous with change. People change all the time—by imitating others, because of outside pressures, by pretending, by accident—but none of these changes should be called transformation. They are all outside a person. (17)

"Transformation" seems to refer only to change that is initiated and directed by an individual. This kind of change, however, is major, because most changes in individuals are generated by "outside" influences. The goal of such transformation as they posit it is

> [t]o live from within yourself, to live truthfully and fully. . . . In some ways this goal is more familiar as a religious rather than a therapeutic goal. Psychotherapy has replaced religion and philosophy as the major institution within which people search for personal meanings. But most psychotherapies have not gone far enough in this direction. We know that a therapy must be more than an impersonal theory or technique, and it must also be more than a personal therapy or belief, applied caringly. Psychotherapy must engender the personal and social contacts that are missing in the community. When a therapy does create the possibilities for a person to feel himself and live his own feelings, that therapy becomes transformational. This is the proper goal for a complete psychotherapy. (18)

This quotation also situates the group relative to the mainstream of psychotherapy. In the ongoing debate about what the discipline is and should be, Feeling Therapists unquestioningly accept an answer that deems psychotherapy an art rather than a science. This notion, moreover, is expanded to be consciously "religious," in the sense of imparting meaning to individuals' lives. And the particular meaning Feeling Therapists seek to impart is that of the value of community in constructing personal identity.[9]

Feeling Therapy in Practice

Given the desirability of a complete psychotherapy, how does one apply it to individuals? Two important concepts used to describe the routine practice of Feeling Therapy are the "feeling moment" and the "cycle of feeling." The "feeling moment" is seen as a critical point of choice for a patient, an instant when she or he can decide to move from insanity toward sanity.

> The feeling moment is the beginning of Feeling Therapy. When a person senses that his feeling is incomplete, it is possible to help him move from defending to feeling. Without this sense it would be impossible because defenses would be entirely unconscious. The feeling moment is available to everyone, at least fleetingly. . . . To begin therapy, each person has his incomplete feelings verified in moments of choice. The verification forces him to choose between believing a partial truth or allowing himself to feel what half-truths do to him. In that moment of choice, the patient either feels how he defends, or by choosing to continue the defense, he feels the moment of openness close off to him. (20)

So, the first task of the Feeling Therapist is to move the patient toward a feeling moment, the recognition that his or her feelings are far less than they could be. One then moves toward feeling by choosing to experience one's defenses. The therapists define defenses as substitutes, as images that do not match inner sensations, meanings, or expressions.

> A defense is the opposite of a moment of choice. There is nothing special anyone has to do to defend because defending is going on all the time. To enter a moment of choice a person must experience a match between what he feels on the inside and what he shows on the outside. . . .
>
> A *defense* is a substitute: a substitute meaning, sensation, or expression which takes the place of the original components of a complete feeling. . . . The function of defensive substitutes is to hide and reduce feelings that could not be expressed. At times it is difficult to detect reductions; substitute expressions may look and sound more intense than the real expression they conceal. Substitutes are detectable because the dramatization does not match the sensations and meanings they are supposed to express. The mismatched expression is not felt and expressed, it is imagined and presented. (28, 29)

When an individual repeatedly feels his defenses, he feels how he is now the one keeping himself crazy. This realization affords him the chance to go beyond craziness and move toward change and "sanity." He learns to recognize his defenses by reference to his bodily state, for pain indicates some awareness of a defense in use.

> In every feeling moment there is a felt meaning which generates an impulse toward active expression; gesture is the natural language of the body. Activities are symbolic when they are indirect expressions of an impulse. Any indirect or symbolic activity generates tension because the organism

must establish a holding-in or mediating response while finding acceptable
indirect outlets for the energy of the original impulse. The momentary
holding-in is tension producing. Eventually a child's system learns to hold
in any kind of response. In therapy when this holding-in is felt, the
individual experiences discomfort. It is not painful to feel and express
feelings—complete feelings in themselves are natural; what does hurt and is
unnatural is the holding-in associated with incomplete feelings.

Pain—stomachache, headache, tight neck—can be a good sign because it
means that a person is not symbolizing away his feelings. He is closer to
feeling expression than he would be otherwise. Of course, discomforting
sensations generated by blocked impulses are themselves substitutes, but
they are closer substitutes than are fantasy or acting out. . . . Pain is a signal
that "my expression is being stopped." (30–31)

Thus there is a hierarchy of expression: complete feelings at the top; then
painful sensations, based on their potential for leading to complete feelings;
and finally "fantasy" and "acting out." All but complete feelings are substitutes for the real, or are seen as symbolic ways of expression in comparison
with the direct way of expression of complete feelings. Accordingly, all are
"defenses" against real feeling.

Unlike other theorists discussing defenses, Feeling Therapists are not
interested in exploring their complexity by describing their multiplicity or variety. They go the opposite route and simplify understanding of defenses,
characterizing their activity as deflating conventional wisdom. They offer two
general criticisms of other ways of conceptualizing defenses.

Iconoclasm One: Defenses and types of pathology are simply states of incomplete feeling. . . .
Defenses, even in their overwhelming variety and complexity, are very
simple to understand. All Feeling Therapists and co-therapists ask themselves
"What is this person doing not to feel? What must he do to feel?"

*Iconoclasm Two: Most therapists do not know what integral feelings are and therefore are
unable to identify what nonfeeling is in themselves and their patients.* They can easily point
out defenses and categorize symptoms, but they rarely move the patient
from nonfeeling to feeling. To do this requires identifying and tracking the
feeling through a series of moments, focusing the feeling, and finally aiding
expression of the feeling. And this is possible only when the therapist lives
integral feelings from himself. (34–35)

The notion of "tracking [feelings] through a series of moments" is very
important in understanding therapeutic sessions. What might seem like immense
arrogance on the part of the therapist is conceptualized as this tracking of the elu-
sive feeling, which hides behind a myriad of defenses. Indeed, this is what Feeling Therapists think is repeatedly occurring—the therapist, sanctioned by the pa-

tient's seeking therapy, tries to force him to confront his defenses time and again until the patient "chooses" to move beyond them into the unknown. Both are seen as necessary for a beneficial therapeutic result: the patient must choose to feel his defenses, and he must choose to move to the "unknown," relying only on the therapist's implicit reassurance that there is something better beyond it.

A story from Rob provides an example of a patient's being forced to recognize his defense by a Feeling Therapist. (21–23). On his twelfth day of intensive therapy, his therapist did not come out to the reception area, where Rob was waiting at the appointed time. Finally, Rob recalls, he looked for him in the therapy room:

> He was sitting in the room talking as if he was doing therapy on me already. So I took off my shoes and began bitching about his not coming out and getting me. He said, "You're so nonexistent, it's the same whether you're in the room or not." I thought he must be a complete nut. He couldn't do therapy if I wasn't in the room! (21)

For the three days preceding to this session, Rob had discussed his feelings for his father and his fears of being a homosexual. He thought he would continue talking about these topics. Instead, the therapist talked about a house Rob and some other new patients had tried to rent, unsuccessfully. The landlord said he would not rent to singles. To this, the therapist said, "That was a good idea. You'd probably screw up the house." Therapist and patient begin a dialogue where the therapist points out repeatedly how Rob missed out. The dialogue closes when the therapist comments, "Well, since you can't get anything in your life, I doubt there is anything you can really get in therapy. I'm going to rest." The therapist, according to Rob, went to sleep.

After twenty minutes of silence, the therapist said to Rob, "Early in therapy it was very fearful for me to be who I was"; he then went back to sleep. This remark prompts Rob to talk about his fears of telling the landlord how he felt, as well as his fear "of becoming a person who I didn't know." The therapist interrupted him with the question "How does it feel to come and go, to fluctuate between being you and not you?" before again going to sleep. This question generates the feeling of insight in Rob:

> Everything I had been talking about crystallized in that one moment. I could feel myself going in and out of knowing my feeling. I started to talk louder. I said, "I know what to do. It just seems so hard. I feel like an asshole talking to someone who isn't in the room. It seems crazy." Then he said, "Be crazy." I said, "I want to talk but I'm afraid. I keep letting it all go by. I do want that house. God damn it, I want that house."

I continued yelling and hitting a mat on the wall until I could feel me. I felt complete. The more I felt the more I knew there were other things I wanted to say. I didn't want to be close to "someone." I wanted a woman to love me and to love. I wanted good sex. I was screaming from deep within myself. The words flowed out of me. I didn't think or hesitate. I had been joking about being a queer with the other patients. I was talking in a loud voice saying "that's no joke." I have real feelings about that.

What amazed me was not what I was saying, but that I was feeling bad and giving shit answers, and then I really started to feel what was going on inside me. Later when I thought about it I wondered how my therapist could seemingly be asleep and then pop awake and say the right thing at the right time. Usually he was very active with me—but on this day he let or made me do it myself. When I remember how much he helped me I feel warm feelings inside me. (23; emphasis added)

What most amazes me about this account is Rob's belief that the therapist was not "active" in this session, and that he "let" or "made" Rob do all the work himself. The therapist's seeming indifference "forced" Rob to "feel" his defenses, presumably those of passivity and homosexuality. Of course, one could also say Rob wanted to change the therapist's response from one of indifference to one of approval and support, and that he thus acted in a way to elicit these responses—that is, by acting very forceful and repudiating homosexual desires or fears.

Retrogression

If a patient does not move toward expressing complete feelings, he "retrogresses": "Retrogression is a person's *manifest* insanity in contrast to counteraction which is expressed and felt insanity" (139). This appears to be unconscious insanity not yet recognized by the patient. It seems very similar to the concept of "resistance." Feeling Therapists describe eight ways of retrogressing: enactments; physical distortion; confusion; going crazy; double-think, double-talk; laughing it off; reporting; and shifting a feeling. Anything a Feeling Therapist does not consider expression of real feelings can be classified as one of these eight ways of retrogressing. Here are some brief definitions from *Going Sane* of the meanings they give these terms.

To Hart, Corriere, and Binder, "enactments" are

symbolic acts of generalized sensation to which a generalized meaning has been applied; in short, they are figured out in one's head. (145)

Of "physical distortion" they say:

What a patient's body does can be either retrogressive or transformative. Remember that sensations reside in the body; when the cortical meaning does not match, it will be manifested in incongruous physical expression. Inharmonious physical expressions are retrogressive. . . . When we look at our patients, we look at everything about them—body shape, facial expressions, gestures, vocal responsiveness. . . . We strive to order feeling, and often we apply physical pressures to our patients' bodies. (146–47)

"Confusion" on the part of patients often occurs as a result of "intensification."

Now the patient will slip further away from feelings into games and roles while his feelings are being pressurized into a smaller and smaller area until they either break out randomly and symbolically or are expressed. In his demand for a feeling reality, the therapist is pushing the patient to this crisis—a pressurizing of feeling until there must be expression. The therapist will not accept any of the substitutes. He will not believe in the patient's apparently distressed situation. . . .

What confusion means is that the patient has resorted to defensive substitutes to balance out expression and experience, but he does this by introducing mismatches and time disorders. . . . At this point in retrogression, the therapist will intensify his responses until the therapeutic ordering is unavoidable. (147, 147–48)

"Going crazy" seems to be an intensification of confusion:

Some patients will go completely into their nonsense layer and act "crazy"; this is a defense against feeling. It is certainly not feeling one's craziness. Such patients will babble, make nonsense sounds, gesticulate wildly with their arms and legs. A person may yell out, "The whole world's crazy—so what does it matter if I am?" Others will scream, "I'm gonna kill you," or maybe "I'm gonna kill myself." All their twisted crazy thoughts and actions will spill out, but again it is retrogression so that other feelings can be held in. Patients will say positive crazy thoughts too. "I'm okay now, I have nothing left to feel. My session's over for today." (149)

"Double-think, double-talk"

are all the endless pronouncements, judgments, projections, introjections, announcements, vacillations, and denials. It doesn't matter what label we apply to them because they all have the same effect upon the patient—they move him away from feeling. (142)

"Laughing it off" means exactly that: "Laughing or joking can ward off complete expression of feeling . . ."

"Reporting" involves looking at one's self from the outside:

Few people are ever able to detect in themselves or others that what is being said is not an expression of inner feelings but an outside reporter's view. People who report feelings are adept at communicating a full picture of detail, and they are able to do this because they are so outside the feeling in the experience they are relating. (143)

Finally, "shifting a feeling" is "moving into more symbolic forms of retrogression" (144).

In discussing retrogression, the authors of Going Sane remark on individuals who claim they do not want to be in therapy:

By suggesting that he doesn't really want to be here, a patient denies that he has been waiting six months or more to get into therapy and that all the money and thought put into arriving at the Center were meaningful. What is happening is a complete giving over to the defensive process. The patient allows what he has known all his life to take over—disordering. The patient turns the therapy into some symbolic activity other than feeling what it really is—a place where people can help him. (144)

Luckily for these recalcitrant, retrogressing persons,

[t]herapists do not accept this as real. The patient comes in for therapy and must begin to fight his disordering from the very first day. The beginning of therapy and the beginning of feeling are not simultaneous. To begin therapy is to begin to fight. . . . A patient begins to fight when he begins expressing what is happening inside, and sharing that fight with his therapist as an ally against his craziness.

By countering the patient's defenses and demanding a feeling present, the therapist gives direction. The fight has no meaning unless the therapist, by being an ordered human, can help the patient know when he is being taken over by disordering and when and how he can begin to fight for himself. If the patient chooses not to respond to the therapist, he removes himself one step further from the present. In doing this, he gives in to insanity and nonsense; he has less expression and less feeling. This is quite different than when the patient fights for his feeling—then he feels the strength and magnitude of his own disordering process. (144–45)

Completing Feelings

The "cycle of feeling" is a four-step process involving what Feeling Therapists call counteraction, abreaction, proaction, and integration. Patients must go through it in order to complete feelings. The entry to each "process" is a "definite feeling moment during which the patient must choose to go further with his feelings or leave himself incomplete" (39). "Counteraction" is the "process of feeling and expressing the defenses which keep a feeling incomplete" (40). "Abreaction is feeling the source of defenses and expressing past feelings which were blocked. . . . In abreaction the patient looks, acts, and sounds like a child" (40). "Proaction" is the "first movement back toward feeling in the present. The patient cannot function in the world if he stays in the regressed position of the child. He must give adult expression to feelings which were blocked off to him in the past" (41). The last step, "integration," is "living from the new level of feeling awareness and expressiveness which is now available after completing a feeling. . . . If the patient does not support his new openness and respond from it he will not transform his life" (41).

The "cycle of feeling" is seen as the means to personal transformation. In the process, the individual moves from "outside" to "inside" himself, for

> [i]ncomplete or disordered feelings contain defensive substitutes; a person does not choose these substitutes—they come from outside himself. When a person moves inside himself he can then express his internal reality, free of disordering externals. (41)

What does this feel like? As one patient describes it,

> When I'm outside myself just "feeling bad" I don't know anything—I just keep trying to find answers, "What to do?" or "What's wrong?" Once I feel myself again the answers and questions disappear. I'm just feeling me, moment-by-moment. (43)

In each session, the Feeling Therapist tries to get his patient to complete feelings. "Simple" feelings can be distinguished from the completion of a feeling cycle by the presence of *conscious* regression (in the latter) and an increased feeling level stemming from the release that occurs in regression. When the patient is fully expressing all his feelings, he is able to move from one feeling level to another, higher level.

In order for patients to accomplish this, they must "consciously regress." This is the place of Primal-like catharsis in Feeling Therapy. The individual "regresses" and remembers an event or events from the past that now seems to be the origin of his present defense. Feeling Therapists then "help" patients to "connect" this past feeling to present-life feeling, usually by an act that symbolizes (although they do not see it as "symbolic") the completion of the past feeling. An example of therapy with an "experienced" Feeling patient illustrates the process. The patient, Dominic Cirincione, is one of the founding therapists, as is the therapist (of this session), Lee Woldenberg.

Dominic was concerned because he felt his defenses were impeding his handling of a patient. Dominic was afraid to beat the patient as hard as the person needed to be hit (to generate the needed hostile response from the "deadened" patient); he feared the individual could and would strike back so hard that he, Dominic, would be physically hurt. Lee probed what he saw as Dominic's real feeling—the fear of following through on contact with people.

Lee made Dominic realize his defense and "feel" it by having him repeatedly swing his arm at a wall, stopping just short of hitting it. This continued until Dominic whimpered in pain, saying how much his arm hurt. Dominic then "realizes" that he "holds himself back" repeatedly in relationships with people, and that this is extremely painful to him.

After this realization, Lee has Dominic "regress" to a past situation where he hesitated to show his affection for others, especially through touch. The situation that Dominic chooses is the time he spent as a seminarian in a Jesuit seminary, where all physical contact between seminarians was prohibited. Dominic now feels how painful this situation was for him.

Beyond the catharsis is "proaction." In the present, Dominic must come out of the regression and complete his previously blocked desire to follow through on affectionate feelings: here, to touch and hold Lee. From this touch, Dominic realizes how nice it is to complete affectionate feelings.

"Integration," or living from the "new level of feeling awareness and expressiveness," seems very similar to the process of integrating insight into one's life. That is, one lives informed by a different sense of oneself and is freed to be able to make new choices.

The "cycle of feeling" is a mechanism of continued change for individuals. As persons complete each cycle of feeling, they are "spiraling upward," reaching higher and higher levels of feeling. As a result, the therapists hypothesize that experienced patients are living in a social world completely different from that of inexperienced patients.

The Feeling Therapist

Patients are supposedly prevented from figuring out what "right" behavior is and engaging in it to show the therapist it doesn't work by the unpredictability of Feeling Therapists. As an example of what this looks like in practice, the authors mention one evening's Feeling Group. Here,

> one patient was told to listen to the air conditioner; another walked through
> the rooms saying, "I'm twenty-six years old and I don't deserve anything";
> another was ignored by the therapists; another was held close and taught
> how to hug his friend; another was told to go home; another was helped to
> feel the weakness in his legs, "I can't stand up for myself"; another was

helped to feel the disorder of never having a mother who let her be a girl, "I just want to be a girl. I want all the things girls have"; another felt the pain of never playing; another felt the hurt of not being able to say a feeling from inside herself, of being trapped in roles that were no longer satisfying. There were sixteen patients and fifteen therapists at that group—thirty-one different lives in movement. That evening will never be repeated. The feelings each person felt or did not feel will never come again. What the therapists did and what the patients felt will never occur again. (Hart, Corriere, and Binder, 1975:417)

The metaphor of the therapist as "lie detector" permeates their theory and practice. The authors remark at one point that the

Feeling Therapist performs his craft from an internal position of "know-ingness" that may sometimes seem awesome or even arrogant. Patients sometimes say "How can you know?" or "You weren't there, how can you say what's true and what isn't?" The therapist's knowingness derives from his depth of feeling. He is a multi-faceted lie detector who can feel the dissonance of his patient's mismatched words and the discord of his actions. (128)

Later on they say:

Our therapists do have one very special capability: they can feel completely and discriminate mixed-up feelings from ordered feelings. They are also very carefully trained; it takes about three years to be fully trained as a Feeling Therapist. (461)

Stan, the Passive Virgin

I will illustrate the ability of Feeling Therapists to discriminate between ordered and disordered feelings with a brief case history. Stan, a new patient going through his three weeks of "intensive" therapy, is described as "a 29 year old virgin and passive" (151–55). At the Friday session of his first week in therapy, his therapist, Riggs Corriere, told him to have sex over the weekend. The transcript from which I quote records the first session of the second week of therapy. Stan told Riggs that he had not had sex that week-end, but that he had spent twenty hours taking care of a female patient be-cause she was going crazy. In response, the "therapist busted through this story line and demanded the truth" (151). It appears that Stan, attempting to carry out his weekend assignment, called another patient, Molly, with the intent of having sex with her. Molly apparently said she did not want to see him. Stan tried unsuccessfully to pick up a waitress, went to a massage parlor where he got "ripped off" (no sex), then returned to the hotel to see Molly.

When I told her I wanted to stay with her she started freaking out—quivering and screaming. She told me she didn't want to fuck because she was raped as a child. I told her I wouldn't do anything like that. I just wanted to be with her. (51)

Therapist and patient then start a dialogue:

T: You just wanted to be with her! You're lying. You lied to her and now you're lying in here.

P: I wanted to be alone with her!

T: More stories. Still no truth.

P: Okay. Maybe I did want to fuck but I was afraid of being rejected.

We are told that the dialogue went on for fifteen minutes, and that the patient continued to "move away from his feelings." The therapist "confronts Stan's reasonable case with blunt responses and then offers Stan chances to say his feelings" in the following way:

T: You're full of crap. You still aren't willing to talk for yourself.

P: Okay.

T: Okay is more crap. It's okay to be a dead virgin? What could you have said?

P: Molly, I'm lying. I really want to fuck with you. I don't want to take care of you. I really want to fuck. Yeah, that's what I really want. I want to suck you, touch you, put it to you.

T: Put it to you? It? What is "it"?

P: My cock, I guess.

T: You guess? Well is it your cock? or is it your big toe?

P: You're mocking me. I—

T: You're mocking you. Is your cock an "it"?

P: No . . . I don't know. I didn't want to screw. I told her it was my assignment. I told her I had to do it for my therapy.

T: You liar. You still aren't willing to say it like it is for you. You complained for a week that you wanted to fuck and she wanted to fuck. Now you squirm out of saying something honest by blaming it on the therapy.

P: I feel tired. I feel dead. I can't move my arms and legs.

The authors of Going Sane say of Stan's behavior that as he "begins to say his feelings he begins to collapse. He tries to go into the past to avoid feeling his collapse in the present." He acts like a "robot," his body is listless, his voice flat. A fearful Stan pleads with his therapist:

P: What's going on here? Riggs, tell me why you're having me do this. What are you trying to do to me? Really, I mean it. Please tell me and then I'll do what's right.

T: You're not willing to say how you feel. You want some intellectual harmony. Either you face your feelings with those girls or you'll stay a zero.

P: I'm afraid.

Of Stan's fear, the authors comment: "The patient is genuinely afraid, but he is still in retrogression. He hasn't yet felt the crisis that his life isn't his own and is run solely by defenses" (153). Riggs, the therapist, then has Stan make sounds to match his feelings when he is with girls. Stan reluctantly makes sounds, until he "begins to feel the crux of his retrogression, which is to be afraid to start and afraid to stop. He collapses whenever his own feelings come up." The final segment of the transcript shows Stan's realization of his fear with women:

P: I was afraid with them. I was afraid to ask to fuck because my cock always softens. I never can fuck. I never could. (crying)

T: Face those girls and tell them. (softly)

P: I'm afraid my dick will get soft, Molly. [His voice is roaring from his body. He is moving, kicking, and thrashing.] I *do* want to fuck. I *want* to fuck. I'm afraid that my dick won't work. I *do* want to fuck.

The authors describe what Stan and Riggs have done in this session, which lasted two hours. They say that

Stan now has a feeling present. He has chosen to show all his feelings. His therapy session actually took over two hours to move from retrogression into the feeling present. . . . [In] Outside therapy with other insane people, Stan got by; in therapy, Stan allowed himself to be affected. (154)

Of the therapist's behavior with Stan, they say:

Stan's therapist continued to respond firmly. He could see that his patient had little more life in him than a corpse, but beneath that passive exterior was a frightened, hurt person who wanted more for himself. He was not hard on Stan, as some readers may conclude; he was hard, even unrelenting, with Stan's *insanity*. We supplement therapy sessions by assigning activities which counter a patient's placid insanity. We make him respond to a more challenging level of feeling expression both within a session and outside the therapy.

Throughout retrogression, a Feeling Therapist pushes the patient toward a point—a moment in which the choice to feel can be made. That moment leads to a beginning of ordering; it is the accomplishment of complete feeling expression over defendedness. Without moments of choice, therapy is ritual. For us, choice means an individual has complete responsibility for himself. A patient must know that he wants therapy for himself and that he must fight for *himself*, not for us. Without that realization, a patient always has escape routes to flee from his feelings. We do not want this to happen because we invest our lives with each patient. And there is no amount of money that can buy our commitment. Feeling Therapy takes place when two people are fully involved—the therapist and the patient. (155)

In sum, Stan was forced to "choose" to feel. He "recognized" his defenses, and he chose to fight them. Riggs was unrelenting in his attack on Stan's "insanity," and he eventually succeeded in making him "feel."

Faked Performances

Feeling Therapists can also discern when people are performing to impress rather than expressing real feelings. Two examples of faking, called "enactments" by Feeling Therapists, are those of Barry and Pat (ibid:145–46). As Barry is speaking of his fear of the ocean and his inability to swim, he begins to look like he's swimming, moving his arms and legs and gurgling. When the therapist asks what is going on, Barry replies that he was feeling himself as a sperm. "Sperms can't talk English," the therapist responds, "[s]o quit it." .
Another therapist says of Pat:

I was working with Pat in group and she was talking about how her father constantly browbeat her when she was about ten or twelve. Her feeling level was torporous, and after spending about fifteen minutes I told her to simply make sounds for how she felt and that I would come back. While working with another patient a few minutes later I heard Pat screaming "No . . . no . . . no . . . " and uttering garbled sounds. I went back into the room and saw her with her arms spread wide, on the tips of her toes with her back against the wall as if inching up it. Apparently she sensed me standing close by and opened her eyes. "What is it?" I asked. "My father," she answered. "I feel him driving me up the wall with his constant browbeating."

Of these incidents, the authors of *Going Sane* say that "the therapists didn't simply stop their patients from enacting a feeling—they had to go beyond symbolic portrayals of generalized sensations and meanings and help their patients recognize real feeling."

An Alternative Perspective

In strong contrast to Janov's Primal therapy, Feeling Therapists emphasize therapeutic community as being central to their theorizing and practice. However, even though they make "therapeutic community" the keystone of their theory and practice, Feeling Therapists never mention or realize the effect of group properties of influence on members' behavior. Yet, part of their reasoning in support of the importance of therapeutic community seems to reflect their recognition that groups influence the behavior of individuals and to express their desire for this outcome. Such a position has significant implications for Feeling Therapists' theorizing and practice. In contrast to their overly psychological and individualistic point of view, my critique will emphasize these unnoticed characteristics of the group as being essential to individual changes that occurred.

It is crucial in understanding Feeling Therapy's theoretical framework to appreciate sufficiently how it was derived from the practice of its founders. The founding therapists derived what they considered a plausible explanation of what they had observed happening with their patients. Their understanding of what was happening intra-psychically and inter-personally was substantially influenced by their previous experience with "alternative" therapies like Bioenergetics and Primal Scream. This experience shaped their theorizing in two important ways: first, it provided the basic "hydraulic" model of personality; second, it allowed them to see the limitations of a therapy. With these two understandings, they constructed a therapeutic program and only then imposed upon it an elaborately constructed theoretical structure.

Intentionally or not, they retained many elements of the Primal Scream approach. First, they kept the notion of a bifurcated self—the "real," always knowing part, and the "unreal," completely unknowing part. As in Primal Scream, the words "direct" and "symbolic" characterize these two aspects of self. They added their own terms, "insane" and "sane," to describe the self before and after therapy. The "insane" self is a mix of real and unreal, mostly unreal; the "sane" self is less of a mix and more of a pure essence. Second, the child's point of view—that of an imposed-upon victim, for the most part "determined" by parents—predominates here. Third, catharsis is accorded great value in practice; the founding therapists even acknowledge their debt to Janov for teaching them the importance of this process. Fourth, a hydraulic model of intra-psychic processes seems most important in their theorizing about personality. Accordingly, they retained the concept of tension and its physiological indicators as their chosen outcome measure in testing their therapy's efficacy. This was particularly true over their first several years. Fifth, they use a similar metaphor for the notion of "feelings"—feelings are like a locked cupboard of spices.[10] They are individually bounded and always retain their own identity. One simply needs to figure out how to unlock the cupboard door; once open, true feelings await one. Like spices not used for a while, unused feelings are not as potent as they are when "fresh." Unlike spices, one can potentiate "unused" feelings. In both therapies, the door to the cupboard is brutally wrenched open. *Sixth*, Feeling Therapy retained the format of Primal Therapy, wherein a person undergoes three weeks of intensive individual therapy, followed by her being placed in a group for sessions several times weekly. (This group therapy was supposed to continue for several months to a year.) *Seventh*, and finally, neither therapy acknowledged any aspect of influence or persuasion as inherent in its practice. Although the rhetorical strategies differ, both therapies stress that the individual is a potent, autonomous actor.

I think that the founders of Feeling Therapy added three elements to this array. The first was their replacement for the notion of "cure." In theory, they conceived of no endpoint to therapy: one could never reach a "growth" limit. So, the idea of limitless change supersedes that of a delimited cure. The second added element follows from the first and translates the notion of unlimited growth into practice. The founders decided to establish a "therapeutic community" to sustain the changes made in patients and to keep limitless change moving. I hypothesize that they added a third element—an intensification of aggressive attack on individual defenses—because of their experience with Janov's therapy. There they realized that people faked or performed to appear to be making progress, and that such changes as were displayed did not necessarily indicate "deeper" changes. In other words, these changes were not necessarily long-term or even consistently shown. I term this insight their realization of the limits of a therapy. Their gradual recognition of the limits to Primal Therapy, however, did not suggest to them that all therapies may necessarily be limited in what they can, and should, accomplish.

The Feeling Therapists' theoretical rationale, and especially their therapeutic practice, closely resemble the process of identity change described by Lifton (1961) and Schein (with Schneier and Barker, 1961). Lifton studied Chinese Communist "thought reform" of Westerners in prison and of Chinese in schools. Schein looked at what he termed "coercive persuasion" of Western prisoners of war in Korea. These theorists examine an extreme change situation, where change is forced in a completely controlled environment. Their investigation of such situations offers some idea of the potential to produce extreme identity change, as well as of the limits to change that exist even in a totally supervised environment.

In the prisons, where individuals did not seek change, a key problem lay in motivating persons to change in the way that those controlling the environment desired. Lifton's and Schein's analyses thus deal with how unwilling people can be motivated to take an active part in a coerced process of change. A process of personality breakdown motivated by fear for one's life proved effective. Once the personality had been broken down, behavior, thought, and feeling could be shaped as desired. This shaping culminated in a third process, the solidification of these changes. Schein refers to these three stages as "unfreezing", generating the change, and "refreezing." Lifton's similar depiction of the change sequence can be fit into this three-stage process. In addition, Lifton delineates a set of eight psychological themes to distinguish an "ideologically totalist" environment from other persuasive environments.[11] For both analysts, the role of the group in generating and maintaining change is paramount. The group constantly monitored one's process of change through unceasing surveillance. It also presented itself as being in unanimous agreement on all aspects of life.

Feeling Therapy as Thought Reform

The authors' copious use of transcripts from therapeutic sessions in *Going Sane* allows the construction of this alternative analysis. I will discuss their therapeutic practice by reference to Schein's three-step model of change: an assault on the individual (unfreezing), shaping desired behavior, thought, and feeling in patients and therapists (the generation of change), and arranging of the environment to stabilize such changes (refreezing).

The first two processes, the assault on identity and inducing desired changes, begin in the initial period of therapy. (I will discuss both in more detail in Chapter Four, "The Intensive.") All the steps the therapist takes work to generate an extreme crisis of identity in the patient. A supremely confident therapist immediately begins the attack on the individual's "defenses." Everything that happens is done in the name of "helping" the patient. The effect of such aggressive attack sounds very similar to the confused state reported by Lifton and Schein. Indeed, Feeling Therapists incorporate the notion of a necessary period of confusion and "craziness" as a normal part of "going sane" into their theoretical rationale. Time and again in the transcripts, patients report feeling confused, feeling crazy, feeling completely out of it. Feeling Therapists normalize this response by terming it a period of "open-endedness" of feeling, similar to early childhood. They believe it is a necessary part of going sane, and accepting it without question is seen as accepting the challenge of growth.

An important rhetoric justifying the immense arrogance of therapists toward patients is that it is necessary and desirable for them to be extremely unpredictable to prevent patients from putting on an act, from conning their therapists or themselves. Moreover, unpredictibility is seen as an appropriate modification of the therapist's behavior to fit each individual at any moment in his level of feeling. The only person who knows *where* the patient is at any moment in his feeling level is a Feeling Therapist. Unquestionably, this keeps patients off guard, unsure of what to expect. Sessions, for example, can take any shape or form, depending solely upon the therapist's assessment of what is required.

Judging from the transcripts, crises occurred regularly. Patients seemed to resolve them by deciding that they were "living from real feelings," or "going sane." That is, patients adopted and voiced the rhetorics used by therapists to describe what was happening to them as patients. (The second step of Schein's model, the generation of change, was going smoothly.) This resolution seemed to produce at least a temporary state of euphoria, which I illustrated earlier in the example of Rob, "feeling his me." Once patients had adopted the "correct" demeanor and vocabulary, they entered the co-constituted social reality of being "feeling," "sane" people.

Once the assault on identity had separated the patient from past points of anchorage, the third step in Schein's model, solidification of changes, furnished new points to which the individual could anchor his changed identity: therapists and other patients bound together in a "therapeutic community." (In Chapter Five, "Careers as Feeling People," I analyze this stage of the process in depth.) For Feeling Therapists to incorporate this notion into their theoretical structure and practice gives inadvertent recognition to the difficulty most persons have in achieving major personal change. No amount of simple "understanding" in the form of "insight" or the reflection back to patients of their feelings could produce the fundamental changes Feeling Therapists considered appropriate and desirable. In the short term, individuals were not very successful at changing themselves so as to solve their self-identified problems. In fact, many seem not to have recognized their insanity. Yet they responded to Feeling Therapists' arrogant tactics, and they appeared to make dramatic changes. Recognizing that a community could better sustain changes—without recognizing that this could mean constant surveillance and punishment for deviants—they set up their community, theorizing that it would be in everyone's best interests.

The essential difference between this change situation and the prison settings of thought reform and coercive persuasion described by Lifton and Schein is that individuals voluntarily sought help from the Center for Feeling Therapy. This fact, of the individual patient coming to the Feeling therapist, was never forgotten, and it was woven into several rhetorics that emphasized patients' voluntary participation and acceptance of all that occurred therapeutically. Although these rhetorics appeared to stress individual autonomy, something very different is not far from the surface. Every objection to therapists' behavior seems to have been met by one response: You decided to come here, You sought help. In other words, because of that initial decision no objection to any part of Feeling Therapy can be valid. Choosing to enter becomes equivalent to giving full and informed consent to all that followed. Every point of the therapeutic process is depicted as being a moment of *individual choice and responsibility;* the options are portrayed as choosing to move ahead or choosing to remain mired in purely "defensive" behavior.

What I see as most problematic about Feeling Therapy's theoretical structure is that it invalidates any conception of harm because of the misuse, intentional or unintentional, of therapeutic authority. There is no recognition that a therapeutic relationship involves the use of authority, and that authority is always subject to misuse. Everything that happens at the Center is justified theoretically in the name of helping patients. Only abstract entities "harm" anyone: person's defenses prevent them from living fulfilling lives. All attacking behavior, of therapists and co-therapists, is legitimated because it is an attack on behavior, insanity, and defenses—not on people. The therapists do not recognize that people have a hard time recognizing the difference between "behaviors" and "self." "Authority" and "power" as normally used have no name in the Center's theoretical and therapeutic structure. Thus, authority relations constituting a social system can not be subject to scrutiny and rearrangement by the group as a whole, contrary to their claimed democratic ethos.

Reinterpretation of Feeling Therapy Practice

Here, I will briefly examine some of the examples of practice that I mentioned earlier. I argue that discovering so-called true feelings can be analogized to the process of extracting a "confession" from prisoners of war. In both cases, individuals have to produce something that conforms to environmental demands while also reflecting their own beliefs. In this process, individuals have to be "deep" actors, that is, they must present performances that convince themselves as well.[12]

Consider the example of the session with an "experienced" patient, that of Dominic and Lee. As described from the transcript, this session supposedly is an example of how the therapists continued receiving therapy to help them in better treating patients. Here, the same process appears as occurred with patients. What seemed to be a true feeling, Dominic's fear of being hit back by a patient, was accorded secondary status and was termed "defensive." What was deemed the "real" feeling was Dominic's fear of following through on contact with people. The entire session was dedicated to getting out this real feeling and to working with it. One can look at this session as revealing how the therapists bolstered their belief in Feeling Therapy when their conviction about the right thing to do flagged. Here, it was a question of Dominic beating another human being as hard as he could to arouse a response from this "dead" patient. Outside the world of Feeling Therapy, the response of reluctance to hit another person might be deemed the "right" feeling, given the therapist's role.

Both Lee and Dominic completely agree that hitting a patient as hard as one can is the correct response. Neither one suggests changing Dominic's therapeutic activity to get the desired reaction from the patient. This example hints at the difficulties involved in eliciting behavior. Neither Dominic nor Lee stops to consider that the "dead" behavior Dominic sees might be a protective response to his present activity. Instead, they think of it as only indicating the essential problem with this patient, a generalized "deadness." In this way they adopt an extreme form of transference. In their view, patients express themselves in therapy in ways indicative of their problems, not ever in response to therapist behavior. No relationship between therapist and patient exists. Patient behavior is only a projection of the patient's feelings and attitudes about others, including parents.

I argue that this conception of therapist's and patient's behavior acts to confuse and confound the patient. Nothing she or he says, does, or thinks will be deemed "right" unless it directly coincides with what the therapist deems right. However, the same behavior can be deemed "right" by one therapist and "wrong" by another.

Consider now the example of Stan, the twenty-nine-year-old passive virgin. The therapists' interpretation of this session accords heroic stature to Riggs for unceasingly demanding Stan's acceptance of his real problem. Riggs will never settle for less than the "truth," so much does he care for Stan's mental health. Riggs's unceasingly ruthless behavior is rewarded by an end many would accept as valuable, the recognition of insight: Stan "recognizes" his defenses, "chooses" to "fight" them, and "feels" something he has not felt before.

My interpretation, however, is that Stan has no way out of this therapy session unless he divines what it is that Riggs thinks is correct behavior indicating awareness of his problem. He arrives at this by trial and error during the session, his effort culminating in a performance that wins Riggs's approval so that the session can end. This performance expresses two "insights": that Stan wants to fuck, and that his fear that "my dick won't work" has kept him from achieving his desire. Presumably, when Stan attempts to incorporate these insights into future behavior, he will attempt in a more wholehearted way to fuck someone.

These so-called insights, however, are achieved only by humiliation and psychological coercion by the therapist. I have no confidence that the "insight" and "feeling" Stan experiences at the end are "authentic." This performance forces Stan to give up any other interpretation he might have of why he is a virgin at age twenty-nine. Also, the therapist completely accepted that to be a virgin at that age reflects a problem. There is *no* good reason to be a virgin at twenty-nine.

Feeling Therapists thus made the claim that what Feeling Therapy offered was an experience unlike anything to be found in other therapies. Anyone may benefit from Feeling Therapy, for everyone is "insane." Ultimately, the ground for their claim rests on Feeling Therapists' personal encounter with, and transcendence of, "insanity."

The same criticisms, and the alternative perspective of what occurs in therapy, that I made of Primal Therapy apply to Feeling Therapy. Both therapists and patients are engaged in intense participation in defined roles. Changes that occurred, or appeared to occur, were the product of a state of intense social influence. The changed sense of self created in the therapy was then sustained by the Feeling Therapy community. The sociologist Richard Ofshe would term this change "situationally adaptive belief change," by which he means "attitude change that is *not* stable and is *environmentally dependent*" (1992:213).[13]

As I have pointed out, not many attempts of patients to feel are accorded the status of "real" feeling. Therapists call certain attempts "enactments," signifying unauthentic performances. From an examination of the Feeling Therapists' literature, little separates these performances from ones they term authentic. I argue that the examples given earlier—of Rob, yelling and hitting the mat until he "could feel me," and of Stan, yelling "I *do* want to fuck, I *want* to fuck, I'm afraid that my dick won't work"—are no more "authentic," no more expressive of "true" feeling than those of Barry feeling himself a sperm or Pat feeling herself browbeaten. What they do illustrate, however, is that the *therapist* is accorded the ability to call some expressions of feeling true, valid, or real, and others false, invalid, or unreal. The *therapist* judges reality. The patient yields to this judgment or is said to be "retrogressing."

Four
The Intensive

Two things most consistently drew people to the Center for Feeling Therapy: Arthur Janov's *Primal Scream* and some form of personal contact with the Center. Having read *The Primal Scream*, many of the men and women I interviewed had become interested enough to contact Janov's institute. For a variety of reasons, however, they wound up at the Center for Feeling Therapy, not the Primal Institute. Several mentioned that they were too young, or that Janov was accepting only psychology professionals; several others said they were referred to the Center by the Primal Institute. One person noticed an ad in the *Village Voice* advertising a talk on Primal versus Feeling Therapy. Since the day for the talk was past, she contacted the Center and received a brochure that claimed Feeling Therapy was better than Primal Therapy. The Center's first book, *Going Sane*, published in 1975, itself brought in two individuals.

Personal acquaintance with a member of the Center attracted the bulk of those I interviewed.[1] Relatives, lovers, and friends who had some experience with Feeling Therapy all encouraged individuals to look into the Center. One person who had left the Center re-entered when Feeling Therapists encouraged his wife to come for what they claimed would be a specially designed (for her) one-month program—they spent the last three years of the Center's existence there together.[2] As this example indicates, the Center often sought out likely prospects, mostly by phone calls.

As the Center grew and became institutionalized, it devised a series of programs designed, according to many of those I interviewed, to "funnel" persons into the Center. These programs were intended to stimulate prospects toward increasing levels of involvement, leading to an interest in and a desire for Intensive therapy; undergoing this therapy led to becoming a member of the therapeutic community. The case of one of my interviewees illustrates this process of increasing involvement that culminated in becoming a Center member. He heard of the Center through a friend, and he read *Going Sane*. He first participated in the "Associates Program," in which he wrote two letters each month and received two letters and a phone call a month from someone

63

at the Center. He found this too limiting, and he then entered the Clinic for Functional Counseling and Psychotherapy. After a short period at the Clinic he decided to join the Center, paying $4,500 for his Intensive. He was at the Center for one year before it collapsed in November 1980.

Preparation for the Intensive

After a person established contact with the Center, and before she or he arrived for the first day of the Intensive, many things occurred. The application process required writing an autobiography; this necessarily revealed much of oneself, and marked the beginning of the Center's "cult of confession." The persons I interviewed recalled answering a series of questions in constructing these autobiographies. Some of the issues included were attitudes about homosexuality, the nature of the problems causing one to seek psychotherapy, relations with parents and siblings, and relations with lovers, spouses, and children. Several people told me that they were encouraged to write their autobiographies in the worst possible light, overemphasizing what they considered problems. Several more commented that writing their autobiographies was a wrenching experience, which forced them to give an accurate picture of what they considered very painful facets of their lives and of their conception of themselves.

Prepayment was required. In 1971, the three-week Intensive and a month of twice-weekly group therapy cost $2,500. By 1980, the fee was $4,500.

Not all of my interviewees could easily pay the fee, and they resorted to a variety of endeavors to save the needed amount. One worked for two years, setting aside much of what he made to pay the fee. Another, who entered the Center at the incessant urging of her boyfriend, who had been involved there for six years, had no money, having already borrowed from her sister for outpatient therapy at the Center. Her boyfriend took out a loan for $5,000 to pay for her Intensive; when I interviewed them, four years after the demise of the Center, they had only paid off the loan the year before.

A third interviewee asked her father for a loan to pay the fee. He refused, and she decided she could best save the money by teaching. In order to teach, she needed a teaching credential, which she acquired in record time. The week after she got her credential she accepted a teaching job in northern California, moving there for one year and saving $500 a month. She then went to Los Angeles and entered the Center.

Most of the people I interviewed thought that they would be in Feeling Therapy for six to nine months. They based this expectation on their knowledge of Primal Therapy; indeed, many of them mentioned that its claim of a cure in six to nine months is precisely what attracted them. As one of the women I interviewed put it, she thought that it sounded like an efficient and economical way to help herself, rather than spending years in therapy, as in psychoanalysis.

Accordingly, most of the people arranged to spend some time in the Los Angeles area, with their therapy at the Center being foremost in their lives for this period. Others, already living in or near the city, set aside time for the initial three-week Intensive, not necessarily intending to leave jobs or school.

Arriving for their Intensive, they first moved into housing suggested by the Center (in the early years, hotels nearby). As the Center grew, people stayed in buildings owned or rented by the Center. The requirements for the twenty-four hours immediately preceding the first day of therapy sound identical to those of Primal Therapy. People had to be alone and not engage in any of their usual habits, like drinking, smoking, and watching television.

The next morning, the group of people scheduled for the Intensive arrived at the Center. The therapy was so emotionally draining for the therapist, it was claimed, that each therapist could only handle one patient during this three-week period (after which she or he took a vacation week). Interviewees reported arriving and then waiting as a group for the therapists to come out to pick up the patient. Some persons I interviewed who became involved during the Center's later years mentioned filling out tests and other materials before their initial meeting with their individual therapist.

The Intensive

Each therapist had his or her own room at the Center building for doing therapy. These rooms had padded walls and contained beds or mattresses. Individual therapy occupied the mornings and was structured by the therapist entirely as she or he chose. Afternoons and evenings were occupied by "assignments," done individually or in groups, again depending entirely upon the therapists' decisions. Group sessions also began in the Intensive. Many of my interviewees reported learning here that all of the therapists seemed to know all about one, not just one's own therapist. One man I interviewed gives some idea of how therapists came by such information.[3] "I was," he recalls,

> a snitch. My therapist would say, you can help your fellow patients by telling us what's going on. In the groups, there became pacts not to talk. I became aware of that and I started snitching on the groups [during Intensive], then they'd have to admit to it to the therapists and their behavior would somehow be curtailed. [What kind of things did you pick up on?] Whether they did their assignments or not. What they thought of their therapists. All nine people in

the group had the assignment to be isolated. I did that assignment well. Also by not bringing it up I didn't bring wrath on myself. I was saving my ass by having the therapists focus on them. This wasn't a thinking thing, to snitch. I had the idea that this would help them and me.

In these group sessions, any therapist could respond to any patient for any reason.

On the first day of the Intensive, many persons found their expectations that they would receive Primal Therapy, or a facsimile, rudely smashed. What they experienced was a very confrontative and disorienting therapy session. One of my interviewees reported being told to stand with his back against the wall and shout everything he said to his therapist. This was because he was soft-spoken.

Many people reported that they had little knowledge of what occurred in others' Intensive sessions. They did, however, observe the disarray of those leaving sessions. They assumed that most sessions were individualized, and that what happened there in some way related to what persons had defined as their problems. Just how it related was never made clear, for the most part. Everyone I spoke to said that therapists never explained what they were doing or why they were doing it. Many people inferred that it, the therapists' behavior, related to characteristics of them, the patients.

The Intensive: Five Vignettes

Martin

Martin entered Feeling Therapy because of a friendship with one of the founders, whom he had met at the Primal Institute. Martin had spent four years in Primal Therapy, just before entering the Center. He had a master's degree in counseling and an interest in drama. When he made the decision to go to the Center for Feeling Therapy, he did so trusting his friend's word that the Center was "light years ahead of the Primal Institute." He was also feeling at loose ends because he had given up being a therapist, partly at the suggestion of those at the Primal Institute that he do physical instead of intellectual work.

Martin was assigned to the therapist he had hoped for, one of the founders, a man he had known at the Primal Institute. His first impression of the Center was shaped by seeing his therapist throw a shoe at a man running down the hall. Soon after, he had his first session. Martin recalls,

Somewhere during the course of that session, he pulled me to my feet, bouncing me off the wall. There was something he was trying to tell me about talking. What he would say is, "You're still not talking." I would deliver a sentence, I would say anything I could. "You're still not talking. You're not talking." I wasn't sure what "not talking" was or wasn't. But he seemed to have a very clear picture of what it was he was after. He would get physically rough with me. At one point I remember he was doing this to me. Had me on the couch and was slapping me on the face and busted a blood vessel there and [gave me] a black eye. I also remember him sitting behind me.

Yet, during this same session, his therapist broke into tears listening to Martin talk, and Martin interpreted this in a positive way.

I said something about him [another founder] being my friend, and maybe I even said something about when we went to camp together, and he broke into tears. So he was listening to me as a therapist and crying. I did not, I didn't know what the hell the Center was about, but it seemed to me that my therapist, I certainly respected his reputation. The fact that he cried in a session, somehow I interpreted it in a positive way, and I didn't understand what it was he was trying to get me to do when he talked to me about talking. I kept trying to come up with stuff.

There were seven patients and seven therapists when Martin was in his Intensive. The atmosphere in the group sessions reminded Martin of what he had experienced when he was a member (for several years, before Primal Therapy) of Synanon.

The feeling, the flavor was very Synanonish. We were told when we were stupid, we were sick, I was dead, someone was schizophrenic, someone else was paranoic, someone was crazy. Labels would be thrown out very strongly.

He recalled when he got a sense of doing something right during these three weeks:

We were always told "respond, respond fully, respond fully." The key word is "respond." Your full response. I said something to one of the patients, and I remember a therapist looking at me and then to one of the other therapists smiling and nodding his head and I thought, "I've just done something right." I wasn't certain what it was I did that was right, but I interpreted his response as [indicating] I had done something right.

At the end of the three-week Intensive, Martin had several responses to the therapy:

Confused like crazy. I'm certain that I was very much afraid. I have never thought of myself as an angry person, but I'm sure I had some anger. If I was a genuinely angry person I probably would have left much earlier.

It was taking the worst thoughts and fears I had about myself and confirming them. You can't say anything to someone with low self-esteem that can make them feel worse, or think worse about himself, than they already do. When the three weeks was over I was totally disoriented and I was totally confused. It was like where the hell am I and where do I go from here? Disoriented is the primary word that I had. I just didn't know what I'd do from that place.

Martin stayed at the Center for Feeling Therapy for the next seven years, until it fell apart in 1980. Although he described himself as the "great resister," he achieved some status, rising to Group 1 when the groups were reorganized and given a hierarchy in 1978. At the end, he was training to be a therapist for the Clinic for Functional Counseling and Psychotherapy.

Larry

Larry became associated with Feeling Therapy in 1974, at the age of twenty-two. He was living in New Jersey and working in a promising entry-level job in his chosen field. Having read and been impressed by *The Primal Scream*, he inquired at Janov's institute and was told he was too young to be accepted. In the *Village Voice*, he read that some Feeling Therapists were coming East to lecture; they said their approach was even better than Primal Therapy. At the lecture, Larry felt they looked and sounded good, and he decided to go to their Intensive therapy. (He had the time and the money.) Larry described his expectations, based on his knowledge of Primal Therapy: "After I'm through, I could charm the birds out of the trees, get anything I want." His main problem centered on being shy and feeling awkward, and wanting to get a girlfriend.

Larry began his Intensive at the end of May, along with nine other patients. As he remembers it:

> My first session with my therapist, he sized me up, asked a few questions, asked if I was a tough guy, because I had a New Jersey accent, I said I wasn't in a gang. He sat on top of a chair, with his feet on the seat, a mattress on the floor, kind of spartan, cork walls. He said he chose me because he identified with me. I liked that. I also heard my therapist was the leader, the top psychologist, . . . and I was pleased to be picked. I don't remember much else.

Most of what happened during his Intensive therapy was confusing, culminating in what he now calls a "nervous breakdown" in one of his later sessions:

> I walked two or three miles home, planning on leaving. I packed my bags, but I decided to give it one more try. I went to my session the next day, and my therapist was all smiles. He said "Hi, Larry, how are you doing?" and I just went into some kind of fit. I started waving my arms and yelling "I don't know what's going on!" That was a relief. I said I don't know what's

going on. My therapist said "That's great, we're going to tell you now. That's the first real feeling you've had so far."

This kind of comment reassured me. God, I didn't know what was going on. My whole body was shaking. You know, help me. Yeah, it reassured me to know that this was kind of planned, that it was part of the normal routine. That's what brought me over the edge. I don't know exactly what happened in some of those other sessions. I was still rebellious. I wouldn't write in my notebook and I told him that and he would just walk out. He'd say well, if you're not going to help yourself, then I'm not going to help you.

Then he beat me up. A problem with a chess game. My therapist said I set up a patient I was to play with. Then I said something like, I knew this was going to happen. I ran over to the corner of the room and I covered myself. You know, you almost expected to get hit. Then he started hitting me. I had bruises on my arms and legs. Then I was going to fight back and he knew I was going to fight back. Then he said put all that anger into pounding on the wall. So he diverted it all. Then the session went on like nothing ever happened. I walked out with my shirt torn. No one ever noticed. He gave reasons for doing it but I don't remember them. You know, I'm really caring for you, I'm doing something extra for you.

Larry was able to play the tape of this beating for me, since he was recording the session as required. He said that for years after this incident, when he replayed the tape

> I'd hear how bad I was and how strong my therapist was, so I wasn't thinking properly. I idolized how strong and powerful my therapist was, and how much I wanted to be that way, and what a wimp I was for getting beat up. That's how I heard the tape for years.

Much of what happened was strange, as this description of his first night at Lie-down group illustrates:

> Each patient was with a co-therapist, the therapists were wandering the room, they told us, me and Joe, another therapist's patient, that much would be strange, would take a while to understand. They told me to draw, one thing I drew was my therapist throwing a woman up against the wall: she thought she was having feeling for him that he was her father. I drew another guy singing Frank Sinatra, "Fly Me to the Moon." No one was listening to him. There was another guy with two pairs of socks on his hands saying, all I can feel are these socks and he was crying. It was bizarre. I was so out of it. I thought I didn't know what was going on.

In the eyes of his therapist, Larry did come close to experiencing a "big" feeling during his Intensive therapy:

> There was a woman in the Intensive Group, who jumped up and called,
> yelled at me: "I want you to be a giant prick," several times. . . . I was being
> very quiet in group, my legs felt shaky, I fainted. They left me lying on the
> floor, stretched me out, and my therapist came over to me and said I was
> having a big feeling come up, but I was too young, too inexperienced to
> deal with it.

This was among several experiences that convinced Larry by the end of the Intensive that "I felt I was fairly close to big feelings, because of the intense experience I'd had."[4]

Mike

Mike began his Intensive in May 1975, aged twenty-two. He went to California from the East Coast at the urging of his brother, who had entered Feeling
Therapy two and a half years earlier. His brother had told him of all the changes
he had experienced, and to Mike the changes seemed to be for the better. In
Mike's eyes, his brother had been a "mess" when he entered therapy, partly the
result of his military service in Vietnam. His brother had read The Primal Scream,
and he had been referred by Janov's institute to the Center for Feeling Therapy.

Six others started the Intensive with Mike. His therapist was the sister
of one of the founders. He describes his first impressions of therapy:

> I was kind of horrified, that was really my first impression, because my
> therapist immediately just started assaulting me, physically even, she wasn't
> real abusive, because she was very small, and she would concentrate on
> pounding on my chest and my arms. She'd leave me black and blue, but it
> was no more than I'd experienced in my past, so that's why it didn't seem
> strange, because my past was worse, okay, you know. It was kind of
> explained, it was like, because, well, one of the things was that I was lying,
> you know, and to be honest, I don't even know what I was lying about, she
> just kept screaming, "You're lying, you're a liar, everything about you is a
> lie. This is a lie, the way you sit is a lie," those kind of things, nonverbal
> lies. I don't know how to classify it, it was mostly for that kind of thing,
> "The look on your face is a lie, the way you're holding your posture is a
> lie," things like that. That happened right away.

Mike himself did not think he was lying.

In this first session, one of the issues was Mike's weight (he described
himself as then being about twenty pounds overweight):

> My first session, I had a diet when I walked out of my first session. She said,
> "You can decide your diet, all I want to see are the results." So I was scared
> shitless, so I couldn't eat anyway, you know, that's one of the reasons I lost
> weight, 'cause I lost my appetite when I hit that therapy, because I had

never, you know, I was, I mean here I was living at home two days before, and then two days later I'm in that.

Mike lost fourteen pounds in the first three weeks of therapy. He attributes part of this weight loss to losing his appetite and part to giving up alcohol when he began his Intensive. His heavy drinking for the past eight years had been a reason he had entered therapy.

One of Mike's daily assignments during the Intensive was to run around the block five times with the others in his group. He liked this assignment. But one time he lied to his therapist about exercising. He describes her reaction:

> So that was one of the times she started pounding on me, and she started screaming, "You're never going to lose weight." And she made me stand there with my hands behind my back, and she made me catch M & M's in my mouth, she was throwing at me, and she was calling me "fatso" as she would throw each one. And I had to eat the whole bag that way, oh yeah, it was pretty depressing, M & M's, *peanut* M & M's, I remember that. Well, it was a long session, three hours, or something like that.

I asked Mike whether his therapist had explained why she was doing this:

> They never explained much, they never really *said*, you know, this is why I'm doing this. They mostly just did it, you know, the truth was, the whole time I was there I really don't remember much in the way of explanation, when it came to one on one. They had these lectures, and they had things like that, where they would explain their *theory*, but a lot of the time when it came for me, anyway, for one on one therapy, it wasn't really explained, it was "you do this, you do this," and a lot of the time, if you did ask why, you'd get *screamed* at. So I just stopped asking.

Mike knew very little about the individual therapy of the six who began their Intensives with him. He saw them in a group session one night a week during the three weeks, and in the evenings he spent time with them doing assignments. Several of the assignments stick out in his memory. For example,

> Eating, without your hands, with your face practically in the plate, or eating without talking, just making sounds, like grunting sounds, or something, and maybe, we'd have to go to movies together, things like that.

Mike's individual assignments mostly concentrated on his losing weight and not drinking.

Although the first week was the worst for Mike (he felt his therapist "lightened up" during the next two weeks), he was relieved when his Intensive ended.

> Very relieved, oh relieved, oh yeah, in fact, one, me and this one guy who I
> was already closer to than the rest of the group, sort of celebrated in *secret*, see
> this is where it already started, celebrated in secret that it was over—we didn't
> want to admit how relieved we were, but we were *relieved*, let me tell you, and
> uh, so we had our own little celebration, we just went out somewhere, and I
> don't remember what the hell we did, I didn't drink, that started later, I started
> that again, but for seven months I didn't, so I was "good" for seven months.

But he had no thought of leaving therapy at that point:

> Yeah, the two months were paid for, right, so after the three weeks of therapy,
> even though I was relieved, I had no thought of leaving, once, ever, once.

I asked whether he had felt as if he had made progress with some of his problems: "Yeah, I did have that feeling at the time, yes."

When Mike says "see this is where it already started" in the transcript
he is referring to his pattern of behaving secretively to the point of lying. Most
of his lies were directed at hiding his frequent heavy drinking, which (except
for the first seven months) he continued for the rest of his time at the Center.

> I was good at lying and hiding, I was excellent at that, I went into the
> Center an amateur liar, and I emerged a professional. Absolutely. I learned
> pretty early on what I could get away with, so I decided to get away with it.

Even though Mike lied a lot, he did not experience a great deal of guilt over
his lying, only occasional guilt feelings. Yet even though he lied, he still believed in the therapists, still thought he had problems and that they were his
fault. He did, however, have doubts and fears about how fast they were going with him, therapeutically.

Unlike Martin, Mike did not ascend in the Center's hierarchy. When
the groups were reorganized, he was placed in Group 5, the "Tombstone
Group." The largest of all the thirteen groups (estimates of membership
ranged from fifty to ninety), this group was specifically for people who had
been at the Center for a time and had made no progress. Mike was placed in
yet another group within this group, one for men only, again because he was
not making progress. He remained in both groups until the Center's breakup
in 1980, which means he was there for five and a half years.

Cristina

Cristina came into the Center for Feeling Therapy in September 1977, intending to be there for one month. Therapists from the Center had come to see
her in the state where she was living with her husband. He had left the Center
after several years of participation. Cristina's husband told me that the therapists

made a special appeal to her in order to get him to return to the Center. He owned a business taking in a million dollars per year and had been generous to the Center during his own participation; presumably, the organization did not want to lose him. The therapists told Cristina they would design a special one-month program for her. Her husband pleaded with Cristina not to go, but she thought she could improve her relationship with him by leaving for California.

Cristina, a social worker with a master's degree, was then thirty. When she entered the Center, she was ten weeks pregnant with their first child. She and her husband had planned this pregnancy for two and a half years. She says, "The first thing my therapist said to me was 'The only thing we're going to talk about is your having an abortion; you're not ready to have a baby.'"

Cristina was told to buy the biggest baby doll she could find and to strap fifteen-pound ankle weights onto it to get a sense of what it would be like carrying a baby. She recalls:

> My therapist had me carry around the baby doll, and she made me feel
> proud of what I was doing. So, when people asked why I was carrying this
> doll around, I'd say, "Because I'm having an abortion to save my
> relationship with my husband." It was the most intensely humiliating
> experience, and they'd make you feel proud of it. People would say, "God,
> that's really wonderful. You must feel wonderful to do that."[5]

After two weeks of carrying the baby doll around, and continual discussion of the need for her to have an abortion, Cristina decided to end her pregnancy. Immediately after making this decision, while her husband was out of town, she had an abortion. Her husband was very upset at the news, and her unilateral decision greatly strained their relationship. The therapists then told her she needed to remain in therapy to save her marriage.

In addition, Cristina stopped doing social work: "I was so convinced I was crazy, that I believed I shouldn't be working with people. I didn't want to inflict my alleged insanity on anybody else. The only way to control my insanity was to stay in the [Feeling Therapy] community."[6]

Cristina and her husband (who went through a second Intensive when he returned to California) were together at the Center for the three years preceding its disintegration in November 1980. Both regretted her decision to have an abortion.

Rachel

Rachel's path to the Intensive illustrates well the later years at the Center and the increased pressure put on clients to bring others in. She met Julia, a woman from the Center, selling plants in the garment district of Los Angeles, where Rachel worked. They became friends and she went to an open house with her. Rachel decided to seek counseling at the Clinic for Functional Counseling and Psychotherapy because she was contemplating a career change.

At the second or third session, her therapist spent half of the two hours trying to get her to sign a paper committing herself to a set period (Rachel thinks it was for eight months) of psychotherapy. At the end of the session, she signed. She remembers asking her therapist about the other therapists' qualifications and being told that "they are all trained professionals." Rachel had lived alone in a suburb of Los Angeles quite happily for several years. Rachel's therapist at the Clinic began to talk about how alone and lonely she must be; since this was true occasionally, she began to consider what her therapist was saying.

While receiving counseling at the Clinic, Rachel met the man who became her boyfriend and later her husband. She encountered him by chance, when she went to dinner at her friend Julia's house. Julia was not home yet, so Rachel went next door to another Center house, where Dan lived, and waited. Eventually, Rachel began going out with Dan, and she became friends with his three male roommates.

Soon, all four began pressuring her to join the Center. Their tactics included physical violence by Dan, which led her to call the police on one occasion. Eventually, although she felt no particular desire or need for such therapy, she gave in and decided to enter the Intensive, in order to retain her romantic relationship.

Her foremost initial impressions of the Center were that the therapists were very nice, and that the language of the Center people (which included liberal use of profanity) was not and that she must be a "dud." While she was with Dan at the Center, before entering the Intensive, all the therapists were very friendly to her. She assumed that this would be how they would act in therapy.

One incident before the Intensive also reflects her understanding of therapy at the time, and illustrates a point I will make in Chapter 5. Rachel and Dan went on a camping trip, intended as a minivacation, with another couple who were members of the Center. Like all their activities, it had to be scheduled around work and therapy, so they got a very late start.

As they began hiking up a hill, Rachel's friend Julia started walking slightly ahead of the other three. She was very excited and enthusiastic about the trip. As she rounded a bend in the trail, her boyfriend grabbed her, threw her to the ground, started screaming at her, and sat on her. Rachel, upset and crying, found this so bizarre that she began running down the hill to get help for Julia. This was the first time she had experienced anything like this that involved the Center.

Her boyfriend stopped her and tried to explain what was happening.

"Julia was in her shit," and "she was trying to show people up." When Rachel tried to defend her friend's behavior, Dan responded, "No, you're wrong." Julia herself was kicking, screaming, and crying violently. Eventually, she gave in, and later she even tried to explain to Rachel what had happened. But the explanation, couched in the Center's ideology, made no sense to Rachel. This incident set the tone for the camping trip, which she describes as "the worst camping trip of my life."

For more than a year, Rachel resisted pressure to get her to come into the Center. She says that her final excuse was that she lacked money. However, her boyfriend was told, "If you want the money, you'll get the money, you'll find a way to do it, if you want her bad enough, you'll get the money." Dan went around to about fifty people at the Center, asking each to co-sign a loan for him; eventually, someone did. Dan and Rachel finally paid off the loan four years after the Center went out of business.

Rachel began her Intensive in February 1980. On the first day, her therapist was markedly cold, in contrast to how she had earlier perceived the therapists. He asked her why she was there, and she said because of her boyfriend. The therapist then threw a pencil at her, yelled, and went into another room where there were two other therapists. One of these was Dan's group therapist. She remembers her therapist yelling to them, "Do you know why Rachel's here?" Rachel felt very bad.

Rachel's Intensive was so difficult—she was not making progress, or, as her husband put it, "they weren't making headway with her"—that they brought him into her Intensive to go through it with her. He spent Mondays through Wednesdays with Rachel; Thursdays and Fridays she was alone. From her description of her response, it sounds as though Rachel withdrew into herself very quickly in the Intensive, giving little apparent response, and that this was the reason the Center attributed no progress to her.

Rachel's case is unusual in that she is the only person I interviewed, and the only case I heard of, where the Intensive was arranged to include, as a routine feature, another person. Since I interviewed both Rachel and Dan, I also got the perspective of an older patient on Intensive therapy.

During this Intensive, her therapist brought out a chart depicting all the major areas of life, life "dynamics."[7] He used it to examine each area, to assess where Rachel was on each, and to pinpoint areas for improvement.

Three other incidents during the Intensive made a significant impression on Rachel. One involved the care and feeding of her cat. Dan had promised to feed him regularly during her Intensive, even though this involved a drive of at least forty-five minutes (one way) to her house. Having found that he had repeatedly failed to feed her pet, she asked to be allowed to bring the cat to the house where she was staying. Eventually, after much fussing, she received permission.

Next came a discussion and ridiculing of her, before a group of about forty people, based on things she had told her therapist about her sex life. She was mortified. This event illustrates the private becoming public, making the individual accessible to group influence.

The third incident was an assignment Rachel was given by her therapist. She was to move out of her own house (where she had lived happily for seven years) and to move into a house with the other members of her Intensive group, all within a month. The move would enable her group to surveil her everyday behavior, another part of the private becoming public. The prospect of moving in with people she did not know appalled her so much that she considered moving in with Dan and his three male roommates. Even though the thought of one woman living with four men was not in line with her conventionality, her distate for the therapist's plan at least made the thought worth considering.

After the Intensive, Rachel and Dan were assigned to work together; they did landscaping, which they both enjoyed. They also found a house in the Hollywood hills, but the $500 deposit, the $1,200 monthly rent, their therapy bills and loan payments consumed most of the money they made.

The Center disintegrated a scant eight months after Rachel's Intensive. When it collapsed, she had moved up to Group 11, from Group 12. This move does not seem to have had much to do with her behavior; she felt it was more related to a new group coming in after her. Her boyfriend (now husband), Dan, however, never made it out of the Tombstone Group he had been placed in when the groups were reorganized in 1978.

Discussion

When individuals arrived for their Intensive at the Center for Feeling Therapy, they were already in part committed to the therapy. Writing the autobiography required for application was the beginning of the person's participation in the patient role. For most, this was also the beginning of opening oneself to group influence. This set the stage for public presentation of the patient self. Those who had to go to great lengths to acquire the money for therapy were becoming committed to the idea of being patients. Finally, having paid in advance, individuals were committed for the duration of the Intensive and the first month after. For these reasons, it is unlikely that many persons would choose to leave the Center early, no matter how uncomfortable they felt.

Social psychologists describe how important it is for influence professionals to gain a commitment in order to gain compliance:

> Not surprisingly, . . . feeling committed to one's freely chosen actions is ingrained in us early. Being *consistent* in words and deeds is a related social value learned young. The key psychological process at work here is the binding effect of an earlier commitment on subsequent behavior; the second act naturally follows from the first in this consistency play. This is especially true when the initial behavior is public and freely chosen, or people have the illusion that it is. (Zimbardo and Leippe, 1991:79)

In addition, "self-attribution" came into play as individuals worked to gain entrance to the therapy program. That is, looking at the steps they took and the money they paid, they inferred that *they* really needed and wanted what was offered by the Center for Feeling Therapy. As I shall point out, this sense of individual motivation and choice in selecting therapy was crucial for therapists to maintain their roster of patients.

The five vignettes I have presented illustrate seven key features of the Intensive period of therapy. First and most important, the Intensive broke a person down and then bonded her or him to an abusive therapist. It was not the beginning of momentous individual "transformation" that the therapists claimed it was. After three weeks the person—crushed, uncertain, "broken"—was placed in a group, and it was here that most therapy took place. By and large, patients no longer had regular individual sessions with the therapist who had "done" their Intensive (although some did see them fairly often around the Center). Social psychologists have shown that the severity of initiation processes increases the commitment of new members (Cialdini, 1984:95–96).[8]

Second, I think it crucial that this initial breaking down occurred when the individual was alone. All those who sought Feeling Therapy were expecting to go through an intense experience with an individual therapist and were therefore expecting a lot of personal attention. They were also expecting this individual attention to be structured around a Primal format, so as to include discussion of one's very early past, including one's birth trauma. This experience was supposed to be intense, involving the whole use of the body in primaling, and was not supposed to be simply a matter of "talking" about one's problems. Thus, the Intensive initially conformed to patients' expectations, an important reason that people stayed through this period.

Additionally, in individual sessions the new patient was broken down in isolation, with no support possible from others. If the therapy had occurred in a group composed only of new patients, some might have mistakenly tried to intervene, as Rachel did when she first confronted an example of physical violence in handling another's "shit." Such support would impede the "destruction of defenses," the breaking down of the person.

A therapist in an individual session could thus devise quite potent "therapeutic" reactions to people, relying on their vulnerabilities as revealed in their autobiographies. Consider, for example, a man I interviewed who was very afraid of total darkness. He was finally broken down by sessions conducted in the dark, including a final session where it was pitch black and where he broke down and cried hysterically. At that point, however, his therapist instantly became supportive, praising him strongly for his behavior. Thus the Intensive format allows for great tailoring to the individual, in a way that a group setting cannot, so that persons can be broken down and rebuilt according to Center norms and values.

Although patients were not expecting the abusive treatment they got, another feature of the Primal Scream approach was readily available to them as an explanation, even if it was never articulated. This is my third point, and I think it is extremely important in explaining why people stayed through abusive treatment. This was the understanding that things are not always what they seem, that much behavior is a defense. After reading and accepting The Primal Scream, many people were prepared to adopt this idea as valuable and potentially useful. Anything and everything might be a defense, and only the therapist could distinguish between behavior that was defensive and behavior that was not.

Some of the things that occurred in the Intensive were so humiliating to patients that they never shared them with even their closest friends until after the Center's demise. Several persons could not discuss these events with me when I interviewed them. One woman, for example, burst into tears when I began asking questions; she could only continue the interview by discussing the experience of others and her own understanding of Center norms.

My fourth point is that everything that happened in the Intensive seemed to indicate that anything was possible at any time. This was disorienting to all those I spoke to, as they tried to figure out what was happening, why it was happening, and how they could be "good" patients. This feature, which I call "arbitrariness," was introduced in the Intensive, and it was a prominent feature of Center life throughout the institution's history. The only constant was change.

While the therapist might do anything, it was an "anything" shaped by some understanding of a patient's fears and vulnerabilities. Yet, it often was a completely off-target approach to a person's perceived problems. Thus, if a woman came seeking help with a spouse, the troubled relationship might never be referred to during the Intensive. Such was the case with one interviewee, who reported getting no help with her husband, from whom she had just separated and with whom she wanted to reunite. Mike received no help with his drinking problem other than the admonition not to drink; he said he was never told he might be an alcoholic, even when he was once taken home in an alcoholic stupor after he had run away from the Center.

A fifth key element introduced in the Intensive was the pervasive Center norm that the private must become public. Everything an individual felt, thought, and did was supposed to be revealed to the group: there were to be no secrets. This seems to be putting Lifton's (1961) "cult of confession" into practice. All those I interviewed commented that they came to recognize this norm during the group sessions held during the Intensive. This revelation of intimate details of individuals' lives to the group was mortifying to many, as in Rachel's case. This element, too, characterized the Center's entire history. It extended at one point to the practice of taking off one's clothes and having the group "poke at" the body, as one interviewee put it. Others mentioned individual sessions with their Intensive therapist where they disrobed and "encountered" their bodies.

A sixth significant feature of the Intensive and all Center therapy was that problems were interpreted in very literal ways and assignments to tackle them were made very concrete. Thus, one's defenses could be "beaten" out of one, because defense was interpreted very literally, concretely, so that one's whole appearance was a defense. One could "batter" it, deflate it, by random attack. One woman's therapist asked her, when she was feeling very confused after several weeks of "busting" in individual and group sessions, what she felt like doing. The woman said she felt like throwing herself against the wall, implying (to me) her extreme frustration. The therapist told her to go ahead, and she bounced off the wall for about two hours. Yet these literal ways of conceptualizing a problem and its therapeutic solution are all *symbolic*, something not recognized by either therapists or patients. These seemingly concrete behaviors were all based on a symbolic understanding of what was happening, so that as one grew accustomed to Center life one came to accept very bizarre behaviors at something other than face value. Physical abuse came to be interpreted as something good for one, as helping one's friends, as forcing a person to abandon a "defense." Patients emulated therapists in adopting these behaviors, a process that began in the Intensive.

This point can be applied more generally: as one accepts the norms of any group, what appeared strange may come to be taken as normal. A striking example appears in Bent Corydon's *L. Ron Hubbard, Messiah or Madman?* (1992), a book about his experiences as a Scientologist. Corydon describes how a four-year-old boy was placed for almost two days in the chain locker of a boat L. Ron Hubbard was living on, merely because he had eaten strips of yellow paper from the telex machines. Corydon (1992:29) describes the chain locker as "dangerous."

> Located at the very bow of the ship under the water-line. It was the place where the section of the chain not in the water was stored. When the entire chain was brought up it filled most of this comparatively small, wet, dark, and sometimes rat-infested locker.

The child's mother had been gone on a "mission," and she was shocked to hear of her son's ordeal. But Corydon explains that "[s]he was 'handled' . . . with explanations about how 'out ethics' and 'down stat' Tony had been. 'He is really a very old thetan [spirit] with a young body,' she was told. 'He should not be permitted to use that young body to stir up sympathy.'" In this instance, accepting the group's ideological notion of "thetans" justified what might otherwise seem to be child abuse.

Seventh and last, whatever the initial drive, desire, or need of patients when they applied for therapy, it was translated in the Intensive into a specific need for Feeling Therapy and for the Center.[9] Rachel's story illustrates what this was like in the last year of the organization's existence. In her case, the therapist brought out charts, and he used them to assess her life on all fronts. This approach removes the power to define from the patient and gives it to the therapist. The patient was expected to conform to the Center's idea of perfection, "going 100%" in all areas of life. Can anyone ever feel she or he is meeting that goal?

This approach broadened the standard against which patients compared themselves to an impossibly high, unattainable ideal. In so doing, Feeling Therapy makes a patient out of anyone. Anyone is vulnerable, regardless of accomplishments and skills, to an assessment of self as needing improvement in some way. This also broadens the category of who is a desirable patient: again, anyone. In this way, too, the focus was shifted away from the patient's particular reason for seeking therapy.[10]

Yet, the "hook" for many persons was that there was always a kernel of truth—somewhere. When her Clinic therapist was giving her the by then standard line that living alone, and outside the Center, was bleak, Rachel reflected that she did sometimes feel alone and lonely. Mike *did* lose weight rapidly, and he stopped drinking during his Intensive. Another man I interviewed, who sought out the Center because of his unhappiness with his homosexuality and his obesity, *did* lose 110 pounds and did act heterosexually from the time he entered until the Center fell apart. These examples illustrate how easy it was for patients to attribute to therapists and the therapy credit for all assessments of self that they considered accurate and credit for all positive changes that occurred.

While individuals were being "broken" and systematically robbed of all supports for their identity as it had existed before the Intensive, they were engaged in zealous interaction with the members of their particular group. They had to live together, at least during this initial period; afterward, they were strongly encouraged to live together, although as Rachel's case illustrates they did not have to, so long as they lived with Center people. They were routinely assigned to do things with their group. In addition, living under the same roof they could have less-organized but still continual contact with each other. This structure fits with Schein's three-step model: breaking the person down, inducing the desired change, and maintaining the change (Schein with Schneier and Barker, 1961). The aggressive, confrontative therapists broke the person down, showed the way to be a "good" patient, and then maintained this new patient identity by using a therapeutic community to ceaselessly reinforce the norms of Feeling Therapy.

The intensity of the initial therapy rubbed off onto these relationships: patients had gone through a momentous thing together. Thus, there was the potential for strong bonding with these other individuals, which often seems to have been realized.

It appears from the experiences of the men and women I interviewed, and from the stories they told about what they observed of others, that a frequent response to the Intensive was a defensive retreat into oneself. Such withdrawal was certain to bring down "busting." The "busting" could be justified (if necessary) as an attempt to bring someone out of "deadness." Any "deadness" observed in an individual was always assumed to be something brought in from the outside world, from one's past, and was never considered to be a response to the "treatment" therapists or patients gave. To be a quiet, shy person was never acceptable. One always had to be acting against tendencies to be quiet or to withdraw within oneself, in order to avoid the attack of others.

The individual who became involved in Feeling Therapy was a person in a particular condition, not just anyone. There was a certain "fit" between the new patient and the organization as far as goal. The individual had decided that she or he was in need of expert help, and that Feeling Therapy was an appropriate source of that help. Moreover, the individual had already gone through a series of steps to become a member: the process of applying could be intense. Most had read The Primal Scream and thought they could be helped by this approach. So, they arrived convinced both of their poor condition, their need, and of their belief in the effectiveness of this therapy. This was in contrast to, say, the Moonies, whose catch-as-catch-can recruiting strategy meant that they began the main work with a diverse group of individuals, not all equally accessible. The Center worked with a more homogeneous group, very accessible to influence; accordingly, it was more likely that those involved would become committed to the therapy.

My point is not that influence procedures are so powerful they can work on *any* individual. Rather, there must be an initial fit between the individual and the group, an overlap of interest, to begin an interaction. Then comes a need to elaborate and develop this interaction. Even when the influence process is buttressed by force (as in a prison), there are limits to its effectiveness. It may exact compliance, out of fear for one's safety, but not attitude and behavior change. Of more value in effecting the latter is setting a situation up so that individuals "choose" to do something—if persons believe that what they do is done freely, commitment is likely to be great.[11]

The first reaction of patients—that they were going crazy, were confused and disoriented—that Hart, Corriere, and Binder mention in *Going Sane* (1975) is what many of the persons I interviewed recalled as their experience of the Intensive period of therapy. The Intensive clarified one understanding above all: one was in even worse shape than one had realized. One felt in great need of help, and felt that this help could only be obtained by continuing therapy beyond the initial period covered by the first fee.

Thus, the Intensive socialized individuals into the "patient" role, concomitant with their accepting extreme therapist authority. As a patient, one was "crazy." The entire organization of the Intensive period of therapy made it very likely that individuals would acquiesce in this definition. In answering the question of what makes a deviant label stick, Schur (1980:16) quotes John Lofland as saying that "other things being equal, the greater the *consistency, duration* and *intensity* with which a definition is promoted by Others about an Actor, the greater the likelihood that an Actor will embrace that definition as applicable to himself." From the day they entered Feeling Therapy, individuals were consistently and intensely labeled as "crazy." Even though progress was claimed, members were still seen as "going sane," not sane; feeling confused and disoriented only seemed to validate the claim that "you're crazy and you need our help." That is, patients' needs for therapy were graphically demonstrated to them. The sight of others (including the therapists) "making progress" also seemed to validate the effectiveness of the therapy, further pressuring individuals to believe in its efficacy.

This process rests on what Cialdini (1984:117) calls "social proof." The principle

> states that one means we use to determine what is correct is to find out what
> other people think is correct. The principle applies especially to the way we
> decide what constitutes correct behavior. We view a behavior as more
> correct in a given situation to the degree that we see others performing it.

When does the principle of social proof work best? "[W]hen the proof is provided by the actions of a lot of other people" (119). Further, "In general, when we are unsure of ourselves, when the situation is unclear or ambiguous, when uncertainty reigns, we are most likely to look to and accept the actions of others as correct" (129). "Especially in an ambiguous situation, the tendency for everyone to be looking to see what everyone else is doing can lead to a fascinating phenomenon called 'pluralistic ignorance.'" (129) And finally,

> the principle of social proof operates most powerfully when we are observing the behavior of people just like us. . . . We will use the actions of others to decide on proper behavior for ourselves, *especially when we view those others as similar to ourselves*. (142)

Five
Careers as Feeling People

One's life after the Intensive therapy program began with a move into community housing. Many persons reported that they, and others they knew, moved into housing with people from their Intensive group. This was not true for all, however, as exceptions might be made for various reasons; for example, a woman leaving the Intensive might move into a house with her boyfriend, who was a several years' patient. Three women I interviewed reported that this happened with them. After the initial three-week Intensive, people could return to jobs, or find jobs enabling them to stay in the Los Angeles area. For both those who came from out of state specifically to enter therapy and those already living in the area, this was a time of rebuilding one's life, with the Center for Feeling Therapy at its core.

Relationships

In the early years of the Center, rebuilding one's life entailed cutting ties with family members and friends. This was not always a deliberate strategy on the patients' part, but often the effect of behavior so offensive that great breaches in relations resulted.[1] Parents were a particular target of attack, since one was encouraged to see them in large part as the cause of one's problems. Many interviewees reported being told to call parents and scream at them, for a variety of reasons. People did so, sometimes reluctantly, sometimes believing in the activity, but certainly to demonstrate their commitment to personal development and their seriousness in therapy. One burnt one's bridges behind one, making it more difficult to return to old relationships during and after therapy.[2] Remarks by two men I interviewed illustrate this point:

> At first I was very arrogant to them, busted my parents a couple of times, for being deprived as a child. Then, when the Center attitude changed, I tried to get them to come to things, they wouldn't. I tried to get my sister to go to a lecture, she didn't. I was not in too much contact with my parents during, so I didn't tell them much, didn't talk about it much after.

My parents didn't want me to come out here, the therapists told me to call
them during the Intensive, about what they'd done to me, I didn't, my
mother didn't want to talk to me, because she thought I, it was really
insane, I thought it was normal, she got upset, wouldn't talk.

When I came back the second time, I had to have $3,000. [Where did
you get it?] My group leader said to get the money any way you can, I got
my parents to put in $1,200, the rest I'd saved, my whole life was therapy. . . .
I lied to my parents to get the money, I knew they'd give me money if I had
a medical problem. . . . I've never told them I was in a cult, because they're
in the[ir] 70s and maybe they'd say "I told you so," and I don't want to
hear that. . . . I burnt a lot of bridges with them, because every time I called,
I would ask for money. Now I talk to them and I have a good time with
them, it's getting better with them.

One's Center life revolved around relationships with other patients and
with therapists. The therapists in particular were regarded as more "feelingful" people, and being in contact with them reputedly sustained one's development of feeling. Living with other patients was conceptualized as necessary
to sustain this feeling development—these others were also more feelingful,
in comparison with people "on the outside." None of the patients, of course,
had yet made it to being completely feeling people; only the therapists had
achieved this state. People outside the Center could lower one's feeling level,
could make one "dead," or lacking in feeling. Therefore, ties with non-Center
people (NITs, or not-in-therapy individuals) were often voluntarily relin-
quished as being no longer worth one's while to maintain. Initially, in keeping with its early 1970s' origin, the Center was nonmonogamous and countercultural in attitudes toward love and romance. The Center ideal then was
that of a single, adventuresome young adult, unfettered by marriage or parenthood in pursuing her or his development. People who came in romantically involved, wishing help with this relationship, were given little aid and
were sometimes discouraged from remaining with their partner(s). Patients
were encouraged to go out with a variety of men and women. Sexual and romantic experience was considered desirable and was constrained only by the
requirement of heterosexuality. The Center, like Janov's institute, was insti-
tutionally homophobic, using the term "fag" contemptuously. From the day
one became a Feeling Therapy patient, one could only behave heterosexually.

Parenthood was never accorded respect at the Center. According to my
interviewees, no children were born during its nine-year history, even though
the population was composed primarily of young adults. Several persons I interviewed spoke of women who gave up their children, having come to believe themselves unfit to be parents.[3] Others mentioned their own abortions

or women they knew who had undergone abortions. Again, women had abortions because they believed themselves unfit to be parents, in spite of strong desires to have children.

The Center ideology governing decisions about birth control was that Center people, products of an insane culture, were not fit to be parents. Even to think of making the choice to conceive a child was construed as an indication of selfishness—one was thinking more about oneself than about the child who might be born. The understanding was that at this point in people's lives, given their insanity, their smartest choice was to decide to work full-time on combating that problem. Children were not highly valued, anyway. They were a "drag," a hindrance to one's development.[4] Several of the women I spoke with mentioned mourning the passing of their childbearing years while they were in the Center. Others mentioned that a lot of people (including some of the therapists) had had children in the first year after the Center broke up.

Indeed, the Center's prohibition of childbearing was probably made easier to achieve because some women stopped menstruating, according to interviewees.[5] One woman mentioned that she stopped menstruating for five years (until after the Center fell apart), that she knew one other woman who had stopped menstruating, and that she, my interviewee, felt this reflected her psychological inferiority. Accordingly, she did not mention this fact to others. When she learned after the Center's collapse that this had happened to many women, she was shocked.

In contrast to this woman's interpretation of and response to the cessation of menstruation, a second interviewee said she stopped menstruating for two years, and that she knew many other women who had stopped menstruating and who had consulted medical doctors. This woman interpreted the cessation of menstruation as "the price of the intense life we live[d], going 100% in all areas of our lives." Periods returned to her and her friends "within three weeks" after the Center's disintegration. I think the difference in interpretation is partly explained by the second interviewee's recognition that she was not alone and by the development of agreement on what cessation of menstruation meant.

The notion that being single was the ideal status eventually gave way to a strong emphasis on (heterosexual) coupled relationships, although marriage was not allowed as a general rule, even for most of the therapists. Riggs Corriere and his girlfriend Konni married in the summer of 1976 (the first marriage within the group); the remaining coupled therapists married during the summer of 1980 (Mithers, 1994:291). The therapists had very strong influence over whom one should get involved with, stay involved with, or leave. One man spoke of the forced relationships, the "Chinese marriages," he knew of; everyone I interviewed knew of people who were "helped" into these artificial relationships. One interviewee mentioned marrying a woman in his group to allow her to remain in the country; he estimated there were ten to fifteen marriages in name only (he was never romantically involved with his "wife," although she was one of his housemates).

Once involved in a relationship that one's therapist sanctioned, one had a very difficult time getting out of it. Persons were told they would experience the same problems in any relationship, so they should face them now. "Try harder, try differently, give it one last try"—some variant of "trying" was the usual advice when patients mentioned wanting to leave relationships. Therapists gave women and men a multitude of assignments to help relationships along, including sexual assignments.

It seems that placing couples under the close scrutiny of the therapists could be experienced as good and bad. Two women I interviewed spoke of feeling they could get continual help with their relationships; as a result, they felt that they were in a community that cared about their happiness.

From other interviews, I got a sense of how "trying" could be a process of sheer misery, of butting one's head against a wall with little return. One man recalled that two of his roommates, to make them feel more "together" to help their relationship, were assigned to tie themselves together for most of their waking hours. My interviewee estimated that this assignment continued for several weeks. Partly as a result, the man in the couple ran away from the Center (he later returned).

Many of these forced relationships dissolved very quickly on the demise of the Center. Persons who had been trying very hard, and in good faith, were left with a sense of "it's all been fake."

Work Lives

The attitude toward earning a living seems to have changed during the almost ten years the Center existed. The early view seems to have stressed finding fulfillment at work by acting as feeling people there, consequently improving the "feeling tone." Exporting the feeling norms to work does not seem to have accomplished its goal; rather, it seemed to have led coworkers to say "you're crazy," thus putting distance between Center people and their colleagues. Many persons reported experiencing work difficulties, as they acted very arrogantly and attempted to be feelingful at all times. Part of this "feelingfulness" involved the use of strong, expressive language, including profanities. Several of those I interviewed reported holding a string of jobs during their time as feeling people; in retrospect, they think their attempts at feelingfulness made them trying to coworkers.

The later years saw a change in approach from seeking self-fulfillment at work to being "functional." Now the emphasis was not on whether one's job was fulfilling, but on whether it paid enough to enable one to maintain the appearance of a materially successful individual.

I hypothesize several things about this shift. Being feelingful all the time in the world outside the Center handicapped one as a worker in that world. Center people did not seem to be making much headway in reshaping the world by their individual behavior in workplaces. Being "functional," on the other hand, at least enabled them to maintain work lives outside the Center. This shift quelled people's expectations for great changes in work satisfaction through changed individual behavior. In other words, the new approach reflected an organizational understanding that the outside world was not so malleable as had been assumed.

Center people did not seem to have become model workers, however. Along with the change in attitude toward work came a far greater effort by the Center to attract outsiders to a variety of programs it had created. Patients were strongly pressured to proselytize at work, to get coworkers to attend open houses, lectures, "Psychological Fitness Days," and so on. Such behavior introduced yet another kind of tension into work lives. Again, the effect seems to have been to put distance between Center and non-Center people, although many of my interviewees did manage to get coworkers to attend Center events.

A number of patients worked at enterprises that sprang up at the Center. Persons were encouraged to start businesses together, the rationale being that these would enable people to work with friends, with those who were similarly concerned with being feelingful, and hence would raise everyone's feeling level. Additionally, patients were told they would all become very wealthy as the businesses prospered. As in all that occurred at the Center, the therapists oversaw the activities.

Patients, primarily women, worked at the Center doing clerical and low-level administrative work. They were paid very little, $400 a month according to several persons I interviewed. Sometimes, if boyfriends were able to support them, women worked without pay; several interviewees recalled this factor being taken into account when wages were set. In any event, the figure of $400 a month is clearly insufficient when one notes that everyone in the Center paid a monthly therapy fee of between $225 and $250 throughout the organization's existence.

The trade-off for such low wages was that one was "working at the hub of the universe," as one interviewee put it. Compared to patients working at jobs in the world outside the Center, one could have more-frequent contact with the therapists and with people working to increase their feelingfulness.

I think that the Center businesses were useful in employing people who had lost jobs or who needed jobs after moving to Los Angeles. One business in particular, the Plant Pusher, seemed elastic enough to absorb a changing labor force. Employing members for very low wages, sometimes having them work for free, meant profit. How much, and what happened to it, are a source of debate, according to my interviews and to the "Cult of Cruelty" broadcast, a five-part series on the Center's demise produced by the local CBS affiliate in May 1981.

In addition to those who worked at the Center or in a business affiliated with it, many persons (all of my interviewees among them) routinely volunteered for various activities and projects at the Center. They received no reduction in fees in return for these hours: this work, too, was construed as being part of their therapy.

Expansion

Initially, the Center's emphasis seems to have centered on work done in the therapeutic community, that is, doing therapy on patients and developing the therapy. Founding therapists lectured and spoke in various contexts, touting Feeling Therapy and proclaiming its unique value. The early years, accordingly, saw a consolidation of the organization's identity, with outreach efforts intended to attract people to the Center.

As the community grew, an emphasis on spreading the word and the work to different parts of the country and the world developed. Centers were set up in Canada, Boston, and Germany; these "satellites" were viewed as only the start of the growth of Feeling Therapy. Feeling Therapy was going to have a momentous effect on therapy and on society. As part of this expansion, the name of the approach was changed to "Functional Therapy," to avoid the touchy-feely connotations of "Feeling Therapy," according to several of those I interviewed.

The name change was only part of the effort to put Feeling Therapy into the mainstream. The major part of this public relations approach was to push programs that would not entail moving into the therapeutic community. "Dream Maker Awareness Training" and "Psychological Fitness Training" were two such programs, with benefits supposedly comparable to those received from work done in the community; the Clinic for Functional Counseling and Psychotherapy, begun in late 1978, made similar claims. All of these efforts seem to reflect the understanding that most women and men were not interested in Feeling Therapy programs entailing community living. According to my interviews, however, the new programs were also designed to funnel the best of these clients—young, intelligent, and well-to-do persons, who were also mentally healthy in the conventional sense—into the Center.

Patients were extremely important in promoting the development of these new efforts. Some persons were encouraged to get degrees from educational institutions outside the Center permitting them to do therapy (although there was no push for patients in general to get degrees). These people (along with those who held degrees when they arrived at the Center) then did therapy, mostly at the Clinic. They worked long hours for very low wages. When the Center broke apart, the Clinic reputedly had an outpatient load of six hundred (Horowitz, 1981; Morain, 1981). Patients also staffed the educational letter and phone program known as the "Associates Program."

Besides staffing these programs, members publicized *Going Sane, The Dream Makers,* and *Psychological Fitness.* Interviewees reported that their groups were given quotas for handing out cards advertising *The Dream Makers.* In order to meet these quotas (in fact if not in spirit), several men and women I interviewed told of going on weekend evenings to the Westwood district and handing out the cards to people standing in lines for movies.

As was the case with anything else they did, persons would be "busted" for how they performed this volunteer work. One interviewee recalled being responsible for setting up the podium for an open house, including providing a pitcher of water. Being late one evening, she had to walk on stage with the pitcher after the audience had arrived. She was later busted for this, for always "having to be noticed."

The Center's various outreach programs affected members in ways besides their volunteering. Although the therapy at the Center was influenced by each development in theory, this seems to have been a matter of passing fads. For example, the literature implies that dream analysis came to play a large role in Center therapy. Interviewees, on the other hand, report a sudden, intense interest in dream analysis, lasting about a year, but not uniformly put into practice. This was followed by an enthusiasm for "Psychological Fitness." Patients I interviewed report having experienced these programs as part of the ever-changing therapy. One person mentioned that the programs seem to have been an attempt by the therapists to create a technique or program that they could market, one that would be as successful as Primal Therapy. However, to the therapists' disappointment, neither their books nor their many media appearances generated the large following or public interest that *The Primal Scream* did.

The Clinic for Functional Counseling and Psychotherapy, on the other hand, appeared to be quite successful, perhaps having the possibility for achieving greater public attention. There too, however, the potential was undermined by internal dynamics, as counselors at the Clinic were pressured to maintain every patient, with any departures being interpreted as a reflection on the inadequacy of the counselor. Once again, here is a reflection of the ideology that the message, the therapy, was so valuable that it alone could retain people, and that it was the inadequacy or mistakes of the individuals putting it into practice that resulted in losing patients. This view reinforced the overall ideology that the theory and therapy were more important than the individuals within it, an illustration of Lifton's (1961) theme of "doctrine over person."

In all the founders' publications on Feeling Therapy, including *The Dream Makers* and *Psychological Fitness*, this message comes through: *what* we have to say is more important than *how* we say it. Note that this is an implicit message; explicitly, they assert the opposite, that process is more important than content. The therapists argue that anyone, from a participant at a "Dream Maker Awareness Training" session to an individual reading *The Dream Makers*, can achieve what they have, if only they follow their suggestions. The founders do not realize that the "transformations" they have seen at their Center do not result from individuals incorporating the *theory* into their lives, but rather result from the particular *interaction* they as therapists set up at the Center. Without this interaction, individuals will get the same benefit from their suggestions as they would from following any regime of self-help or personal change—if they have the discipline to stick with a program of personal betterment, they may see results.

Center expansionism was also responsible for new attitudes toward family members and former friends. This change occurred during the Center's last three years. It involved encouraging patients to get back in touch with family members and friends, and then urging those persons to come to the various programs, particularly the "Psychological Fitness Programs," which were designed for the public (around a flat $1,000 fee). Several women and men I interviewed reported success in getting family members, friends, and coworkers to come. One woman remembered how her boyfriend at the time succeeded in getting his mother to attend a "Psychological Fitness Week." The high point occurred when she was able to express her dislike for her son's girlfriend. His mother was seemingly impressed by this program; my interviewee was humiliated.

Invest in Your Future

Richard "Riggs" Corriere's dream appears to have been the creation of a community whose members had a future together. According to interviewees long associated with the Center, he twice made a pitch to the members for money to buy a property. The community would retreat there for rest and recuperation in the present, and the members would retire there in the future. Both times, his proposal met with less than a fervent response. According to men and women I interviewed, the first appeal was perceived as unrealistic; Center members were not rich enough to live well, let alone to invest in the community in a large way.

The second pitch, several years later, was better received—people did contribute money. But this proposal only succeeded in revised form, contribution to the "gym fund." It was billed as an effort to raise funds to build a gymnasium near the Center, and individuals contributed money specifically toward this end. The members' subsequent discovery that this money had been used to buy a ranch in Arizona was instrumental in the disintegration of the Center.

At a certain point in the organization's existence, patients were encouraged to invest money only under the supervision of one of the therapists. The rationale was that individuals had been making bad investments, and that it was in their best interest to consult with this therapist. One woman I interviewed reported that the new policy led her boyfriend not to buy several properties that he had carefully investigated; rather, he invested his money in the "gym fund." In this way, the therapists created yet another filament binding persons to the Center.

The Cult of Masculinity

Part of what initially interested me in this organization were newspaper reports of a group ethos that sounded decidedly "masculinist": for example, an aggressive, attacking method of therapy; a leadership that was all male; a concentration of female patients' attention on their appearances; and a prohibition on nurturant behavior, especially as expressed in the forbidding of childbearing. Traditionally, therapists have reinforced the reproductive aspects of women's roles, so to see this group emphasizing femininity without nurturance surprised and interested me.

The sociologist Lewis Coser, in Greedy Institutions (1974:106), explores how demanding organizations like religious and political sects prohibit family relationships as a means of developing exclusive commitment:

> Since outside contracts necessarily detract from the members' obligations to the group, sects have looked with suspicion at family responsibilities. Just as celibacy was one of the means by which the Church attempted to insure total allegiance of the clergy, so the sect will look with disfavor at the kinship and other social obligations of its adherents. Sexual promiscuity, so frequent in the Communist Party and other radical organizations, has often had the same function as celibacy in the Catholic clergy—lasting attachment to "outsiders" and permanent outside social obligations could be reduced to a minimum by celibacy in one case, by promiscuity in the other.

Benjamin Zablocki, in The Joyful Community (1971), offers additional examples and discussion of the equivalent function of these two different organizations of sexuality.

The last three years of the Center for Feeling Therapy saw an extreme emphasis on the physical appearance of therapists and patients. Both men and women were encouraged to buy very expensive clothes and to wear them, even while selling plants. But women in particular were pressured; they were told to adopt an ultra-feminine appearance, which was a time- and emotion-absorbing process. In this way, women's concerns were narrowed to an intense preoccupation with their appearance. In explaining to me the "atmosphere" of the Center, a female interviewee commented that

> their [the therapists'] values were like the worst taken right out of American popular culture—"Women should have big boobs and be as thin as possible and be very pliable so we can screw them when we feel like it"— and that's a real woman, and she should like to cook and she should defer to her man.

From about 1975 on, many Center women were placed on diet and exercise programs to attain very low weights. Many persons I interviewed (both men and women) remarked on the details of these programs. Several women reported binge-and-purge eating cycles—that lasted for years—as they tried to reach what seem to have been impossibly low weights. One woman, for example, reported that in her group, Group 1, headed by Richard Corriere, all the women had to maintain their weight between 96 and 98 pounds, regardless of body build. Weekly weigh-ins were held before the start of a therapy group. My interviewee recalled that for one week of the month she was permitted to weigh as much as 98 pounds; for the other weeks, she paid a fine of $500 if her weight exceeded 96 pounds.

Women had "diet coaches" to monitor their weight, as well as diet and exercise strategies they followed to lose weight or maintain weight stability. Other women most often served as these "diet coaches." In the twice-weekly group therapy sessions, women reported to the group. "Discipline" for infractions of these therapy assignments could be immediate and humiliating: several people mentioned the night in a therapy group when a woman was told to crawl around the therapy rooms on all fours "mooing" because she was a "fat cow." Another interviewee mentioned a woman who never lost weight, despite her best efforts; she was referred to as "Madame von Blimpenberg."

Women had to maintain very high standards of personal grooming, learning how to apply makeup correctly, growing their fingernails long, wearing skirts and dresses made of expensive and fragile materials. One woman I interviewed, who sold plants, described how she tried to maintain a "dewy" look by making up her face once every hour. According to my interviewees, far more of women's therapy assignments centered on diet, exercise, makeup, and clothing in the Center's last few years. In addition to meeting demanding standards of physical femininity, women were encouraged to be feminine in behavior, to be deferential to their men.

Leadership by women at the Center was minimal. With the ouster of the two female founders complete by 1976, the most important therapists were all men. Two other women later attained prominent positions as therapists. One was Konni, the girlfriend, then wife, of Richard Corriere. Several of the persons I interviewed theorized that she was the "model" to which the female patients were to be shaped; in fact, she had at one time been a model.[6] This woman was uniformly described as being very beautiful. She was not, however, described as being very intellectual or intelligent. The other woman rose from patient to therapist while obtaining a degree in psychology. Note, however, that according to my interviewees these women were not seen as being as powerful as the founding, male therapists.

Demeaning certain activities usually associated with women—nurturant behavior in general, and mothering in particular—was prominent in the Center's redefinition of female behavior. The aspect of femininity most emphasized in the redefinition was appearance and physical beauty. Weight and attractiveness is certainly a general concern for women in our society. In fact, I think few persons would have seen much "wrong" with the women at the Center had they simply observed them, since their behavior was but an accentuation of traditional prescriptions for women. I would argue that this is part of the reason these emphases were chosen: they resonated with women's felt inadequacies. I argue that this cultivation of femininity worked as a form of social control, making women more susceptible and malleable for the therapists.[7]

One of the themes of the contemporary women's movement has been the analysis of femininity as social control. Feminists have seen the concept of femininity as limiting women to particular behaviors, personality traits, and social roles, or, as Friedan (1963) terms it, the "feminine mystique." These behaviors, traits, and roles are devalued in comparison to those defined as "masculine." Friedan sees the acceptance and cultivation of this notion of femininity as resulting in the "problem with no name." Much of the feminist critique has consisted of "naming" this problem, delineating the elements and dynamics of the mystique. Thus, "femininity" is a crucial element contributing to the maintenance of a male-dominant society.

The feminist analysis of femininity has criticized social assessments of women that are primarily of value to men. This value seems to center on female youthful attractiveness, particularly sexual attractiveness; psychological responsiveness; and reproductive abilities. Feminists have criticized our society's dominant view of female attractiveness as one exalting an unrealistic slenderness. They have emphasized how cultivating physical attractiveness can waste time and emotional energy. They have also pointed out that it is futile in the long run, as physical attractiveness diminishes with time, unlike more "durable" assets such as intelligence.[8]

Black Thursday

This world came to a sudden end over three days in November 1980. Following a week at the ranch in Arizona without Riggs (and Werner, the second ranked therapist), the other therapists returned to Los Angeles to "bust" him, thereby equaling out the by now quite uneven arrangement of power. During the course of the ensuing turmoil, several things became known to the patients. Chief among these was that Riggs had used the "gym fund" money to buy the ranch. This report spread among the patients, along with the rumor that the therapists had been doctoring the research results and that, instead of Center patients becoming more relaxed over time, they were becoming more high-strung, coming to resemble "Type A" personalities.

Although the therapists who brought Riggs into Group 1 (and Werner into Group 2, his group) for criticism did not intend this to be the end of the Center, patients' responses led to the demise. Patients exploded with recriminations against all the therapists. Some therapists admitted to making "mistakes," but said they were going to and remedy them and change things. Therapist solidarity broke down under the weight of patients' criticisms, and all appeared confused, uncertain, or crushed. Although some founders tried to return to their Intensive patients the day after Black Thursday, clinic therapists stopped them. Clinic counselors called their clients; calls went out to the satellite centers, which closed within days. Patients' responses to the demise were varied, ranging from shock, dismay, confusion, anger, and fear to euphoria, as they learned much previously unknown about others' experiences. Patients also learned they were not alone in their doubts about therapy, which in fact had been widespread. People who had been like gods to them were now seen as concerned more with self-interest than with patient interest. Some patients immediately began talking of lawsuits.[9]

Six
From Culture to Cult

I will now explore the social world of the Center for Feeling Therapy, seeking to explain how it allowed the therapists to exercise such great influence over patients. I believe six characteristics of this culture were crucial in generating extreme control of patients: the role of the therapist as authority, a therapeutic ideology, a "confrontative encounter" form of therapy, the creation of a therapeutic community, the arbitrariness of Center life (the only constant is change), and the intensity of Center life. Although I think that the notions of the therapist as authority and of therapeutic ideology go hand in hand, each is discussed in a separate section, as are the other characteristics. Considered together, I believe these characteristics explain the Center's path toward becoming a cult.

Therapist as Authority

Although the group's literature claimed that diverse perspectives were in play at the Center, such was never the case in the actual psychotherapeutic practice. The founders began the Center with a narrow outlook. Their previous experience of therapies seems to have consisted of many instances of a particular kind of therapy, that characteristic of the human-potential movement. Their work with alternative therapeutic practices, and the large number of founders (nine), did not result in an attitude of toleration for difference. Rather, the founders were rigidly convinced of the ultimate rightness of the therapeutic approach at the Center. This does not mean that theory and practice became ossified, for the Center was constantly changing. However, each new direction in theory or practice was rigidly proclaimed to be the only principle or technique that could be effective.

A liberal give-and-take among therapists of varying persuasions, which would contribute to a richness and completeness of theory and practice and would also safeguard patients against the harms arising from the human failings of therapists, never appeared in the Center's organizational structure and routine. Instead, a rigid hierarchy evolved among the founders. One individual, Richard

"Riggs" Corriere, rose to prominence and then achieved absolute power within the Center. He was thus able to shape the organization according to his ideas, with very little input from other therapists or patients. The patients formed the large rank of those at the bottom of the pyramidal structure that evolved.

Corriere seems to have achieved this position by the force of his "charisma"; time and again in my interviews, he was described as a charismatic leader. People seem to have meant various things by this description, but they consistently recall him as a forceful personality, dynamic and enthusiastic. Many found him extremely attractive; some expressed fear of his physical strength; others mentioned that he could be deeply insightful and empathic, as well as extremely brutal and bullying.

Attractiveness and self-confidence, however, seem foremost among the personal characteristics that led to Corriere's being termed a charismatic leader. This general position is shared by other researchers. The social psychologist Robert Cialdini, in illustrating the importance of attractiveness in leading one person to like another, remarks that

> it is apparent that good-looking people enjoy an enormous social advantage in our culture. They are better liked, more persuasive, more frequently helped, and seen as possessing better personality traits and intellectual capacities. (1984:168)

The political scientist Ann Willner, in *The Spellbinders* (1984), subtitled *Charismatic Political Leadership*,[1] says that the individual qualities of a person may cause him or her to be seen as superhuman. She finds that being perceived in this fashion constitutes one of three dimensions in the process of charismatic legitimation. She explains:

> A leader may be seen by those around him to exhibit some quality or perhaps several to a degree far beyond that considered "normal" among men. The quality itself may be shared by hundreds or millions of individuals; the exceedingly large measure of it in the person of the leader sets him apart as especially endowed. . . . [A] number of the charismatic leaders dealt with here, as well as others who were probably charismatic, shared certain characteristics, such as *supreme self-confidence and exceedingly high energy.*
>
> It is not only the possession of qualities that are themselves judged supernatural or close to it that lends some individuals the aura of the superhuman. Perceptions of an individual as transcending the normal and even the unusual among humankind can arise if that individual has or is held to have an extraordinary amount of an attribute that many people share. This is especially true if it is an attribute that is somehow associated with power or latent power. (140; emphasis added)

Willner names the following attributes as being important in perceiving the individual as transcending the normal: determination; energy, or vitality; composure, or presence of mind; intellect, or learning; self-confidence, or self-assurance; and the physical feature of "eyes of a certain quality" (149).[2]

She emphasizes how these characteristics are subject to cultural context for their power. For example, in discussing self-confidence Willner comments:

> It can be argued . . . that an extreme degree of self-assurance in a political leader is acceptable and admirable in an American context, provided that self-assurance is communicated in a relaxed and occasionally self-deprecatory or self-teasing style. In the same context, Hitler's mode of communicating self-confidence is likely to be seen and rejected as brutal arrogance, even though it might provoke some awe. (146)

Despite the egalitarian claims of what therapeutic community would involve for members, a hierarchy was clearly present at all times at the Center. It consisted of the seven remaining founders at the top, with "second generation" therapists as a supporting (and usually much less powerful) tier. The founders exercised great and arbitrary power, based on their claims of expert knowledge. An extreme sense of deference to therapeutic authority was generated, and every aspect of Center life buttressed this authority.

As I have mentioned, the founding therapists claimed to be the world's foremost authorities on therapy. They had doctorates from reputable universities and (eventually) state licenses to practice. The founders developed a body of published research that they claimed scientifically proved their therapy worked. They wrote and publicized a series of books that spread the word to the general public. They appeared on national television and radio programs, as patients watched and listened. The scientific and popular recognition implied by academic and mass-market publication seemed to validate the therapists' claims to legitimate expertise. On all fronts, it looked to patients as though these were professionals, who could honestly call themselves experts in therapy.

The therapists also made a claim to uniquely personal authority, based on their successful experience of their own "insanity." They declared that their therapy worked, and offered themselves as exemplars: they appeared attractive, happy, and "feelingful," in addition, of course, to being brilliant. They made the claim, which was seemingly validated by patients, that they were successfully treating all members of the therapeutic community.

Thus, the founders presented themselves on all fronts as experts with special technical and personal authority. If people deferred to this authority, then they had the chance to be like the therapists. I think this successful proclamation of therapeutic authority is the single most important feature of the

Center that allowed for extreme control of patients. It alone, however, could not do the job.

Arbitrariness of Therapeutic Authority

The crucial factor contributing to the arbitrary nature of the therapists' power was the understanding that therapy could be anything: it could be undertaken in any place at any time by any one, including a therapist who had never worked individually with a person. Anything the therapist did was therapeutic; she or he never acknowledged mistakes of diagnosis or treatment. The therapists' work in this regard resembled little that many practitioners would recognize, as all individuals were judged "insane" until they had passed through Feeling Therapy's therapeutic community. Everything a person presented as the self was considered a "defense," one that needed to be demolished. This was true whether a person appeared to be confident and doing well in most areas or whether she or he was in need of help with a particular issue like homosexuality or alcoholism. Everyone submitted to and presumably profited from a therapeutic regime characterized by "confrontative encounter."

A second important element of arbitrariness was refusing to explain what was given as therapy and inducing patients to accept this. The proper response was simply to "experience," not question, therapy. There was a distinct prejudice against "intellectualism." The shared understanding was that "simply" thinking about personal change got one nowhere. Most therapy, the founders implied and stated, was just this: it concentrated on "insight" rather than action or behavior. At the Center, in contrast, one should act or experience and only then think about it (presumably). Time and again, those I interviewed reported that they did not know why they were told to do things; many times, however, they led themselves to attribute reason to assignments.

What a person might be told by one therapist might be completely reversed by another, or reversed after a time. For example, one couple I interviewed remembered that for the first year and a half of their time at the Center they were pointed out and described as the worst couple there. During the next year and a half, however, they were pointed out as the best couple. Both felt that their behavior had not changed so as to merit this new assessment. In retrospect, they felt they had no real communication during these three years; they did not talk to each other as they had before and after their time at the Center. However, when they were suddenly deemed the "best" couple, they began to act affectionate and romantic in group and to consider themselves extremely lucky. My point here is that they acted up to, and in accord with, the Center's characterization of them, which had abruptly been reversed for no reason they could discern. One can take this as an example of the creation of a self-fulfilling prophecy.

In another case, an interviewee told one of the therapists that he was having trouble with sex, and that he did not want to be pressured about sex. He reported that this therapist was very sympathetic and did not push him in any way. For some reason, however, his group therapist was not so sympathetic. Instead, he gave him an assignment to have sex twice a day with his girlfriend. He estimated that this assignment lasted for two months.

"Real" Feelings Subject to Therapists' Approval

What determined whether a feeling or a performance was labeled authentic? Above all, if a therapist responded to a feeling as "real," then it was deemed real. In lieu of his or her approval by word or gesture, the group would determine what was real. Persons of low status, those who had made no progress in spite of some time at the Center or those who were new to Feeling Therapy, were usually those least able to have much say in naming their feelings as real.

The major effect of this facet of arbitrariness was that persons could not form a stable sense of self, even patients who had been at the Center the longest and those who were deemed more "feelingful." Women and men always had to act with an eye to the group, but most especially with an eye to the therapists' response, which was deliberately capricious. Although the role that was supposed to be enacted was that of a very arrogant individual, no strong core of self underlay the performance.

Therapeutic Ideology: "Responseability"

The Center emphasized a concern with "feeling," not with "right" or "wrong." *Going Sane* (1975) spoke of the "responseability" of their therapists. What this seems to have translated into in practice was that what was good for one—oneself or others—should be done, regardless of other considerations. What was good for a person's mental health was determined by "experts" in Feeling Therapy. The ethical values a man or woman brought to the Center— let alone individual preferences, abilities (as in work), or responses—were not relevant. Underlying this belief is the assumption that one was too sick, too "insane" to know how to make reasonable choices.

Thus, the therapists' authority was enhanced still more. Any activity could be "therapeutic," even if it was painful, even if it was humiliating, even if it was dangerous. If an activity was termed "good" for one, one had to defer to the therapist and do it, regardless of objections or feelings. A state of continual deference to authority was thus built up and sustained, all in the name of one's "best" interests.

A notion of "expert" knowledge was generated such that it overrode commonsense ideas of appropriate behavior. Therapists presented themselves as experts in an area where people often feel experientially ignorant, where they feel they do not understand themselves fully, let alone others. This notion of therapeutic authority undermined individuals' moral values, making persons more pliable under the therapists' influence and making certain brutalities acceptable. Women and men might still fear what could happen to them, but they became less likely to object to what happened to others. And what happened to oneself and others was often bizarre.

Confrontative Encounter: "Busting"

The key characteristic of the system of therapy offered at the Center was what I have referred to as "confrontative encounter." Within this system, actors, both therapists and patients, could perform helpful or supportive acts, but the Center did not encourage this unless it was part of a good cop/bad cop sequence.[3] "Bad cop" behavior was the confrontative attack on the patient to induce a "feeling" response. "Good cop" behavior occurred when the "feeling" occurred, when an individual broke down and cried, for example. One man I interviewed recalled:

> Physical intimidation occurred at the Center constantly . . . , I saw a therapist once with a new patient, literally wrestle the patient to the ground, get him in a headlock, all doing therapy. And at some point, the kid began to talk and cry. As soon as he broke and started crying, the therapist let him go, and would get the guy to talk from his sadness. When he did that, he invariably felt better. The technique used to get him there was extreme physical violence.

The good cop/bad cop approach was used to the Center's great advantage, for example to retain patients who seemed to have reached the end of their endurance of the institution. One interviewee, placed in the Tombstone Group when the groups were reorganized and remaining there until the end, began to feel he was going crazy and to think about committing suicide. He started to think of leaving the Center and told his therapist this. The therapist said, and acted like, he really cared about him; he also gave him the assignment of having no assignments. The man remembers this as the "only time I felt really good about myself at the Center."

His assignment went on until the end of the Center (it began in the last year). After some time, however, my interviewee was told that if he really wanted to be a success he would have to choose to be a success, and he was pressured in various ways to choose. In this way, when the habitual harsh treatment brought him to the point of thinking of leaving, his therapist switched his approach and allowed the pressure to be lifted. Not all of it, but the pressure of always trying to conform to the group's norms appearing to make progress.

Therapists were never totally harsh toward patients. Their abusiveness was relieved by moments of affection, tenderness, compassion, understanding, and friendliness. Patients also interpreted responses that might be ambiguous as reflecting the therapist's good intent. For example, Martin in Chapter Four interpreted his therapist's tears at hearing him talk about his friendship with another founding therapist "in a positive way." Individual therapists seem to have had favorite patients, and they probably gave them more benign treatment. The therapists, however, were still acting within a system characterized by "confrontative encounter." This form of "therapy" acted both to open up individuals to change and to generate continual fear of physical or psychological assault, by individuals or groups.

Harsh Treatment of Deviants

Persons having trouble conforming were often punished swiftly and harshly. The punishments often made the recipients stick out to all, as in the example of a patient given the "Turkey of the Week" button and assignments that accompanied the award. Several people recalled the same incident as being the most frightening or humiliating. In one instance, everyone in the group was urged to tell his or her most secret thought. One man recalled that he had been thinking that Riggs was a megalomaniac. He did not want to report this, but after much prodding he did. He was harshly busted by being screamed at by several therapists, and he was given an assignment to stand on a chair while in group for several weeks, since he considered himself so much "above" the others. The effect on those observing this incident, who related it to me, was to make them generally fearful and to make clear the norm of unquestioning support for all that therapy entailed.

A less harsh but no less swift response was made to a male interviewee who had wondered aloud what the Center had become:

> I was afraid it was a cult like Jonestown, I was told it wasn't, Dominic came into the room, several others, and asked "Where are the bars?", said Riggs is not alone, he's getting help, implied not like Jones . . . meeting where Riggs ended it by saying there's Kool-Aid. [making a joking reference to the poison Jonestown members took]

Another assignment that several people mentioned as particularly frightening to them was the case of a man who was assigned to behave like a baby, since he was acting like a baby. He had to wear a diaper, eat baby food, sleep in a crib (he constructed a cardboard facsimile), and not have sex with his girlfriend. This went on for several weeks, according to my interviewees. Mike (described in Chapter Four) was a friend of the man; he thought this assignment was so horrible that he avoided his friend for the duration, so as to spare him further humiliation. The man himself did not know, however, why he had been given this assignment. Several others mentioned that they thought it was to force him back to work at a Center-affiliated business (he had left with plans to return to school). As a result of the assignment, he did return to the business for a time.

This kind of harsh punishment makes it unlikely that someone would make a gesture of support to an individual being attacked; rather, it makes it likely that someone would make a gesture indicating support of the attack, in order to avoid the same fate. Mithers (1994:145) describes what occurred as the development of a Save Your Ass ethic. People became accustomed to a certain level of humiliation of themselves and others as a given of social life. Yet, extreme forms of humiliation retained the power to shock and cow members, as did less extreme forms of humiliation that were keyed to an individual's particular vulnerabilities. The more extreme forms of humiliation seemed to impress many people, to the extent that a number of persons told me of several of the same extreme incidents.

Tombstone Group

The Center needed a place for the "hard core losers," as one interviewee put it. I think an important function of the Tombstone Group was to shape up the resisters and to remove those whose presence cast doubt on the therapy from the sight of others making progress. This group was the largest at the Center; estimates of its size vary from fifty to ninety. One of the lowest ranked therapists headed this group. Several women and men I interviewed saw his position as an assignment, perhaps even a punishment. One interviewee suggested that he had been given the group because "he'd been from a loser background, and had pulled himself up to this incredible level of metaphysical efficacy"—in other words, his past paralleled the path that the other therapists wanted for members of the Tombstone Group.

The therapist led the group from the stage of the auditorium, with members in the hall's seats (at other groups, therapists sat on chairs and patients sat around them on the floor). As noted in Chapter Four, Dan, Rachel's husband, was in this group from its origin until the Center's collapse. His story illustrates what happened to persons who were naturally rather shy and quiet, as well as how the Center could become a patient's obsession.

Dan describes an incident that occurred early in his therapy. He was waiting for a "lay-down" session, standing in a casual posture (one foot up, a hand behind his back, and leaning against the wall), when one of the therapists "came up to me, told me I was completely out of it, and *wham*, he hit me in the chest as hard as he could, very hard, until I cried." When Dan said he was always afraid of the therapists when he came to the Center, his therapist responded, "Well, you *should* be afraid!" Although Dan was able to ignore other incidents, he says of this one that "it *really* hit deep with me." When I asked why he thought this particularly affected him, he replied:

> I was exhibiting a behavior more natural, I wasn't just acting completely broken down, I was acting in a way I'd act before I came to the Center. I wasn't just a cowering ninny, I was acting kind of confident, sort of cool, whatever. So from then on I acted like a cowering ninny, just to get by. From then on, I was kind of a tense person all the time, they never could force me to function in some wonderful, dynamic way, so that I could be promoted into another group, I just stayed in Group 5 [the Tombstone Group], I was one of the failures, right.

Dan describes the atmosphere in this group in vivid detail:

> all vying for attention, [yelling the therapist's name], you had to speak out in group each time or you'd be fucked, if you didn't, you'd be ghostly and pale, because you didn't express yourself in group, and you'd be awarded a Turkey button. . . . It said "All American Turkey," with a picture of a turkey on it, and you'd be "Turkey of the Week."

Patients receiving the button had to wear it for a week, "gobble ten minutes of every waking hour," and eat turkey for one meal a day. Dan was unfortunate enough to receive this "award" two times in a row; the second week, he also had to eat Spam for one meal a day.

How could fifty to ninety persons express themselves every week in one meeting, usually lasting between two and three hours? According to Dan, most patients got about ten seconds to speak, and what they said was something like "I'm going 100% this week." His therapist usually picked one person to work on for an hour or so, in addition to hearing how the rest of the group was doing. Dan remembers that

> if somebody gave up and became ashen, then they'd be really screwed, and they'd get a few words of disapproval at the end[;] quite frequently that was me, because I was one of the more shy people there, so it was a big effort for me to try and talk every week, and . . . but that was one behavior that they actually forced me to do, try to talk, because I'd rather act like an idiot trying to talk, than be awarded the Turkey button, or have that horrible feeling of having been quiet all night.

Deciding what he would say in the Tuesday and Thursday night groups consumed much time and emotional energy, as both Dan and his wife point out. Rachel mentions that Dan began worrying about Tuesday night on Sunday night, and she describes how distressed she was to see him so upset. She tried to coach him on what to say, and she tried to build up his confidence. Dan recalls what he would begin to worry about after Tuesday night was over:

> If I had talked, I felt wonderful relief . . . if I hadn't talked and hadn't been busted, I would feel horrible anyway . . . if I hadn't talked and had been busted, I would feel extra horrible, so I had this horrible malaise going on most of the time. . . . I would only feel ecstatic if I had talked and been praised.
>
> Thursday night was one more time to talk, I still had the pressure to get in there and get something in there, or else feel like a failure and feel terrible for the rest of the week.

This example illustrates how therapy-induced concerns—the need to speak up in group—were generated and how they then became preoccupations, here consuming much of both Dan and Rachel's time and energy. Dan reports that he also got no real help in trying to deal with his feelings of shyness. Striving to meet this norm generated an intense, daily anxiety in Dan, which helped keep therapy in the forefront of his life. It was as if Dan were on a treadmill: he would never get beyond his "problem," because the "treatment" for it was patently absurd. His unceasing anxiety could be quelled momentarily by only one thing: speaking up in group for at least ten seconds.

I believe that this anxiety accounted for some of the fervor with which Dan tried to pressure Rachel into coming into the Center. It is easy to understand how he might have felt an urgent need to do something to alleviate the intense anxiety generated in him by the Center, something clearly appropriate when so much was unclear to him as far as its appropriateness. Pressuring Rachel, and getting her into the Center, were visible, concrete actions. At a time when he seemed so unable to demonstrate his commitment in a way that gained approval and helped him to progress in the hierarchy, they served as signs of his commitment to therapy.

Rachel also recounts how frequently Dan would return from therapy "all fired up . . .[;] we were going to fight regardless of what I wanted . . . and it would usually be a knock-down drag out fight." Some of the energy for busting others thus came from an inability to be angry at one's own humiliating treatment; then, the anger was redirected toward other patients.

Dan watched all but one of his friends leave Tombstone Group and move up into Group 4. He recalls that he and his friend "were like pets in my therapist's group . . . he told us we were like dogs, loyal." Dan remembers his therapist saying,

Now that [the group is] this big, it's even going to be harder for you to be noticed, you're going to have to make yourself noticed . . . if you don't do it you'll just be left behind . . . your friends are gonna go up and you're gonna be still here . . . and if you're left too long, we're just gonna have to . . . you're gonna have to go in the Clinic or leave." . . . [A]nd that was the most terrifying thing of all, to leave, and to go in the Clinic was like a real loss of face . . . "[O]h, you're just a pitiful, poor, brain-damaged person, you have to go into the Clinic."[4]

He dreaded this possibility, but in spite of his avid desire to be "promoted" he could not succeed.

Dan describes his therapist's "therapy" in group as consisting of speaking perhaps one sentence to each person. For example, a woman having problems with her boyfriend might be assigned to "sit on his face every night for a week." In retrospect, Dan saw his therapist as

really off the cuff . . . he'd be really egotistical with his comments . . . like a gigantic rooster sitting up there flipping out comments. . . . [H]is view of himself was that he was really [snaps his fingers], incredibly, that sharp, one sentence would be enough therapy for a week for a person, right, he was that dynamic, he thought, about himself. . . . [E]verybody thought this was really dynamic therapy.

I believe that placing individuals in a group that was stigmatized as "bad," one composed of patients making little or no progress, had the desired effect of inducing these women and men to try to remove their stigma by greater conformity. Bound by rules that prohibited sharing their personal frustrations and doubts, and thus blocked from developing an alternative solidarity and perspective on Center life of their own, they competed with each other to rise in the hierarchy. Another man I interviewed who was in the Tombstone Group illustrates this dynamic. He thought that another person in the group liked him and shared his views. Consequently, he really did not want to sit next to the man in group, let alone discuss anything with him. Instead, he wanted to sit next to someone he thought was acting better than himself. Although he might not be able to act in the right ways, he might at least gain some approval for associating with more "feelingful" people. In other words, at least he could show he wanted to conform to the Center's notion of how to act, even if he himself did not act that way.

Not all dissidents and "losers" remained indefinitely in Tombstone, however. Dan mentions a woman who was eventually sent away from the Center; not only was she failing to make progress, she seemed to be getting worse, psychologically. He remembers discussions in the group over whether she was taking the medication her therapist had prescribed for her. Dan and

Rachel saw her shortly before she left the Center, and both describe her as "real spaced out." Their understanding is that she was sent home to her parents, with the suggestion that she be committed to a mental hospital. In their eyes, and in those of several other interviewees, the Center therapy drove this woman to insanity.

Another interviewee reported being placed in a group called the "losers' group" when he re-entered therapy after an eighteen-months' absence. He remarked, "I didn't have the sense we were losers, we were an example for other patients: 'If you leave here, you come back begging for help.'"

Falls from Status

There were enough plunges from favor that all felt threatened, including therapists. The two female founders were placed within Riggs Corriere's group for therapy, and they eventually "chose" not to do therapy. One of the two Primal Therapists involved at the start of the Center, and thus one of the more powerful leaders then, was "busted" by Riggs and demoted. The reasons were not clear to my interviewees. Some thought it had to do with this therapist's sleeping with some of his patients; others referred to him as often "brutal" before the fall, while after he was more "gentle." The other trained Primal Therapist, also one of the original leaders, was given the "Tombstone Group" of doubters and resisters. The men and women I interviewed listed him consistently as being at the bottom of the hierarchy of founding therapists.

One interviewee (ultimately at the Center for nine years), a model patient, was being trained to do therapy within her first year. Jessie describes an incident that she thinks had a lot to do with her being thrown out of training. Her training therapist had begun to go out with another patient in her training group. Shortly after, he began busting this woman in training, which made her very upset. Jessie protested his busting, saying that he had something he needed to deal with, that he too wasn't saying his feelings. As she saw it, this therapist was taking his feelings, derived from the romantic relationship he had just begun with this woman, and inappropriately expressing them in the work setting of therapy training. Jessie was busted heavily for her action; eventually, the other woman, too, was thrown out of training. Both fell in prestige among therapists and patients.

This man's dating his trainee (who is after all still a patient) is but one example among many at the Center of what therapists call "dual relationships," which are prohibited by most professional codes of ethics.

Another interviewee recalled a man who was busted from Group 4 to Group 5 and told he was "addicted to being a failure." In David's eyes, his friend's fall was very quick—"He'd done well, moved up, he looked good to appearances, he'd gotten a job as a computer operator, he was making money, he had a girlfriend." When David began to hang out with this man because he felt sorry for him, he was "really busted." He was told he could only be with the man for short periods or when others were around. David found this incident very frightening, and he felt the same thing could happen to him at any time.

Another interviewee mentions his co-therapist's fall from grace, which occurred toward the end. He described this man as being one of Riggs's favorites. The co-therapist wanted to get into medical school, and Riggs and the community were supporting him. When he failed to be admitted, he was suddenly out of favor. According to my interviewee, he was not thrown out of therapy, but he was superseded as the most prestigious co-therapist. Suddenly, he was not around much.

In retrospect, what patients experienced as capricious, often not understandable, makes sense. Riggs was trying for, and gaining, control over the other founding therapists. His actions benefited the social structure of the Center for Feeling Therapy (which included the role played by therapists), but not the individual.

Therapeutic Community: *Appearance of Unanimous Agreement*

The next crucial element in establishing extreme control is the communal organization that evolved. This development can be attributed to Corriere, according to several of my interviewees. The founders' original approach—that following Primal Therapy's practice, individuals in the Intensive should live in the same residence, even if they did not interact—grew into the notion that all members of Feeling Therapy should live together in housing located near the Center. As individuals bought up and rented nearby houses and apartments, an inner core developed around an area that became known as the "Compound." This core consisted mainly of the founding therapists, some of the next generation of therapists, and some of the higher-status patients.

According to the founders, the chief characteristics of this community were its "attitude of making the private public" (which one can interpret as being Lifton's [1961] "cult of confession") and its intentionality (Corriere et al., 1980:123). These attitudes are reflected in the actual physical structure, particularly that of the Compound:

> Presently more than three hundred people are involved in our community, over half living within a three block radius. At the center of this circle is the "compound" where the founding members of the community reside. A heavily traveled path runs in front of the compound separating it from other houses that face it in the typical American city fashion. A redwood fence and

thick hedge further define the core of the village forming a large rectangle more than half a block long. Within these confines four houses sit together, unbound by any external divisions. Rose bushes, shrubbery and fences have been removed and a grassy field substituted. . . . The back yards all open together, forming a large field containing an orchard, basketball court, playing area and swimming pool. This large area is shared with and enclosed by the four other homes that face the rear of the compound from the street that runs behind. Since they, too, are connected by a large fence, the eight houses encircle an enclosed courtyard. The houses have been opened to each other. Intervening fences were removed and doors and windows added. Wooded decks and runways were constructed to connect each house and facilitate contact between them. These changes were undertaken step-by-step until the compound achieved a form that we later realized would be more in accord with what the Senoi [an aboriginal group in Malaysia whom Feeling Therapists saw as a model of what a "dreamer" community should be] would find familiar. . . .

The houses were opened inside as well, to match the open spaces that formed outside in the yards. Large living-dining-cooking rooms became the focus for visiting, sharing and working together, similar in function to the communal long houses of the Iroquois and the Senoi. These newly developing structures facilitated our helping each other in a natural way during the course of the day. (123–24, 125)

The "attitude of making the private public" claimed by the founders in their literature does appear to have permeated the organization of the Center, in both the therapeutic practice and the communal living arrangements. Men and women were routinely in a great deal of contact with therapists and other patients, and members of the community found their lives increasingly bound together. This social organization allowed the norms of Feeling Therapy to permeate every aspect of persons' lives. As I have argued, these norms were rigid and allowed little room for individual differences. The style of life at the Center permitted extensive surveillance of members, which was particularly important because the closeness of the community was predicated on strict compliance with the ever changing norms and policies of the Center. Conformity to norms seems to have been most pronounced at the Compound, which fits with Kanter's (1987) analysis of pressures to conform (in the corporation she studied) being greatest at the top.

Development of the Appearance of Complete Unanimity

There are limits to individual authority. A group can enforce a leader's authority. This is where group dynamics enters. The entire Feeling Therapy community, true believers and doubters, bolstered therapeutic authority by presenting the *appearance* of unanimous agreement on the acceptance of therapeutic authority as legitimate, the validity of the therapy, and the value of therapeutic community. This then subtly and directly pressured patients to accept authority and do what was "good" for them.

Creating the appearance of complete unanimity on social reality accompanied the development of the therapeutic community. Individuals conformed or appeared to conform to Center norms for living life as "feeling persons." When one was in accord with these norms, one could feel part of a close-knit community. When one was out of touch with these norms, one felt like a stranger in the midst of a close-knit community—one assumed that "only I" felt estranged. This fluctuating sense of alienation seemed to center on individuals' experiencing doubts or having criticisms of Center life. Even in the midst of a strongly articulated ideal of community, it is striking how successful the therapists were at preventing individual feelings of alienation from being shared. This is partly explained by their ability to push responsibility for therapeutic change onto individuals.

The appearance of unanimous agreement on social reality deceived individuals even as they were presenting the same performance of complete conviction. For the most part, each believed that the performances of the others expressed reality. Each felt she or he alone had doubts. Bainbridge and Stark (1980:132) use the term "pluralistic ignorance" to refer to the process by which the "majority of contactees appeared to believe the claims of the *other* contactees and to think they were the only ones who were shamming." They are speaking here of their research on Scientology. Bainbridge and Stark argue that "pluralistic ignorance" is a widely used mechanism in maintaining faith in cult groups.

Women and men were thus *more* and *less* isolated while in the Center than they might have been outside it. Individuals were isolated in ways that they might not be outside an organization like the Center, while they were in a more dependent relation to each other than they might be outside the Center. On the outside, persons might confide basic fears, doubts, and worries to one or more intimates; they might depend on these intimates in the same ways as Center people, with the difference that the number of intimates was fairly small. Yet, at the Center, it seems that certain things could never be confided to one's friends, even one's most intimate friends (e.g., a lover). Persons seemed to develop secrets that they could not confide for fear that these secrets would be revealed to the larger group. Yet, women and men also had more-intense ties with more people than many had experienced before or would experience after Center life, according to my interviews. These deep ties seemed to be the result of going through an intense experience together and feeling a solidarity because of it, as well as the result of the great many

intimate details of individuals' lives that patients routinely knew. As a consequence, members felt close to each other.

The complete unanimity of the community expressed the conviction that
Center life was the only way to live one's life.[5] Strong negative boundaries were
created between life inside and life outside. Living outside the Center, after one
had lived inside, was depicted as being worse than simply being "insane," as one
had been before: once one knew the "true" state of things life outside the Center would be even more difficult to bear. People dreaded returning to a world
that, as more feelingful people, they would find even more difficult: one would
be even more isolated from these non-feelingful people than when one had been
a non-feelingful person. Since many of those I interviewed had felt themselves
to be loners or to have few close ties before coming into the Center, they dreaded
the thought of returning to a condition of isolation from others.

The psychiatrist Irvin Yalom (1975) mentions that universality is one of
the benefits of group psychotherapy. In the group psychotherapy Yalom refers
to, men and women generalize the connection to people outside the group, that
they too experience individual problems that make them feel isolated. They feel
more connected to people, while also recognizing a certain essential aloneness as
a condition of being human (which he terms existentiality).[6]

As portrayed in their accounts, onetime Feeling Therapy patients are
noteworthy for not feeling this sense of connection either to people outside
the Center or to people inside the Center, at least on the key issue of individual doubt. At the Center, many persons assumed everyone else had a deeper,
more genuine, sense of wholehearted commitment to the therapy and the
therapists. A great feeling of estrangement from non-Center people developed, so that they were never considered an alternate source of emotional sus-
tenance. One gets the impression from interviews of almost tangible barriers
developing; ties with non-Center individuals, although they might be a regular feature of patients' lives (for instance, many kept their non-Center jobs),
never developed "warmth," or attracting power, for Center members.[7]

Making the Private Public

In the Intensive, patients found that all the therapists they were in contact with knew much, if not all, about them. The most intimate parts of one's
identity were revealed; early on, this was taken to the literal extreme of nudity. Patients thus "revealed" all: physical nakedness was equated with psychological openness. Several persons I interviewed reported being in "body
groups," where everyone stripped and made fun of each other's bodies, all,
supposedly, to break down one's socialized inhibitions. (One man recalled
being forced to "show his asshole to his entire group.") Paul Watkins's *My Life*

with *Charles Manson* (1979) describes similar behavior on Manson's part, as he socialized individuals into "overcoming" their socially induced "inhibitions."

Other persons I interviewed described nude sessions with their therapists, who remained clothed. This use of nudity appears to have been more common in the earlier years of the Center, but always intimate details of patients' sex lives were revealed. Additionally, one's vulnerabilities were continually sought out and scrutinized.

Bathrooms were not private places in Center houses, although the degree to which they were public seems to have varied by house. At the Compound, the situation was even less private. Toilets were located right in the bedrooms, as bathroom walls had been torn down. One female interviewee reported visiting the Compound and seeing a therapist going to the bathroom. This therapist gave her a lecture on the naturalness of bodily functions. This understanding did not extend to the Center buildings where there was contact with the outside world, however. It seemed generally understood that some things would "weird-out" the public and that this was one of them. As one man I interviewed put it,

> [They] used to say the public takes more time to get adjusted to their way, used to tell us not to freak people out, and tell them everything, just tell them enough to get interested. . . . I remember one person freaking out a prospect, by telling how people lived together, that it was a big community. Got scolded for doing so, "You know that's going to freak them out . . . you gotta bring them in slowly . . . it takes time to get them adjusted" . . . they said they worked on their therapy, and threw out the ones that didn't work, that didn't bring about change.

The admonition that "everything should be shared with one's friends" is one reason underlying the harsh treatment of shy or quiet individuals. It was assumed that these persons were keeping to themselves what they should be sharing with others. One woman who was quiet remembers her therapist telling her "you probably even smell," since she was so secretive.

The result of this norm being put into practice was that there was very little space for what the sociologist Erving Goffman spoke of as behind-the-scenes work on the self, for public presentation of self. At the Center, every waking moment involved a public presentation of the self, even if one was not conscious of intending it. There was no private time in which one could just let down one's face.

A related result is that time for reflection decreased. One always had to have some awareness of others' reactions, be attuned to their responses to one. In addition, others invaded spaces usually considered private, like bathrooms. Houses were often quite crowded, so that one had more contact on a regular basis with people, even in leisure, nontherapy time. One man I interviewed said that he and his wife (then girlfriend) bought a house with six others, including several people he could not stand.

And finally, "making the private public" meant intense scrutiny and monitoring of all members for conformity to Center norms.

Isolation of Individuals

At key points, persons' associations were restricted. Initially, they were only to associate with members of their Intensive cohort, thus isolating them from previous ties and supports of self. This illustrates Lifton's (1961) "milieu control" as part of the therapy structure. Later on, individuals were isolated with their doubts and dissatisfactions about Center life and the therapists. Many of these became "secrets," not shared with friends or lovers. For example, one woman I interviewed was told to choose one person and make her a total confidante. Although she would have liked to have chosen her closest friend, she was afraid this woman would have busted her for diet violations, so she selected someone else.

In the 1978 reorganization of groups into a hierarchy of thirteen groups, a lot of patients who, for a variety of reasons, were not making progress were thrown into the "Tombstone Group" (numerically the largest). Thus, a whole category of patients who cast doubt on the therapy by their lack of progress in spite of years of membership were isolated from other patients. They were cut off both from those above them in Groups 1 to 4, who conformed more to Center norms, and from those in Groups 6 to 13, who were more recent members.

The major effect of these different forms of isolation was to prevent women and men from realizing that others shared their grievances. Without this realization, coalitions could not form. No real questioning was given a place within the structure of the Center, and this opened the way for the increasingly authoritarian environment that developed. Thus, the founders were forever able to turn individual doubt and dissatisfaction into feelings of individual inferiority or unworthiness.

Authoritarian groups have various ways to suppress doubt. One is to neutralize disagreement and doubt by relegating them to a particular place in the social structure. Synanon, for example, relegated these disagreements and doubts to the "Game," where one was then "gamed" about one's problems in understanding. "Negativity" thus disappeared from the routine organization of social life. est handled doubts about its worth in another way. Bry (1976:108) quotes a trainer's response to the question of whether est is a religion: "I got it. It's not and if that's what you experience it's O.K." That is, the trainer asserted the est position while supposedly "accepting" the individual's differing assessment. What he in effect did was to discount the individual's criticism by implying indifference: the question did not deserve discussion or explanation of how *est* differed from a religion. However, Bry sees such remarks as implying a "positive response" to everyone who spoke (44). The *est* way of handling questioning was thus one of seeming to be indifferent to questions expressing doubt or criticism. The individual cannot continue to talk about *est*'s worth in a situation where conventional modes of discussion and debate do not exist. The result is to make the skeptic look like a fool.

A third way of handling doubt is to deal with it outside the group, often in a one-to-one setting like religious confession. Here, one can reveal one's transgressions and receive guidance in dealing with them. This was one of the ways I was treated during my own participant observation of the Moonies: I was often sent to see the leader at Boonville because of the continual questions I asked in most settings.

These various approaches give individuals the impression that all doubt and disagreement are momentary, misguided, gone through. Doubt and disagreement thus come to be taken as transitory and not routine features of social organization. One assumes and fears that "only I" do not completely accept everything. In such an environment, "secrets" proliferate, even as certain "secrets" are regularly revealed to the group (Lifton, 1961:426–27). These new secrets express resentments of environmental controls. They express the emotions one should not feel, the negative evaluations one should not make. The individual is ever fearful that these secrets will escape: he or she knows they must not.

Arbitrariness of Center Life

I have already described the therapists' authority as being arbitrary. In addition, living at the Center seems to have been a matter of great arbitrariness, such that the only constant was change, but not change in any particular, predictable pattern.

This environment contributed to several important arrangements. It kept people continually off-balance, in a state of confusion and crisis. It maintained therapeutic authority and a hierarchy based on it, with the therapists (active) interpreting behavior and acting spontaneously, and the patients (reactive) responding to the therapists' interpretations and actions. Finally, it prevented individuals from developing cognitive maps of their environment, such that they could predict their social world.

The arbitrariness of life at the Center was one of the most striking findings of my interviews. Everyone spoke of being told to do things continually, with no explanation given, no matter how strange the assignment. Explanation did exist, to a limited degree, in the form of weekly lectures by one or two of the therapists. These talks on the theory of Feeling Therapy, or the therapeutic practice, however, were often so abstract, so unrelated to individuals' therapeutic activities, that they provided no understanding of them. Yet, patients often attributed reason to the assignments they were given; when they could not, they assumed that an unintelligible rationality lay behind them. Accordingly, they took for granted that a lot of activity was "good for them" and for other Center members, even when it did not appear so, or even when it appeared humiliating or harmful. Patients thus continually attributed good intent and rationality to the therapists.

Intensity of Center Life

Constant activity from early morning to late night characterized life at the Center for the men and women I interviewed. It seemed to be a part of the organization's intense atmosphere This activity was carried out in a certain way: people spoke very loudly and "feelingfully" at all times. Two persons mentioned that in their neighborhood the members of the Center households were known as the "screamers." Another suggested I interview some of the surrounding neighbors for their perspective on what Center people looked like to those on the "outside":

> [Y]ou ought to, someone should go in and interview some of the people in the neighborhood where we lived, because sometimes people in a house would be screaming at each other for hours, screaming and shouting at the top of their voices, shouting, and the neighbors would call the police, saying "we've got a bunch of lunatics next door."

Although housemates might scream at each other for many reasons, this kind of conflict seems to have arisen from another key norm, that one should express all one's feelings at all times. A couple I interviewed discuss what this meant for their daily life:

> Jane: It's not the kind of fighting people do in real life, it's *feeling* fighting, "That doesn't *feel* right to me," and then they'd go into this whole thing about who feels the rightest, and what really. . . . [y]ou could never end a discussion until everyone felt good, therefore you couldn't resolve it, so you took it to your friends. But that's how you spent your time with people, was, was, you'd come out of a movie, and it'd be, you, "I don't like the look on your face."
>
> Ted: Well, you were supposed to express every feeling and every thought, up to a point, and then they changed it all around, but for a long time that

was the idea. . . . Well, as Jane said, if I didn't like that sweater [referring to a sweater I was wearing], instead of just ignoring it, I'd shout at you, "I don't like that sweater, it doesn't look good on you, take it off, it's typical of you to wear clothes that don't look good on you, you don't take care of yourself," and pretty soon we'd be in a huge fight, I'd be screaming at you, you'd be screaming at me, and it'd be over nothing.

Jane: Or else you'd give in and submit and realize you shouldn't wear a grey sweater.

One could easily, in this way, consume hours of "leisure" time. In this way too, therapy, in the form of attempting to adhere to Center norms, always remained at the forefront of patients' lives, regardless of time or place. The Center was thus a classic example of Coser's (1974) "greedy institutions," taking up almost all of a person's life.

Relationships of all kinds assumed an intensity. My interviewees recall the peculiar nature of friendship at the Center:

Ted: It was weird, you might know the most sensitive things about somebody's sex life, but you didn't know whether they voted for Reagan or Carter . . .

Jane: Or whether they voted at all.

Ted: Or whether they went to college, or if they did, what they studied or what they thought about anything, you know.

Jane: Much interaction . . . revolved around things that would not have existed if we hadn't been in therapy. . . . A lot of the intensity of relationships was around "I don't like it that you always wear grey," and you'd sit around for an hour talking about how you thought a person always wore grey clothes, and grey clothes were the wrong image for the person.

The points that this couple make are several. An artificial intensity was created by the demand for all to express all feelings about a person, so that the most minor feelings emerged as equivalent to major ones. This generated a lot of daily conflict in the form of screaming and yelling in houses, which absorbed a lot of time and energy. Without the therapy, people would have had little to discuss. Relationships thus had an unusual balance: one might know the most intimate details of the sex lives of many persons, yet know very little of their more mundane characteristics, those traits one might learn first when a friendship was developing outside the Center (in the "real" world).

Other interviews yielded the same picture of Center households. One woman lived in a "righteous" house with nine other members, which she called one of the largest households. She described feeling an "edge" when she walked in—it was "punchy," "jokey in a sarcastic way." The television was always tuned to sports. She was frequently busted for "standing up too much in the house," for "being too quiet," and for "moving slowly." My interviewee avoided the house as much as possible. She mentions an assignment that one of her roommates had, to be angry every night, which she fulfilled by busting her. It got so that every night, at a certain point, her roommate would come up and say, "It really angers me that you . . . ," regardless of what had gone on between them, or even whether they had crossed paths at all that day.

All these comments highlight the importance of visible display as demonstrating commitment to the project of being a feeling person and in showing that one was making progress.[8] They also show how little space there was for deviating from Center norms. Even when far away from the Center, as in the story of the camping trip that Rachel told in Chapter Four, people adhered to its norms.

Impact on the Individual

In understanding the Center's effect on its patients, I think it important to re-emphasize several points. Most important is that the individual voluntarily chose to enter the Center for Feeling Therapy. The Intensive period and life as a patient afterward built on the person's earlier assessment of self as in need of help and on his or her choice (for a variety of reasons) of Feeling Therapy as an appropriate source of help. These two assessments that individuals made, even before beginning therapy, gave the Center a great advantage in breaking them down, as compared, for example, to those who were given the task of carrying out "thought reform" of prisoners in China and prisoners of war in Korea (Lifton, 1961; Schein with Schneier and Barker, 1961). By the time they entered their Intensives, persons had already persuaded themselves in great part of Feeling Therapy's value. This initial spirit of volunteering was then manipulated in a variety of ways, so that individuals were continually reminded that they sought out the Center and that they took great pains to get there. In addition, women and men were reminded that they needed the Center's help, rather than the Center needing them. Finally, the therapists implied that the person's initial choice to enter therapy extended to all that occurred in therapy.

The Intensive, then, took an already pliable individual and proceeded to break down his or her sense of self. I hypothesize that the therapists were able to do this by making contact with a person's "negative identity" and magnifying it until it eclipsed the individual's "positive" identity.[9] The person thus emerged from the Intensive with a greatly heightened awareness of his or her deficiencies, and a greatly increased need for Feeling Therapy. One of the men I interviewed recalls:

After the Intensive, I felt that I couldn't hack it, I better stay for help. First few months, loser identity clarified: I really need it, stay with the therapy, when my money ran out, I felt worse, embarrassed, couldn't meet their expectations. I didn't even bring my portfolio out here, eventually I had to send for it, I had not intended to stay, I left it at home. I was feeling so low that I was going for any type of job, grocery store, just to get by, to get the therapy to keep going. When I got out of school [college], I had waited a year to get the good job I had . . . I totally forgot what I'd been. . . . I took any job while at the Center to be able to maintain therapy and then be well . . . just trying to live up to their expectations.

Individuals began their lives as Feeling Therapy patients having been deeply touched or affected by their Intensive therapy. They were then placed within an organization that strongly pressured them to conform to its rigid, unrealistic norms. The sense of individual unworthiness, or inferiority, was thus continually stimulated, and a sense of guilt and shame was continually generated over infractions of unrealistic norms. Thus, individuals' sense of guilt and shame as being in the forefront of their lives was created and maintained from sources past and present.

This continual generation of individual guilt, as patients tried and failed to meet Feeling Therapy standards of behavior, thought, and feeling, made it impossible for them to create a stable sense of autonomous self. As noted earlier, part of the reason for this is that attempts to meet the standards always had to be attuned to others' responses. One performed every action with an eye toward its reception by others, not by reference to internal satisfaction.

Thus, Feeling Therapy patients "performed" as they attempted at all times to live up to the norms of their new reference group. These norms induced many unpleasant individual responses, as arrogance, intolerance, and lack of empathy for others characterized patients' performances, which were modeled on the behavior of therapists. Feeling Therapy norms slighted such characteristics as generosity of spirit, compassion for human frailties, reflectiveness, concern for civilized behavior as symbolized by manners, and quiet, peaceful ways of being.

Negative Identity

The Center made contact with the aspects of an individual's personality that he or she most wanted to suppress and then magnified that to be one's "real" identity. Contact with this identity associated with an early sense of guilt and shame gave the therapists access to the person in a very potent way. It opened up that part of the self that agreed with the Center's assessment of a woman or man's worst. Given the combination of a basic belief in the worth

of therapy with a psychological turning point or a life crisis, everyone is potentially vulnerable to this kind of attack, especially so if one wound up at a
group like the Center for Feeling Therapy.

In this way, valuing what one had achieved, and appreciating one's skills,
talents, and personality characteristics, was replaced by the Center's unrelievedly
grim assessment. For women, this frequently centered on their appearance, particularly their body. When my interviewee Jane (Ted's wife, mentioned earlier)
at first told her husband the Center's opinion—that she was ten pounds overweight, that she was a compulsive eater, and that she had a severe weight problem—Ted responded, "That's not true, you've never had a weight problem."
She, accepting the therapists' judgment, would say, "It's all been secret." By the
time the Center broke apart, her husband had come to think that she had a "raging weight problem" and that she was an "uncontrollable eater." For about a year
after the collapse, when Jane would attempt to have a full plate of food or eat
dessert, Ted would try to take it away from her, convinced that she would soon
"weigh three hundred pounds." Four other women I interviewed described
themselves as afraid they would become "blimps" without the Center; none of
them looked to me as though she should diet, and they reported being about the
weight they were before they came to the Center.

But in all these cases, the deep fear that the Center tapped into was part
of the negative identity that comes with growing up feminine in our culture:
one should be dainty, small, thin, rather than big, strong, or fat.[10] In the case
of women and dieting at the Center, to begin the struggle was to lose it continually. Accepting an assessment of themselves as "really" compulsive eaters
meant that they were more ready to take extreme action to rectify this problem, for it had assumed a greater magnitude.

This also illustrates the principle that one way to get a person to perform an extreme action is to place the action in the context of an even more
extreme action. Suppose, for example, that one is in the Moonies, trying to
decide whether to stay with the group and to give up other options to do its
work. This choice pales into insignificance beside both your eventual reward
(eternal glory for you as one who heeded the call, plus access to this glory for
all your successors based on their relationship with you) and what is about to
occur: the final days of the world as we know it. Pursuing normal activity now
looks absurd; one is concerned with pursuing a career that will never be because the world is about to end. At the Center, concern with polite ways of
dealing with people—family, friends, strangers, coworkers—looked insignif-
icant indeed compared to *saving* your own life.

Rather than "weigh three hundred pounds," women tried to stick to
600-calorie-a-day diets and to rigorous exercise programs, for years. Their

diet coaches continually rebuked them for their failures, which were many. These women reported falling into "binge and purge" cycles lasting for years.

In this way, a sense of urgency was created—you need to do something now about this problem. When one acts, the effect is twofold: it shows one's commitment and good intent, and it starts one on a fruitless pursuit.

Women and men were in a new social world. They had a new reference group by which to compare and judge their self, that of Center patients and therapists. And, as in any social world, they desired to make progress, to achieve status within that world. At the least, they desired to avoid disapproval, expressed in the form of "busting." Yet this desire to achieve status looks like an infantile desire to win approval from hypercritical therapists-as-parents.

Men too were placed on diets, which seemed designed to construct an appropriately "masculine" physique to match the "feminine" appearance of women. That is, slight men were put on diets to "bulk" them up. Several interviewees reported that they and other slight men were forced to gain weight, sometimes as much as twenty-five pounds. One woman recalled how her boyfriend continually tried to gain weight, eating until he threw up.

By placing men and women on assignments that were so unrealistic, the Center's culture generated continual individual failure. Day in and day out, individuals failed and felt inferior, no good, worthless. This failure often was not even on grounds the individual had previously cared about. But I hypothesize that even though the unrealistic norm might not relate to an individual's previous value system, the therapists had made contact with a "deep" part of the self. It formed from the earliest web of relationships, that of the family and early caretakers, and it was that part of self one had been admonished not to be. By making such deep contact, the Center's therapeutic structure was able to have a more profound effect than the prison on the persons that Lifton (1961) talks about. Therapists were able to make such a contact by virtue of their professional role as socially sanctioned healers. The role carries with it respect and prestige, and patients bring their expectations for help and care, and their trust, to therapists.

Escapes

Yet, people managed to circumvent Center scrutiny in various ways. They "escaped" momentarily, however; they did not leave for good. One woman I interviewed found that, by working overtime at her teaching job, she escaped some leisure activities and even occasionally therapy groups. Another said that she and her boyfriend would go away for weekends with another couple from the Center so that they could all enjoy activities they did not pursue at the Center. Jessie and her boyfriend read and slept; the other man and woman drank scotch. There was little interaction between the couples, except to say "we're fine, how are you?" These couples seemed to share an unspoken agreement not to bust each other for these violations of Center norms. Another interviewee mentioned the same kind of low-pressure interaction involving him and his girlfriend and another couple in the last year of the Center. Two other interviewees mentioned that they went horseback riding together every day at dawn and that this was their only real escape from the Center. As such it was greatly valued by each.

As other examples, the Center rule against smoking meant that when persons did smoke they "sneaked" a cigarette. Some use of alcohol was allowed, but frequent, heavy drinking was prohibited, so, as Mike's behavior (noted in Chapter Four) showed, people sneaked this too.

It seems to me that people who could lie also had an escape. Mike lied to cover his drinking. A second example is that of Joan, a woman who, for the two years she was there (the last two years of the Center), got up very early every morning, went to a café, and smoked and wrote in her journal. She never told anyone of this habit of hers, even though she described herself as being extremely close to her Intensive therapist and to her boyfriend. After this, she would return to her house, go back to bed, and get up with her boyfriend. Joan described this practice as being a continuation of her daily journal writing and her smoking habits. She said that she experienced only occasional guilt pangs over her behavior and her concealing it, but she knew she would be heavily busted if she revealed her activities to either her boyfriend or her therapist. By continuing her habit, she was able to retain more of her old identity. Most of the persons I interviewed, however, said that it did not occur to them to lie, that they usually told the truth, and that they were often busted for doing so, since they revealed their violations of Center rules and norms.

The Exceptions

Only two persons I interviewed reported that, overall, they had a good experience at the Center. These two examples, however, illustrate several things. The first case is that of Joan (mentioned above), who entered Feeling Therapy as a very successful professional. About four years before entering her Intensive, she had gone to a UCLA extension program on Feeling Therapy, and she had been involved for about six months in the "Associates Program." As she saw things at the time, she had sacrificed everything else in her life to become successful, and she lacked intimate relationships. As a result, Joan felt that she was not normal, and she wanted a chance to deal with everyday, "normal" things. She reports that many of her acquaintances perceived her as being "very together" and very independent. She thought otherwise.

It seems as though the Center's underlying assumption, that everyone is insane until he or she had undergone Feeling Therapy, validated her perception that she was not okay, no matter how others saw her. Even though she might appear quite successful, she was unhappy. Hence, Feeling Therapy agreed with her perception of herself.

Although Joan described her Intensive and her therapist to me as "terrific," she ran away once during her Intensive, because of the "increase of feelings that came up." When she got back to her apartment, however, she felt very much alone, and she returned to the Center. She described this as a realization that she "needed" her Intensive.

The therapist mostly worked on getting Joan attached to her and on getting her to do "normal" things, like enjoying people, everyday tasks like doing the laundry, and routine events like going to the movies and taking a bath. Joan reports that her therapist was always available to her and that she guided her in her career and in all aspects of life. By the end of the Intensive, Joan was calling her therapist all the time. At that point, her therapist told her she had to live her own life.

Joan's life after the Intensive was similar in many ways to her life before. She continued her career, which consumed much time and energy, and which meant she was away from Center life a lot. She retained the friends she had. She found a boyfriend at the Center, and she describes this as her first real romance. She also maintained a close relationship with her Intensive therapist for the two years she was there, in contrast to the others I interviewed. Joan said that she always felt special, and she always felt lucky in comparison to the others in her group. She thinks this was because she received a lot more personal attention than they did.

Joan reports not liking going to group and not liking doing assignments; she also said she did not do some assignments. Individual attention from her Intensive therapist, her co-therapists (she had four during her two years), and her special group therapist was what she particularly liked.

Several features of her experience separate her from many people at the Center. When she entered, the Center was emphasizing success in the outside world, and she was a successful working woman. (She continued her career the whole time, and she was not pressured to give it up.) Joan was almost thirty, in contrast to some of the people who entered at a younger age, when they had no firmly established career. She worked in a glamorous field, and Center therapists may have hoped to use her enroll her colleagues. She was pressured to invite people to Center activities, and she brought several friends.

Although they continued to be friends with her, they did not return a second time to the Center; after the organization disintegrated, they told her that they hated her involvement.

Thus, Joan was busy and away from the Center a lot, doing work she had chosen and that she enjoyed. She kept up earlier friendships, and she became involved in her first serious romance. She lived with this man and one other couple, who both worked at the Clinic and hence were usually gone from the house. Thus, Joan enjoyed more privacy with her boyfriend, and she was spared the pressure of being constantly monitored by housemates. In addition, she continued her practice of reserving daily "private time" for herself, and she felt free to use it exactly as she chose. She adhered to Center norms while on private time only to the extent necessary to not flaunt any infractions.

Her boyfriend, moreover, was one of Riggs Corriere's favorite patients. Both Riggs and his wife, Konni, treated Joan with respect, based on her association with a favored, older patient. She reported that the other therapists also treated her well and were available to her if she wanted their help. Her therapist was on good terms with her; in Joan's eyes, and in the eyes of a friend of hers with whom I also spoke, she was one of her therapist's favorite patients. She said that she believed her therapist *understood* her, and that she "always felt taken care of" and "very special." She thought she "was paid full attention to" by her therapist; she felt free to call her at "all hours," although she might have to wait for her therapist to be free to speak to her or to see her. Joan's one fear concerning her therapist was that she would cut off contact with her—that is, she feared the loss of contact that she experienced as always available and always nurturant, even though it might be quite controlling. The one example Joan gave me of suspended contact was that when her therapist knew she had smoked she "cut me off!" Joan would then "waylay her" until she would get some time with her.

Although Joan felt she had a good experience at the Center, some of the things that she later heard had happened there shocked her and changed her assessment of Center therapy. She thinks that many things the therapists did, which she discovered during and after the Center's breakup, were wrong.

Joan's experience at the Center differed in key ways from that of many others. Her special position seems attributable to her high external status, which she retained; to a relationship with a therapist that seems more personal, more individualized than many therapist-patient relationships there; to her involvement with a boyfriend, which was something she had very much wanted; and to an absence of many pressures from the environment, because of her relatively infrequent contact with persons of and at the Center for Feeling Therapy. In addition, she felt little guilt about maintaining in secret a daily habit that was very important to her. This example is only one that illustrates how people's social position in a group shapes their perspective on the group. Joan's relatively privileged position led her to have a benign view of the Center.

The second exceptional case is that of Mark. He, too, came into the Center when he was older (aged thirty), and when he had been pursuing a career for years. He had read The Primal Scream, but it was Going Sane that most interested him and drew him to the Center. Unlike many of the persons I interviewed, Mark had had extensive therapy, dating back to when he was eighteen. He describes himself just before he came to the Center as very discouraged with his therapy and with his homosexuality. His therapist had suggested he accept himself, his family had come around to this perspective, and he had experienced both these responses as ones of giving up on him.

What very much attracted him in Going Sane was the idea of a therapeutic community, or, as he expressed it to me, "their saying no one will leave you ever again." He thought of it as a place where people helped each other, and he saw it as better than weekly visits to a traditional therapist. He understood participating at the Center as "reparenting yourself, letting the Center be your parents," and he said this greatly attracted him.

He was very unhappy with his homosexuality—"[I]didn't know what I wanted, I was a real wreck"—and he was "moving more and more in the direction of male prostitutes." When he and his male lover broke up, he "was in such pain I couldn't stand, I had to crawl," and he felt "I had to do something."

At this point, his father died; he became closer to his mother in the wake of this death. She ultimately helped him get to the Center, because he did not have the money. She told him, "I'm going to do something your father wouldn't have approved of, I've always believed in you, and if you think this will help you, I'll give you the money to go." Mark estimates that she paid $4,500 for his Intensive and first month of therapy.

When he left the East Coast, he was willing to give up his career.

> I just was willing to give up everything and come out here. I was willing to give up anything it took. It was a big change, where I was saying, I'm willing to get well, but someone's got to help me with it because, I kept being told I can't. I would read books, you know, and I'd look for myself in books, and you know, by this point I was so convinced of it, that I would just see impossible, impossible, impossible, you are untreatable, or accept your condition, there's nothing you can do about it, and to me that was the most depressing, horrible thing you could say. It was like giving up on me. And I didn't have any, I didn't know what to fight back with, but that's the way I felt, you know, basically people were just sort of, well, you know, treating me that way.

When he got to the Center, he decided he would go to a gay bar one last time. A week before his Intensive, "I picked up someone who pulled a gun on me, took me on a joy ride, made me take off my clothes, throw them out of the car, and was threatening to go home, and make me take him to where my mother lived." He managed to talk his way out of the situation, but this helped to convince him of how much he needed the therapy he would receive: "So, I arrived at the Center knowing that this is what I needed."

There were five people in his Intensive cohort, in 1975. He explained his understanding of the requirement for initial isolation of his cohort from others:

> To me, they were, they were confining you, like a hospital, saying they're going to be doing very intense work with you, we don't want you to be exposed to outside pressures, influences, you're a group now, you're entering all at the same time, there were five of us, we were a small group and, uh, that's how it began.

Mark had a difficult time in his Intensive. He got very afraid that he "wasn't going to make it again" because he wasn't "responding." His therapist repeatedly left the room, and Mark thought it was to ask for help in treating him. The therapist kept trying to get him to "react," "to fight back":

> He kept coming after me, one time, I remember it because it was an upsetting time, he jumped on top of me, and started beating me. I just started crying "why are you doing this?" I'd been picked on before. He said he was trying to get me to react, to fight back, and when I didn't, he actually got extremely upset because he had done something which had a reverse [effect] on me.

The therapist explained that he was doing this to get a reaction,

> because I wouldn't fight for myself, I would just sort of look and say why? I was a total wimp then by this point psychologically, and just, I really didn't, I felt very helpless, and he wanted me to start fighting, to do something. He had a lot of trouble treating me, and he said later, I had him all along, and I really liked my therapist, but he had a lot of trouble with me, he said later, "[W]e share some things that are in common, and I have a real problem, a real blind spot, and I need to give you to other people." But constantly when he'd run into trouble he'd go out and get help for himself, and I was always impressed with that.

Mark said he just knew his therapist left sessions to get help in treating him; the therapist never told him this.

Besides his homosexuality, his weight was a major issue, and this too was dealt with in the Intensive:

> We had a session with my body, because I was overweight as I am back
> being overweight now, where I had to take off my clothes and stand in
> front of the mirror and look at myself and talk about my feeling about my
> body, how I really felt, not all the reasons you tell yourself when you're out
> of shape, but how I really felt, and uh there were other things he had me do
> to make me start wanting something different, to make me start fighting,
> because I didn't know what I wanted, and he, they needed to put me on a
> diet, a very, very low-calorie diet, and I lost a lot of weight, almost
> immediately, which was the first time in my life. I was down, I got down
> eventually to around 180, never making the goal which we'd set of 175, I'd
> get close and just freak out and gain two pounds.

His therapist put him on a diet limited to six hundred calories a day.

The hardest thing during the Intensive was an assignment his therapist
gave him. Mark did not understand it, and he thought at the time that it was
a mistake.

> My therapist kept trying to get me to, he discovered very early and he ended
> up being absolutely correct, although I didn't understand it at the time, it
> came out after the Center, he said, "You've been seduced by your mother,"
> and he tried to make me insult her, find fault with her, and I didn't
> understand why he would want to do that, because I was feeling very good
> about my mother, her having sent me there, and I didn't understand it.

Mark qualified his evaluation of this assignment and others he felt were mistakes: "I say they didn't work but I ended up later being affected by things, so
I don't know, if they did work, I question, I wonder what worked there."

From the start, Mark behaved heterosexually, developing a relationship with a woman that lasted for most of his five years at the Center. He also
lost 110 pounds. He describes his career as developing. He was, therefore, a
success in the areas where he had felt he needed help, and he attributes his
success to the therapy.

However, note that Mark's story corroborates the stories told by those
of my interviewees who claim they were greatly harmed by their participation at the Center. He saw and experienced many of the same things, but he
construes them quite differently. Mark recalls events in a way that, for the
most part, preserves the therapists' authority intact and places the burden for
change on individual patients.

Above all else, in evaluating his gains and losses from participating at
the Center, Mark seems to place the romantic relationship he developed—and
the achievement of heterosexuality that it implies—at the top of the list of
benefits. On the other hand, he was almost never appalled:

> Only one time at the Center did I really react and think that was really horrible, and that was when a therapist said to someone, "I gave you your girlfriend and I can take her away."

He thinks this affected him so strongly "because that's sort of in a way what happened with me." This event took place during the Center's last year, and in the "last year a lot of things were not making very much sense." He recalls his internal monologue explaining such events:

> When I would see things like this, and think it looks harsh, my justification of it would be, in my experience, when they'd try things, when my therapist had done that, that, behind that was a saying, "I [the therapist] know you, and I'm not going to let that go, you're not going to get away with that here," and they would persist with people. And some people never gave in in those areas they'd continually get busted in, and then, later, I'd find out when I'd talk to them after the Center, they had never, ever admitted their problems, they'd fight in those same areas.

Thus, Mark in large measure accepted the Center's claims that it was doing what was good for people and that the therapists had correctly divined patients' problems. If they had listened to the therapists, and given in, men and women would have gotten rid of their psychological ills. Yet, Mark also observed many of the same things, and shared many of the same fears, reported by my other interviewees. Like all the persons I spoke with, Mark wondered how much of the change in himself could be attributed to Feeling Therapy as such, and how much could be attributed to living in a community of persons undergoing therapy.

Why Did Patients Remain at the Center?

Despite all the humiliations involved, men and women stayed at the Center for Feeling Therapy for the same reasons people remain in any group: their sense of self, or identity, came to depend on the relationships in which they became involved while at the Center, including those with the therapists. They developed strong links with the leaders and with other members, which ties became more important to them than those with people outside the group, including family members and former friends.

The most important feature of the relationships that developed with therapists was the therapeutic aspect: "I am here to help you, and I can help you," with "You are greatly in need of help, and you can only get it here" being the counterpart. A plethora of understandings arose that placed the responsibility for making progress in dealing with one's problems and for attaining happiness onto the individual patient. The therapists and the Feeling Therapy ideology could help, but only if one cooperated and did one's share. So, "If you're not getting better, you're not trying hard enough" and "If you're unhappy, it's your own fault" were constant Center refrains.[11] Leaving was equated with failure by the person. Individual men and women, who had often entered with a sense of having failed in some way, could not arrive at an alternative interpretation of leaving, and they did not want to fail again. Failure was cast in frightening images: patients were told they would be placed in mental hospitals, they would commit suicide, they would become "homeless bums." One woman I interviewed said she was told she would probably become a prostitute. Often, individuals' worst fears were used to give these images an intense emotional charge. One interviewee reported, for example, that two patients whose siblings had been hospitalized as schizophrenic and who feared the same fate were told that this was very likely, especially if they left.

The arbitrariness of Center life prevented women and men from arriving at clear understandings of how the organization worked. Thus, they were not able to share their insights with others and develop alternative positions. Nor could coalitions of patients develop. Stannard-Friel's *Harassment Therapy* (1981), in describing the ending of abusive therapy practices by the demands of patients as a group, illustrates the importance of such coalitions.

In addition, some features of the Center attracted patients. Chief among these appeared to be its sense of community. Individuals were "real" with each other to different degrees: some seemed to put their hearts into their relationships, others seemed to have simply accepted them, and still others did the minimum to remain involved, feeling close to only a very few persons. Individuals might chafe at the restraints, especially if they were urged to continue friendships or romances in which they were unhappy. Yet, the idea and practice of community was very important for many members. Jerome Frank, describing "demoralization" as the state common to all seeking psychotherapy, says that the "demoralized person feels *isolated*, hopeless, and helpless, and is preoccupied with merely trying to survive" (1974:314; emphasis added).[12]

A sense of being part of an elite also attracted men and women to Center life. The therapists claimed to be a vanguard in psychology and in society; they promised that all, patients and therapists alike, would eventually be widely esteemed as "feelingful" people by the larger community. Members shared in this, feeling that they, unlike the unknowing, were on the road to "sanity." According to my interviewees, the therapists at least looked as though they might be able to achieve this revolution: they were attractive and dressed in the latest of fashion, and they appeared knowledgeable, supremely confident, powerful, and happy. Patients wanted to become like the therapists, to look as good as they did and to be as happy as they were. Persons at the Center were encouraged to attribute these characteristics to Feeling Therapy's influence on the therapists' lives.

Another attractive feature of the therapy was its all-inclusiveness, its emphasis on paying attention to all parts of life.[13] One could feel one was making progress on all fronts. Yet, this sense of mastery was more fanciful than real.

Two other factors made it hard for patients to consider leaving the Center. The first was a consequence of what I have called good cop/bad cop behavior by the therapists. No therapist was described as being always and completely confrontative and attacking. Yet, this style predominated, with gentleness and supportiveness being secondary. Their scarcity made the infrequent displays of warmth and support much more effective and valued. Scarcity is one of the six psychological principles organizing human behavior discussed by Cialdini (1984:230).

The second feature was individuals' general sense of impotence,[14] which I think is covered by Lifton's (1961) term "psychology of the pawn." Patients felt psychologically unable to leave the group, even when they had doubts, even when they wondered whether they were in a cult, and even when they did leave physically. Several persons I interviewed left for a time, then returned on their own. The sense of being impotent to leave the Center was colored by a deep foreboding of dire consequences that would follow any departure. Individuals felt these consequences to be real possibilities.

Both deferring to authority and conforming to peers were important in motivating women and men to remain Feeling Therapy patients. In addition, members "pluralistic ignorance" of others' doubts and dissatisfactions prevented them from forming a coalition that might challenge therapeutic authority and unanimous agreement. The social reality of the Center became paramount to these individuals, making them extremely dependent on Center therapists and Center life.

The organization lost the ability to isolate people in the space of seventy-two hours. This was just long enough for control over communication in the group to break down, resulting in the disintegration of the social world of the Center. Since the Center's beliefs were in opposition to those of the outside world, they could not be sustained in the outside world. Accordingly, members were then left with a set of beliefs that could have no sustaining culture.

The way in which the Center for Feeling Therapy collapsed is part of its uniqueness. Very few cults break apart in such a sudden, cataclysmic way. The more usual way for people to leave cults is as an individual "splittee"— they abandon the group, with the cult remaining intact and authoritative for the majority who remain. In this instance, however, the group lost all legitimacy, and all members, whether unhappy or happy with Center life, were forced to face the end of their world.

The very aspect of social organization that helped to maintain the organization's intense control over members—the network of interaction and communication among patients and therapists key to "therapeutic community"—was also responsible for the therapists' inability to regain control and for the complete destruction of the Center. Rumors spread almost instantly through these networks. Rather than the therapists' word being communicated, what was communicated was that the therapists' word was not to be trusted.

Although many members suddenly "saw the light" and realized that many of their suppressed doubts were valid, they were still "brainwashed." That is, although they were suddenly released from the system of strong social influence they had lived under for years, they still had the set of beliefs according to which they had organized their lives. They did not, in this moment of sudden, sharp realization, revert to a prior state of identity. Rather, they had to reconstruct, yet again, a sense of identity that would incorporate their years at the Center, a task colored by the very painful realization that they had been manipulated in ways not helpful by the very therapists who had offered them help.

Seven
Coping with Stigma: Rebuilding Lives

One of the most interesting phenomena in seeing how the men and women I interviewed reconstructed their lives was examining the way individuals had to explain their experience publicly so as to regain social respectability. Right from the start of the group's being labeled a "cult" by the news media (e.g., "The Cult of Cruelty"), persons had to deal with the "spoiled identity" of being an "ex–cult member." In addition to all the personal problems they had to deal with privately, they also had to confront the public's sense that their having participated in a "cult" indicated that something was wrong with them.

Although at the time of my interviews the vicissitudes of being an "ex-cultist" were largely uncharted, later work is filling this gap. *Recovery from Cults* (1993), edited by the psychologist Michael D. Langone, presents an introduction and twenty articles about understanding "mind control, leaving cults, facilitating recovery," along with miscellaneous articles such as "Children and Cults." The book represents the culmination of years of work by various professionals and onetime cult members to help former cultists recover and adapt to the mainstream. The articles provide useful guidelines for the variety of practitioners who are in contact with former members, as well as for family and former members themselves. Key to their recovery is information on "mind control"; the approach presented is that erstwhile cultists need to understand cognitively what happened to them. Thus, the authors present "exit counseling" (in contrast to "deprogramming," involving forcible abduction) as being most helpful. Imparting information so that individuals can make more-informed choices is crucial to this approach. *Exit Counseling*, by Carol Giambalvo (1995), describes in more detail the actual mechanics and logistics of "exit counseling" (although she would prefer the term "thought-reform consulting"), whose goal she describes as "to help a loved one evaluate his or her involvement in a cultic group" (x). This "exit counseling" is to be distinguished from the more lengthy "post-cult counseling": the former is usually a three- to five-day affair, and it is not to be expected that all possible problems will be resolved during this time. *Captive Hearts, Captive Minds* (1994), by Madeleine

Landau Tobias and Janja Lalich, two former cult members, is another excellent resource, addressing in depth the recovery issues they and others experienced. Finally, Wendy Ford's *Recovery from Abusive Groups* (1993) also provides much information for onetime cultists and their families, based on what she learned during her recovery from her involvement with The Way International. Two videotapes are available to help people who have left cults. Ten former cult members share their stories of recovery in *After the Cult: Recovering Together* (1994), developed by Project Recovery of the American Family Foundation. Margaret Singer (1995) also discusses these issues in *Leaving a Cult*.[1]

I divide the process of reconstruction into the following stages: (1) Leaving the Role of Patient; (2) What Do I Do next? and (3) Time Heals. What did these former patients experience in this process of reconstruction?[2]

Leaving the Role of Patient

The Center for Feeling Therapy continued to exist because of the continual creation of, and maintenance of deference to, therapeutic authority. Throughout its existence, there was very little public challenge to this authority. At the end, the seven male therapists who headed the Center were known as the "founders." While one of them, Riggs Corriere, was widely acknowledged as the head therapist at the time, patients saw all these men as being very powerful. Other therapists stood lower in the hierarchy; they were known as "second" and "third" generation therapists.

The Delegitimation of Therapeutic Authority

Given this appearance of unanimity, why did the Center break up so suddenly? Two things appear crucial in understanding its demise. Both contributed to the destruction of the appearance of unanimity and to the realization that individual grievances were shared by large numbers of patients, even therapists. I hypothesize that both resulted from Riggs's increased control at the Center.

First, and more important, is the split that developed between Riggs and the rest of the therapists, including his wife. He had progressively gained control over the other therapists, and he had placed himself at the top of the Center hierarchy. His most loyal friends ranked below him as heads of Groups 2, 3, and 4. When the groups were reorganized in 1978 the power bases of the therapists were removed.

One aspect of the developing split took shape among the junior therapists as they compared themselves to the founding therapists. The junior therapists were making much less money than the founders; when they requested additional money, they were busted. This caused the junior therapists to begin talking among themselves—which was the first step in developing an alternative perspective on the Center. In several other ways, solidarity grew among this group as they began to share their real feelings, away from the Center. For example, Mithers (1994:29–95) describes the solidarity that grew up among four clinicians who had been assigned to develop an outpost some sixty miles south of the Center. They began communicating during their long commute between Los Angeles and the satellite community.

When the junior therapists arrived at the Doll Baby Ranch, they were assigned to the former cowboys' quarters, away from the main house, where Riggs and the other founders stayed. This seemed to symbolize their status within the organization, as their accommodations were crowded and less grand than those of the main house. Here they began to grumble among themselves—and have fun. All of this allowed for more solidarity to develop among them.

Second, the therapists' monthly vacation week was replaced by a week spent at the Doll Baby Ranch. This time entailed not rest and recuperation (as it had previously) but constant hard work making the ranch fit for the community to use. Thus, therapists' lives came to resemble patients' lives more closely—Riggs might awaken them at 6 A.M. to work on the corral. Center life, for both therapists and patients, had become more intense, time-consuming, and exhausting.

At what was to become the last week of the Center, several founding therapists began to talk to each other about their dissatisfactions with Riggs's leadership. They discovered that they shared similar grievances. They also found they were having fun without Riggs. This discovery came while the therapists were at the ranch in Arizona, and he and his wife were at the Center in California. In Riggs's absence, a coalition grew up among the therapists for the first time, and they developed an alternative understanding of Center life. They concluded that Riggs had grown too powerful and that he needed to be busted to get him to be "more personal." These therapists also recognized that the therapy needed some changes.

They returned to the Center with the idea of expressing their grievances to Riggs as part of busting him. Dominic Cirincione took on the task of busting Riggs, during a week of therapy sessions (Mithers, 1994:306). That Monday, the senior staff held the first "Get Down Group" (therapy for the therapists) in five years; here, they expressed their resentments of Riggs and the number two therapist (heading Group 2), all in a "feelingful" way, as usual. That is, the meeting involved a great deal of yelling and screaming.

The therapists met again on Tuesday. Feeling they had not succeeded in busting Riggs and the second-ranking therapist, they decided to bring them before Groups 1 and 2 (their own groups) and allow the members to express

their resentments directly. This invitation acknowledged to patients that
something was wrong with the Center's functioning, and it gave them permission to voice their dissatisfactions.

The women and men in these two groups might be considered the
most loyal patients at the Center. In both, however, a torrent of resentments
poured out. Leading the attack in Groups 1 and 2 were female patients, whose
status was arguably that of "second class citizens" (Mithers, 1994:307). The
unexpected flood of complaints was so strong that, for the first time in the
Center's history, the therapists lost all control.

Although they had asked patients to vent their dissatisfactions about
the head therapist, these therapists too became the objects of criticism, and for
the same reasons that they were criticizing Riggs Corriere. As one woman I
interviewed, a longtime patient in Group 1, put it, "Nobody forgot *anything*,
nobody forgot anytime they were busted, they *ate* it, but they remembered it,
and all of us it turned out remembered it." What was intended to be a limited
expression of dissatisfaction with the Riggs and the second-ranking therapist,
Werner Karle, enlarged to include expression of resentments against all Center therapists. As another woman I interviewed said:

> When they went to the ranch, one therapist threw out a tiny joke about
> Riggs, they laughed, he started another, they laughed, this was the
> beginning of the end, they had no idea *they* were monsters. . . . The criticism
> snowballed [during the final three days], it turned on Binder, Cirincione—
> they didn't expect it, they'd disassociated [themselves] from Riggs, the
> monster. My house was buzzing when I got home: "[W]e've been robbed."

This woman's mention of robbery refers to patients' contributions to the gym
fund, which appeared to have gone to buy and maintain the ranch, and to
money paid by Center businesses to Center "consultants."

At the time of the disintegration some of the therapists and patients feared
violence might erupt, so intense was the patients' anger. It was as if the therapists
had held a lighted match to a stick of dynamite: the group "blew up."

Lalich (1993:51–84) describes the very similar demise of the political
cult she was involved in for ten years. In this case the leader left, having turned
on her loyal second in command. This woman then initiated discussion of
criticisms of the leader; she spoke first with her cronies, who then raised the
issue in "Quality of Life" discussions (part of a current party campaign). This
marked the first time that members were allowed to criticize the leader and to
express their feelings completely. Of these sessions, Lalich says:

> In a sense the Quality of Life meetings turned into group therapy sessions. Still
> bound by party discipline and riddled with guilt and self-critical attitudes,

militants tiptoed into the unknown. They spoke with anguish about losing friends and families. One woman described how she felt when her husband was put under house arrest [by the cult] and eventually expelled; at the time she had been told not to think or ever talk about it. She never saw him again and her distress at this event remained bundled up inside her for years. Parents shed tears over never having time to see their children. (84)

Singer (with Lalich 1995:223–24) mentions a group begun by two male art professors; it lasted five years, until the older professor died and his colleague was dismissed from their college. The collapse came when the "students exchanged information about their private relationships with the teachers and came to see that the men were not the world-class teachers they claimed."[3]

Even if the therapists precipitated the downfall of the Center for Feeling Therapy, why were the patients so ready to join in? I think the same things that led to the split between Riggs and the other therapists brought about increased conflict and tension among the patients. One additional condition must be mentioned: the absence of the thirteen founding and junior therapists from the Center for two months during the summer of 1980. The therapists were doing training at several satellite centers and taking an extended vacation at the ranch. In addition, the unmarried founders who were romantically involved all married at this time.

Balch (1985) describes a similar absence by the two leaders of the flying-saucer cult he studied, which led to a loss of membership. (This cult gained notoriety in 1997 as Heaven's Gate; Balch's article provides an insight into this group before most of its members killed themselves.)

While the Center's leaders were away, Group 1 patients were in charge of running the therapy. These patients were much less impressive, and much less harsh, than the therapists. Thus, there was a loosening of control that patients enjoyed. Moreover, many older patients could see Group 1 members as their peers, not as authorities like the therapists. Again, this meant a loosening of control.[4]

The reorganization of groups along hierarchical lines, while undermining therapists' relationships to patients and thus destroying their bases of power, also undermined solidarity ties among members. For much of the Center's existence, there was a strong sense of "we" and "they"—"we" in the Center are far superior to those unknowing, unfeeling individuals on the outside. In addition, before the change in groups, persons had been placed with others from their Intensive cohort or with those who had been in the next Intensive. Consequently, men and women in these groups were roughly the same "age," having had the same therapist-leader for years.

Immediately preceding the reorganizing and numbering of groups, therapists had begun rotating among them (they got only halfway before the groups were numbered). After the numbering, women and men were placed according to their rank in the Center. New patients entered the lowest group, groups would keep being added, and individuals would, theoretically, progress up the hierarchy. At the Center's collapse there were thirteen groups. Note that this system introduced, for the first time, an element of explicit competition among members. Now one had a tangible way to gauge one's "feeling" status—one's rank in the hierarchy. Competition for membership in the upper groups was intense, and there was little mobility; this struggle also undermined the members' solidarity.

In addition, patients' lives had become more intense in several ways. One interviewee used the metaphor of a carousel spinning ever faster to describe the last year of the Center. Greater emphasis on becoming a successful, mainstream therapy meant greater emphasis on appearing attractive to the outside world and less attention paid to relations among persons at the Center. Men and women had to "look good" all the time (in spite of how they felt), which became very difficult. The Center had become more of a business, and this emphasis undermined relationships.

A third feature, which again was true for both therapists and patients, was that many "dissidents," when busted and demoted, were retained within the organization. Joe Hart, who left about eight months before the end, was the exception. Taken in conjunction, these four features—the absence of the therapists and the resulting loosened control; the introduction of explicit completion among member; the more intense, exhausting life, with less emphasis on relationships among members; the retention of dissidents—made the Center seem like a powder keg waiting to be ignited.

This sequence of events during the final days of the Center destroyed the image of the therapists as godlike in their authority. It destroyed, too, the image of the therapeutic regime as ultimately benefiting patients. However, the destruction of the Center did not mean that women and men suddenly and completely lost faith in what had become the guiding force in their lives and reverted to their earlier identities. Rather, individuals began a very painful process of discovering what had happened to them.

In the outpouring of grievances that followed the therapists' invitation to bust Riggs (and Werner Karle), the "pluralistic ignorance" that patients had of others' dissatisfactions and doubts was shattered. Balch (1985) would say this was the "crack in consensual validation," which he saw as beginning the process of defection in the flying-saucer cult he studied. Patients at the Center realized that their feelings of "only I am dissatisfied, only I am not progressing" were collective. One man I interviewed expressed his anger and his realization of shared grievance.

> When I heard these like gods, people who could do no wrong, had done wrong, I wanted to leave, wanted to go kill the person [speaking of the head therapist], to believe you were led on, that it was all a trick, everything at the Center was a mystery. . . . I always thought it was just me, turned out everyone else thought this too, I thought everyone else *knew* what was going on, but they didn't know, it was a mystery for them too.

The patient network rapidly circulated the word: what the therapists said was not to be trusted.

Among the accusations against the therapists were deceitfulness, embezzlement, falsification of research reports on the therapy's efficacy, and therapeutic malpractice. These charges seemed to explode the members' trust, based on the therapeutic relationship, that the therapists were caring professionals concerned with watching out for patients' interests. Instead, the accusations revealed the therapists as too little concerned with patients and too much concerned with self-interest (e.g., in buying a ranch for themselves with money collected to build a gym for the community, and in producing false research results favorable to their brand of therapy).

The Center's Social World Comes Apart

Immediately after the collapse, my respondents' reactions varied. The organization they belonged to had disintegrated, and all members had to reconstruct their lives apart from it. Because of the response to lawsuits that were filed immediately after the collapse, none of the therapists could continue to work with the patients. Immediate reactions ranged from euphoria to dismay. Some actions former members took against the therapists impressed me as being similar to those of rebellious adolescents against overcontrolling parents: for example, interviewees reported large numbers of unordered pizzas being delivered to the therapists and rocks being thrown through the therapists' windows. Others reported fearing for the lives of the therapists because of the raging, suddenly released anger of patients who felt that they had been "duped." All this seemed to take place in a generally forbidding atmosphere.

The persons I interviewed all reported being shocked at the speed and totality of the collapse. They reported that they could not foresee the events based on their own internal feelings of dissatisfaction, since they had experienced such feelings many times before with no ill consequences for the organization.

Many romances and friendships seem to have broken up very soon after. This further damaged the organization, since patients lived in group houses—the collapse of the group also meant the collapse of intimate relationships, housing arrangements, and sometimes even the loss of a job (for those working at the Center or at Center-affiliated businesses). These events meant that men and women experienced the end of the Center as the end of their previous way of living. One interviewee described her feelings at the time:

> I felt incredible rage at first, and incredible loss—after almost six years, the
> end was a great loss to me. My relationship ended very abruptly, I had no
> money, no job, no career, no car, no home (my boyfriend owned the house
> and he threw me out). I found I had lost everything.

Several themes characterized these first reactions: intense anger, intense anxiety, intense anomie, or sense of meaninglessness, and mourning—for losses of time, friendships, a feeling of purposefulness, a child aborted. These themes characterized the long-term reactions of the persons I interviewed as well; as the literature on recovery from cults (referred to earlier) shows, these are common responses.

The men and women I interviewed had to deal with an involuntary exit from a social world. Moreover, as part of the process of constructing a new sense of identity, they still had to "exit" the master role of Feeling Therapy patient. At the time of the Center's demise, former members experienced the "vacuum" Ebaugh's (1988:143) exiters faced, in which the majority "went through a period of feeling anxious, scared, at loose ends, that they didn't belong. The experience is best described as the 'vacuum' in that people felt 'in midair,' 'ungrounded,' 'neither here nor there,' 'nowhere.'"[5]

What Happened?

As the Center for Feeling Therapy broke apart, individuals were concerned with asking and answering many questions. This was the beginning of a search for understanding, the beginning of "cognitive reorganization" (Balch, 1985:49), which persisted through the other stages. Perhaps foremost was the question of what the Center was. Was it a noble experiment gone wrong or a cult? Additional questions arose. Was the therapy abusive? Why did therapists do the things (good and bad) they did? What did others *really* experience in their therapy? Why did the Center collapse? Why did "I" and "they" stay in the therapy? These questions remained questions for many. One man I interviewed tried to explain his sudden questioning this way:

> Gold [one of the therapists] said he didn't want to go to jail, Woldenberg
> [another therapist] said they were making mistakes, they hadn't been sure
> of things, and I began to think, "[Y]ou mean maybe my negative thoughts
> were valid. Maybe the people who left Plant Pusher [a center business], the
> 'pirates,' *they* were the successes." So, I wanted to look at all my doubts, and
> see if they were valid. Woldenberg was saying these people [the "pirates"]
> were the successes, and I was one of the "pirates."

One of the major tasks involved in reconstructing their lives was figuring out exactly what their experience in the Center had been.[6] This included
understanding the collapse of the organization first of all, for its disintegration threw major doubt on the value of the therapy, the authority of the therapists, and the therapeutic community that had evolved. Until the Center
broke up, these three elements of life as a Feeling Therapy patient had gone
largely unquestioned in public. Suddenly, from being regarded so highly as
to be revered by patients (and therapists), these elements had become worse
than base metal, in the eyes of some. The persons who led the sharp reassess-
ment were the "oldest" patients, those who had been members the longest.
The "youngest" patients were viewed, by many of my interviewees, as being
more likely to still be enamored of Feeling Therapy at the end, as being harder
to persuade of the new, "real" assessment of things.

If the therapy, the therapeutic authority, and the therapeutic community
were all to be questioned, then what of one's own participation? How was it to
be regarded? The women and men I interviewed reported that, as active participants, they had put the organization at the center of their lives for periods ranging from eight months to ten years; the therapists, who after all embodied the
therapy, were the authorities most important to these persons in living their lives,
more important than the individuals' own feelings, thoughts, or preferences.
This therapeutic authority was referred to frequently, for decisions in all aspects
of life—for example, whether to enter or leave a relationship, have an abortion,
relinquish custody of a child, gain or lose weight.

One man I interviewed said that "maybe being lowest [in the groups]
means not being so brainwashed. I was always a bad patient." Several others
said that they too were consistently viewed as "bad" patients at the Center,
and that perhaps this meant they were less "brainwashed," less controlled than
others.

The Controversy Begins: "Stigma Contests"

The Center's demise, and the subsequent dispute between therapists
and patients as to the relationship between the two groups,[7] showed up in the
pages of the Los Angeles Times. The organization was labeled a "psychotherapy
cult," with all the negative connotations associated with the word "cult."[8]
From that moment, past members had to deal with public perception of their
activities in Feeling Therapy as "cultlike." That is, they now had to be concerned about the stigma of being an "ex-cultist."

For erstwhile patients, this involved problems relating to "spoiled identity." Beckford (1985:196) suggests that because the most popular explanation
for recruitment into and participation in a cult is that of "brainwashing," one-

time members "are stigmatized as people who, probably through no fault of their own, have become unstable and untrustworthy." This rationale gives family members and friends a "kind of moral power over the ex-members." Beckford continues: "In the families of ex-members, the notion of 'brainwashing' has been employed for the purpose of reminding them that their moral capacity is suspect and that they are not to be fully trusted 'until they come to their senses.'" (197). Of course, family members

> claim to know what the relevant criteria of "coming to their senses" are, the ex-Moonies' own judgments are not taken seriously. This has, in some cases, set in motion a vicious spiral of degradation followed by diminished self-respect, followed by further degradation, and so on. (197)

Certainly there is need for more research on how persons who have been in a group characterized as a "cult" renegotiate the passage back to becoming a "normal" individual in social interactions. As mentioned earlier, Langone's *Recovery from Cults* (1993), the videotape *After the Cult*, and Tobias and Lalich's *Captive Hearts, Captive Minds* (1994) provide good information on this process. The problem remains, however, both for those who characterize their time spent in these groups as valuable and for those who bemoan the destructive effects of participation in such groups, for, overwhelmingly, most Americans regard "cults" as bad.

What Do I Do Next?

In the second stage of personal reconstruction, both those happy and those unhappy with Feeling Therapy had to decide what to do next with their lives. The choice to remain a patient disappeared with the Center. Once the collapse was accepted as irreversible, choices arose about residence, occupation, romantic partners, friendships, and psychological help, among other things. Those who had worked at the Center were suddenly out of a job. Those living in groups with other Feeling Therapy patients faced sudden conflicts over who should continue to live in the houses and who should go. Some persons immediately began talking of filing lawsuits against the therapists. Others immediately packed up and returned to where they had lived before coming to Los Angeles for therapy. Some men and women who had been coupled by therapeutic edict suddenly dumped their partners, seeing them as vestiges of their prior lives as a therapy patients.

Thus, stage two of personal reconstruction includes the step of *initial choices made*, which is concerned with such matters as jobs initially taken up, new housing, and returns for "time-outs" with family. Trial-and-error decision making seemed to characterize most of these choices. Two psychological issues seemed central in this stage, trustworthiness and establishing criteria for decision making. Who and what can I trust? Can I trust myself? What criteria does a "normal" person use to make choices? Who does one turn to for help in answering these questions? All of these issues were of great concern to the persons I interviewed.

Recourse to "Experts"

Perhaps the interviewees' biggest problem as a group has been finding sympathetic individuals who can both listen and help them to better understand their experience. Many of the therapists they saw after leaving the Center seemed to understand little of what being in a "cult" entails. They also seemed to impose definitions of the situation on the former members, which definitions emphasized their personality trait of "dependency." This was supposedly what attracted them to the group, in their new therapists' eyes. That is, these experts focused on an explanation in which individual personality was essential, rather than on a situational explanation, in accounting for decisions to enter and to stay with the group.[9] This did not seem to alleviate difficulties of adjustment, for although the former members may have had problems with "dependency," they also had to deal with problems of therapeutic abuse. They needed a cognitive understanding of the ways in which their dependency, and other needs, had been manipulated by Feeling Therapists to their detriment.[10]

In coping with reorganizing their lives, with whom did the Center's past patients consult? Many reported seeking out other therapists, but using different criteria: once-burned, forever shy would not describe these individuals, but cautious and more trusting of "gut" responses would. This latter notion was itself a reaction to the experience, one that came from having overlooked "gut" or internal responses in favor of therapeutic authority or peer pressure while at the Center. One interviewee described trusting and acting on her feelings about a therapist she saw after she had left the Center. When he "came on" to her, "I stopped therapy, yelled at him, and he said I had a problem with anger, I was very vulnerable—'this person is obviously upset'— and he attacked me with sophisticated labels."

Some former patients at the Center went to community mental health services, some to a symposium on cults, some to a psychiatrist affiliated with a religious task force on cults, some to various other therapists, one to Alcoholics Anonymous. Others seemed to rely strongly on ties to others from the group, in their own form of "peer counseling" and support.

Several of those I interviewed reported feeling almost immediately that the Feeling Therapists had harmed them; they filed lawsuits against them shortly thereafter. Others reported that it took a long time for them to feel anger toward the therapists.

Work

For many onetime members, reconstructing a work life was paramount in reorganizing their lives. Persons who had left jobs or careers upon entering therapy at the Center, and who had worked at low-wage, low-skilled jobs for the duration of their stay, wanted to get on with their working lives. One interviewee recalls how she began this part of reconstructing her life:

> I entered wanting help with getting boyfriends and a career, and I got no real help with that [getting a career]. I had an image [at the Center] as a boring, dull person, and I assumed I was dumb. At the end I recognized that I could be a "smart" secretary. One of the therapists told me that when he discovered I could take shorthand. Afterwards, I went to the UCLA Career Guidance Clinic. I paid $400. I was told I was really smart, I could have been a doctor but now I was too old. I got really mad, because I'd believed my negative image all along, and I had gotten no help with this.

The onetime patients often perceived themselves as being behind others their age in their careers; this was still a significant concern at the time I did my interviews. Comparing themselves to women and men of their own age who had not been in a cult, they arrived at largely unfavorable self-estimates. Their reference group had radically and suddenly shifted: now they were no longer comparing themselves to the other members of the Feeling Therapy community with whom they lived, but rather to individuals in a variety of contexts (coworkers, former friends, family members, strangers about their age). Nor were they any longer concerned with the Center notion of how "feelingfully" they were living life. Rather, they were thinking of what they were doing in a career, how much money they made, whether they owned a house (as one man said, "people [at] thirty-three have houses, I'm so far behind"), whether they had other key material possessions like televisions, and whether they had children. SanGiovanni (1978) uses the concept of "age deviance" to explain the feeling the former nuns she studied had of being "behind" peers in their new reference groups.

Reconstruction of Autobiography

In addition to seeing themselves as being behind in the pursuit and acquisition of the middle-class American Dream, in ordinary interactions with individuals they met the men and women I interviewed were likely to feel stigmatized if they said they had been in a "therapy cult." Having become acutely attuned to the responses of others, particularly therapists, while they were at the Center, after its disintegration the past members were acutely attuned to the negative responses of other persons, such as disbelief, hostility, "you're crazy," and blank, uncomprehending looks. As one interviewee said of a therapist he consulted,

> I went to a therapist with an MA, and I had to bring in articles to explain to her, I was disappointed because I expected a remedy, she let me talk . . . no literature on stuff like the Center.

Family members, as well as friends and new acquaintances not connected with the Center, were as prone to give these responses as were new therapists.

At the time of the interviews, individuals were well aware that most persons they met would probably not understand their experiences, and they were selective in revealing them. Yet, their sense of not being able to talk about this past, "contaminated" experience, which was central to their lives, resulted in feelings of distance from the friends they did make. The underlying fear was that if they revealed such experience they would be judged and found deeply wanting. As the man just quoted puts it:

> [I]t isolates you, I keep basically the same friends. I'm real close to people from the Center, I have a real bond with people I've gone through hell with. I don't have those ties with people in the outside world and if I talk about it with them, they don't really understand, they say "you stayed," they put you down for it, don't understand the system. I don't want to get into feelings again, with new people, secret history—you don't go bragging about this, past membership, this isolates you, you're always hiding something, don't think people will understand, but some do. You have to keep taking a chance, because you've already been so humiliated.

The persons I interviewed reported that many individuals responded very negatively when they learned about their pasts. Overwhelmingly, outsiders reacted as if involvement with the Center meant dependence and lack of independent thought, or stupidity. Almost all of their new friends seemed to think "it could never have happened to me, something must be wrong with him or her." Given such a response, it was hard to explain just what the experience had been like, and many interviewees, uncertain themselves how to describe their participation, immediately became defensive and quiet. Indeed, one frequently adopted coping technique was to become highly selective in deciding whether to tell someone, then when to tell someone, and finally what to tell.[11]

In explaining the experience to oneself, the use of the word "cult" revealed much about the cognitive interpretation individuals chose. Some readily accepted the term to describe the Center for Feeling Therapy. Some thought that the word "cult" had negative connotations, and they were extremely reluctant to apply it to the Center. Some differentiated between "religious" cults and their own experience, which, although it might look very similar to an outside observer, was very different in their eyes.

Several persons reported choosing other words to signify the experience. For example, one woman reported that people were more likely to understand if she compared her experience to a bad romance that she should have left sooner. In this way, she avoided strangers' instant imputation of the stigma of being a former cultist, and she maintained communication with her new friends. She could continue to reveal information about what the experience had been like, instead of cutting off dialogue. Yet, others' choice of the word "cult" seemed to be part of a search for understanding of a very traumatic, little-understood phenomenon.

Deliberately using the word "cult" seemed intended to signify the person as having been harmed greatly by participation, or as having been unable to decide freely to be a participant. All of the women and men I interviewed still seemed strongly concerned with explaining this experience to themselves: had only they been uniquely vulnerable, or would anyone subjected to the Center's influence have been vulnerable? The answer chosen contributes to a person's present sense of self-esteem. If one regards oneself as having been uniquely vulnerable, and as thus separated out from the mass of individuals, then one has to discern why one was vulnerable and remove this vulnerability, in order to preclude making other "dumb" decisions. One wants to think one can act in one's best interests; thus, feeling that one made "dumb" choices joining and staying in a cult affords little sense of security about one's essential self. If, on the other hand, one decides that many others would have been vulnerable if subjected to a cult's influence, then one is not particularly vulnerable now, and one does not have to answer the question of "why did I stay" in the same manner. The focus shifts, instead, to attributes of the organization that exerted controlling influence. One's intent then becomes avoiding such organizations and influences in the future, not rectifying some deep personal vulnerability.

Adopting the explanation of having been "brainwashed" by some mysterious, incomprehensible process leads into a continuing dilemma: it introduces doubt about one's intellectual capabilities, which feeds into an unending cycle of self-doubt.

This struggle to understand what happened brings to the forefront the strong American belief in individualism. Persons largely attribute actions to individual intentions; the social situation and its influence on individual behavior is eclipsed. What onetime members of cults are brought up against is this individualism, which they may once have believed but which they now temper with a social situational perspective (what I would call a social influence perspective). Society largely believes that cult members are "zombies" or "brainwashed automatons," that is, the exact antithesis of a normal individual.[12] In a sense, the Center's former patients have developed a more sociological or social psychological understanding of behavior—and this is not a widely shared understanding. In addition, they have not been able to face society in a way that does not further degrade them; for example they cannot say, simply and honestly, "I was in a cult." There is no "status elevation" ceremony, by which they can be publicly "redeemed." So they are left to devise individual strategies to bridge the gap that opens as soon as information about one's past is revealed. No one in my sample used "I was in a new religious movement" as an explanation; even if someone had said this, however, it would not have solved the problem of how to regain social respectability.[13]

Time Heals

In the third and final stage of rebuilding, more-permanent choices were made for "catching up" with age peers—getting married, buying a house and other material possessions, finishing degrees, beginning new careers. The former patients came to a greater understanding of what had happened to them, involving a firming up of the applicable "account" to use when explaining their years in Feeling Therapy.

In this stage of recovery, the search for understanding has resulted in a stable way of interpreting the cult experience to oneself and to others. One might say, for example, "I was vulnerable and these professionals took advantage of my vulnerability."[14]

From Private Problem to Social Grievance

I think that the long period it has taken those I interviewed to rebuild their lives results from their lingering belief that it is they who are primarily responsible for their experience in Feeling Therapy, a belief generated during their therapy there. As one woman I interviewed said:

> [W]hen I first left the Center, I had great trouble in realizing myself as victim[;] among the reasons why I had trouble was because I had gone to the Center. I feel that the fact that the state is backing me [in the license-revocation hearings] is the major thing helping me recover from my experiences.

That it was the individual patient who had sought out Feeling Therapy was never forgotten during the Center's existence. It was woven into several

rhetorics that stressed persons' voluntary participation in and acceptance of all
that occurred therapeutically. After all, they entered voluntarily, and stayed,
often for years, largely in the absence of physical restraint.[15] While onetime
members can articulately describe the feeling of psychological coercion they
experienced, in retrospect they wonder why they were not "strong" enough
to up and leave. Often they assume that others in their position would have
left, especially as all former patients reported experiencing doubts and dissatisfactions, often intense, while in the Center.

Accordingly, in making decisions to sue the therapists or to complain
to the California Board of Medical Quality Assurance, they have had to overcome this feeling of being primarily responsible for what happened. Those
persons who did overcome it came to feel they could hold the therapists responsible for abusive treatment.[16] Usually, coming to this realization involved
exploring what it means to be a professional therapist, including learning
about professional codes of ethics and disciplinary procedures. The California
attorney general's decision to try to revoke the therapists' professional licenses
validated former members' perceptions of having been abused.

Other people, who may feel they were harmed but who have not arrived at an analysis that involves some notion of systematic and injurious manipulation by professional therapists, wished only to put this period of their
lives behind them. They also were extremely reluctant to air their "dirty laundry" in public, as they would by filing a civil lawsuit or by testifying.

One of the ways in which men and women resolved their adjustment
difficulties after leaving the Center was to develop the attitude of wanting to
help others who had been in similar situations and of wanting to prevent future abuse.[17] Many of those I interviewed explicitly spoke of talking to me,
and to other researchers, as one way of informing the general public that most
persons are quite vulnerable to manipulation by authority, particularly expert
authority, and to social pressure. Pursuing the license revocations and civil
lawsuits was described as a way to prevent the therapists from abusing others
and to call them to account.

"Stigma Contests" Continue

In this third stage of recovery, one has developed enough of a subsequent life history so that the identity of Feeling Therapy patient is eclipsed.
Eclipsed, but not forgotten. The ongoing civil suits and license-revocation
hearings clearly kept the Center experience more in the forefront of onetime
members' lives than if these legal actions had not been undertaken.

In this "stigma contest," former patients and former therapists were
engaged in "deviantizing" (Schur, 1980:4–16), or battling over the right to

define what might be termed "deviant" psychotherapy. The Center's past members and the state (in the person of the California deputy attorney general who handled the license-revocation hearings) asserted that the therapists did not provide legitimate treatment but rather developed a "cult," in which patients were unethically manipulated into remaining as patients. In response, the therapists (and some former members) asserted that persons stayed at the Center voluntarily. The onetime patients claimed that the therapy was abuse, that the therapists were manipulative abusers of trust and vulnerability, and that the therapeutic community was a cult. The therapists denied in general what was alleged to have occurred, and they claimed that the "sickness" of patients accounted for alleged harms.[18] "Who will be believed, the therapists or me?" was thus an important concern at the time I conducted my interviews.

When I spoke with persons who had been involved with the Center, the outcome of this contest was far from clear. As the legal proceedings dragged out over years, past members were subject to constant reminders of their failings. They had to reveal their "dirty laundry" repeatedly, in depositions, interrogatories, and in testimony at the license-revocation hearings, and they repeatedly had to counter the therapists' characterizations of them as very ill mentally. Those testifying during the license-revocation hearings had to confront the very people they had once seen as godlike face to face.

Only one of the thirteen therapists admitted the facts alleged against him: Werner Karle. Timnick (1986b) reports that he,

> in an effort to keep his credentials, has admitted to many of the allegations against him and his colleagues and, in testimony and a signed stipulation, acknowledged that "feeling therapy" involved "patient brutality in a cult setting practiced largely by unlicensed individuals." He said he had ridiculed some patients, calling them "stingy Jew," "nigger" and "crazy," and abused, struck, threatened, pressured and had sex with others.

Karle, once the Center's second-ranking therapist, later died in a fall from his roof during an epileptic attack. Charges against him were dismissed.

Social support and validation were important in maintaining the erstwhile patients' sense of grievance and of their right to hold the therapists accountable. Lawyers who handled the suits and hearings provided some of this support and validation, and the informal network that had sprung up among the Center's former patients provided more.

Marie Fortune, in Is Nothing Sacred? (1989a), describes a case of pastoral abuse of female parishioners. Six women came forward to press official charges against the pastor. The process of trying to hold him accountable dragged on for several years. The recognition that there were still more women involved, that their own relationships with the pastor were not "special," was what caused the women to try to stop his abuse. This group support (as well as that of Fortune, who acted as advocate and pastor for the group) is what maintained their determination, even in the face of the pastor's defaming them before the congregation. In the end, it was the women's resolve to see the pastor stopped, not any action by church officials, that caused him to resign voluntarily.

Once again, it is authority (Fortune, who helped the women develop an alternative interpretation of their situation) and peers (who provided social support and consensual validation) that are the essentials in influencing individuals' actions.

After the hearings (and after my interviews), the therapists' licenses were revoked. This may be seen as upholding the patients' claims. The decisions represent authoritative imposition of a stigma: those, particularly its victims, who believed the Center for Feeling Therapy became a cult were vindicated.[19]

My central conclusion about the reconstruction experience is that it is a long and difficult process, involving much pain and struggle. The initial euphoria after the Center's collapse that some of my interviewees mentioned was soon followed by the hard work of rebuilding identities and lives. All of the men and women I interviewed, regardless of the position they took at the time of the interview on the "goodness" or "badness" of the Center for Feeling Therapy, reported that they experienced its sudden demise as a cataclysm that shook their sense of self and their perspective on life profoundly. Moreover, they all reported that it has taken them a long time to begin putting their lives back together.

Fundamental to this reconstruction of identity seems to be re-establishing a sense of trust, both of themselves and of the world. Individuals seemed mortified, in retrospect, at what they did to themselves and to others while involved with the Center, at "how much of myself I gave away," as one interviewee put it. Their long years of "therapy" did not leave them with a sure sense of self; rather, their experience seems to have left them profoundly self-doubting.

Key to successful reconstruction of identity and life is figuring out ways of interpreting their experiences that others can comprehend as being something they themselves might have undergone. Individuals must overcome the public's tendency to "kind of person" explanations of cult membership—emphasizing differences between those who have been in cults and those who have not—by establishing a sense of commonality. In other words, former members must bridge the gap created when the knowledge that one spent years in a group others might label a "cult" becomes public. The women and men I interviewed who were able to do this seemed to make the transition to normalcy more easily than those who were not.

Finally, absolutely crucial for the onetime members in developing a way of interpreting their experiences, and of reconstructing identity and life, was social support. Because there was so little ready support from the "outside" world, the former patients needed desperately to have *someone* who believed in them as "normal."[20]

Eight
Recognizing Social Influence

For the social psychology of this century reveals a major lesson: often, it is not so much the kind of person a man is as the kind of situation in which he finds himself that determines how he will act. (Milgram, 1975:205)

Effective mind control exists in the most mundane aspects of human existence: the inner pressures to be bonded to other people, the power of group norms to influence behavior, the force of social rewards (such as smiles, praise, a gentle touch). We influence one another, intentionally or unintentionally, using the most basic principles of social psychology, motivation, and social learning. It is people in convincing social situations and not gadgets or gimmicks that control the minds of others. The more worried we are about being seen as ignorant, uncultured, untalented or boring, and the more ambiguous the events are that are to be evaluated, the more likely we are to take on the beliefs of those around us in order to avoid being rejected by them. (Andersen and Zimbardo, 1984:198)

Individuals involved with Feeling Therapy often acted in the same way "normal" persons would, but they lived in a very different social world. That social world, I argue, is what we as a society would term a "cult." This was the view of society's representative, Judge Robert A. Neher, who ruled that the Center for Feeling Therapy was a "personality cult." In asserting that the Center was not a religious cult, Judge Neher seemed to be thinking in accord with a perception that cults, by definition, are religious. However, although many cults are religious, many others are not.

I choose to employ the word "cult" because I am interested in explaining the popular conception of what these controversial organizations are. I take this conception to be one of an authoritarian leader controlling most aspects of the lives of his or her followers, who live in an insular group.[1]

My view is similar to the anthropologist Willa Appel's definition of a "cult" as involving, in greater or lesser degrees, an authoritarian structure, the regimentation of followers, renunciation of the world, and the belief that adherents alone are gifted with the truth. All the other qualities associated with cults derive from these characteristics: an attitude of moral superiority, a contempt for secular laws, rigidity of thought, and the diminution of regard for the individual.[2] (1983:16–17)

The Social Psychology of Extreme Organizations

What might be called the social psychology of extreme organizations (cults being one) begins with the analyses of political "thought reform" and "coercive persuasion" by Robert Lifton (1961) and Edgar Schein (with Schneier and Barker, 1961) and continues through analyses of various contemporary social contexts (e.g., Zablocki, 1991; Ofshe, 1992; Singer with Lalich, 1995 and 1996). A range of different ideologically based groups use similar techniques of control, parallel to the political techniques involved in "thought reform." For example, Dennis King's 1989 book about Lyndon LaRouche and his followers describes a contemporary quasi-conservative political movement whose members were controlled in a fashion somewhat like that characterizing the Center for Feeling Therapy. Janja Lalich (1993:51–84) describes a similarly controlling feminist Marxist-Leninist organization led by women (men were also members). Synanon, a drug-rehabilitation center that became a religion, has been portrayed in like fashion (Ofshe, 1976, 1980; Gerstel, 1982). The Sullivanians is another psychotherapy group that greatly resembled Feeling Therapy (Black, 1975; Conason with McGarrahan, 1986; Hoban, 1989; Siskind, 1990). Finally, the renowned Bruno Bettelheim's residential facility for children was described in ways characteristic of the Center for Feeling Therapy by former patients and staff after Bettelheim's death in 1990 (Masson, 1994:301–6).[3]

In attempting to determine why persons stay in groups like the Center for Feeling Therapy, some might assume that physical coercion is necessary. Research, however, indicates just the opposite (Ofshe, 1992; Singer and Addis, 1992; Singer with Lalich, 1995). For example, the physical coercion of being confined in prison indeed underpinned the resocialization of some of Lifton's (1961) subjects in Communist China. But in addition, and most important for my purposes, women and men who were resocialized in revolutionary universities participated voluntarily in the activities available to them—and they experienced the greater change, compared to those confined to prison. This would seem in accord with the finding of social psychologists that "we accept inner responsibility for a behavior when we think we have chosen to perform it in the absence of strong outside pressures" (Cialdini, 1984:97–98). The social psychologist Tony Greenwald, who has written on dissonance theory, comments:

The smallest incentive you can possibly use to get someone to do something is likely to be the most effective in getting the person to like the activity and keep on doing it. The theoretical reason for this is that in the adult human mind, particularly, reward does not operate by instrumental learning and classical conditioning mechanisms, but by cognitive dissonance or attribution mechanisms, whereby people arrive at explanations for their own behavior by taking note of the conditions under which they generate the behavior. So this is a cognitive understanding of the way incentives operate rather than a mechanistic conditioning law. (quoted in Aron and Aron, 1989:116; emphasis added)

While Lifton (1961) provided a compelling analysis of what the "thought reform" world is like, which he still believes (1985) can be applied to the contemporary scene, the social psychologist Edgar Schein's (with Schneir and Barker, 1961) work involving prisoners of war in Korea provides a useful three-step model of how influence is exerted that may be used in explaining many instances of extreme identity change.[4]

Margaret Singer and Richard Ofshe make use of the work of these earlier researchers, while expanding it to apply to the contemporary situation. Ofshe and Singer (1986) argue that "second generation" influence programs employ similar tactics to induce and stabilize change, but they note that these programs have added tactics from the human potential and encounter movements (e.g., hypnosis and emotional flooding) and have focused attention on central (rather than peripheral) elements of self. These additions add to the potency of change tactics. Singer and Lalich (1995:125–81) elaborate on the physiological and psychological persuasion techniques now in use.

Milgram's Findings on Obedience to Authority

In line with Lifton and Schein's conclusions that many normal individuals, not just a pathological minority, were vulnerable to strong and organized techniques of persuasion, Stanley Milgram's now famous studies of obedience to authority began with his attempt to understand how ordinary people could participate in such evils as the Holocaust and the My Lai massacre. Milgram (1975:174) concludes that

processes of obedience to authority . . . remain invariant so long as the basic condition for its occurrence exists: namely, that one is defined into a relationship with a person who one feels has, by virtue of his status, the right to prescribe behavior.

In these situations, the "person responds not so much to the content of what is required but on the basis of his relationship to the person who requires it.

Indeed, where legitimate authority is the source of action, *relationship overwhelms content*" (175).[5]

Milgram began his experiments with the assumption that most subjects would refuse to administer even the first, mild electric shocks to what they believed were other people and would walk out of the lab. He asked psychiatrists, graduate students and faculty in the behavioral sciences, college sophomores, and middle-class adults to predict how other persons would perform during the experiments. All responded similarly:

> They predict that virtually all subjects will refuse to obey the experimenter; only a pathological fringe, not exceeding one or two per cent, was expected to proceed to the end of the shockboard. (31)

Milgram found out otherwise. Roughly two-thirds of his participants were "obedient subjects," administering shocks until their victims were apparently unconscious. From this finding, Milgram concluded that "ordinary people, simply doing their jobs, and without any particular hostility on their part, can become agents in a terrible destructive process" (6).[6]

But once having acted against the victim, many subjects harshly devalued him. They "found it necessary to view him as an unworthy individual, whose punishment was made inevitable by his own deficiencies of intelligence and character"—"he was so stupid and stubborn he deserved to get shocked" (10). The process of "cognitive dissonance" can explain what occurred. To think that they had shocked a helpless victim was not consistent with the subjects' views of self; therefore, they "justified" their actions by redefining the victim as one who merited punishment. I would argue that this process also occurred in the case of the Feeling Therapists: their repeated brutal treatment of patients meant they could *only* see them *as* patients whose brutal treatment was justified, not as peers in a community of equals, which is what they claimed.

What affects obedience? The amount of surveillance maintained by the authority, the role a person occupies in the network of authority, and the level of peer support favoring or opposing the authority. Obedience was almost three times as great in face-to-face situations than when the order to continue was delivered by phone (62). The transmitters were twice as obedient as the executants—that is, persons closer to the authority but farther from throwing the switch were more obedient. And finally, if peers comply with and support authority, this increases the pressure on the subject to comply. If peers resist, the subject will tend to disobey.

No other experiment was as important in demonstrating how the experimenter's authority could be undercut as that in which two peers rebelled. Here, thirty-six of the forty subjects (90 percent) defied the experimenter. Milgram concludes:

> When an individual wishes to stand in opposition to authority, he does best to find support for his position from others in his group. The mutual support provided by men for each other is the strongest bulwark we have against the excesses of authority. (121)

Thus, Milgram's work provided experimental evidence establishing both the importance of authority in commanding obedience and the effectiveness of a peer group in supporting or resisting authority. Asch's studies on conformity, discussed earlier in this book, also demonstrated that one other person standing against the opinion or judgment of the majority was enough to reduce pressures to conform.

Beyond Milgram

Whereas Milgram showed how obedience to authority underlies extreme action, most social psychology has explored obedience to authority in ordinary action. This research concludes that here, too, most of us obey most authorities, that most often we conform to peers' behavior, and that most times this behavior serves us well (Zimbardo and Leippe, 1991:65–76). Thus, the same processes of obedience to authority and conformity to peers occur in both ordinary and extraordinary situations. This is, of course, at variance with what most of us think explains most of our behavior. As a society, we are more likely to focus on individual motivations for action than on situational influences (93).[7]

Robert B. Cialdini's *Influence* (1984) seeks to answer the question of how and why people agree to things. He analyzes the tactics of "compliance practitioners," placing them into six categories. These, in turn, rely on six basic psychological principles that organize human behavior: consistency, reciprocation, social proof, authority, liking, and scarcity. Techniques built on these principles generate an almost mindless compliance, giving their users

> an enormous additional benefit—*the ability to manipulate without the appearance of manipulation.* Even the victims themselves tend to see their compliance as due to the action of natural forces rather than to the designs of the person who profits from that compliance. (Cialdini, 1984:23–24, emphasis added)

Cialdini illustrates how the authority relationship can overwhelm content with an example of a nurse following orders:

> A physician ordered ear drops to be administered to the right ear of a patient suffering pain and infection there. But instead of writing out completely the

location "right ear" on the prescription, the doctor abbreviated it so that the instructions read "place in R ear." Upon receiving the prescription, the duty nurse promptly put the required number of ear drops into the patient's anus.

Obviously, rectal treatment of an earache made no sense. Yet neither the patient nor the nurse questioned it. The important lesson of this story is that in many situations where a legitimate authority has spoken, what would otherwise make sense is irrelevant. In these instances, we don't consider the situation as a whole but attend and respond to only one aspect of it. (212–13)

Pratkanis and Aronson's *Age of Propaganda* (1991), subtitled *The Everyday Use and Abuse of Persuasion*, has a chapter entitled "How to Become a Cult Leader." They suggest "seven mundane but nonetheless 'proven-effective' tactics for creating and maintaining a cult" (240–49).[8] The authors believe that the techniques used by cults are ordinary tactics employed "in a much more systematic and complete manner than we are accustomed to" (241).

What Kind of People Would Do That?

When the public finds out about a group like the Center for Feeling Therapy, the chief reaction is puzzlement. The assumption is that weird individuals were attracted to the group for weird reasons. But when we hear about a group from the news media, it is usually because the group has in some way gone beyond "acceptable" deviance, or (sometimes as a result) has collapsed or gotten into difficulty with the law. For these reasons it is often labeled a "cult" by commentators. We often erroneously assume that individuals were attracted to the group because it provided these weird experiences. However, although these are often the end point in the evolution of a group, they are not necessarily the starting point. Some examples will illustrate this idea.

The sociologist Ronald Enroth, in discussing his research on abusive churches, mentions an evolution of abuse over time, as pastors discover their ability to influence (1992:216). The sociologist Stephen Kent's article "Lustful Prophet: A Psychosexual Historical Study of the Children of God's Leader, David Berg" (1994) provides a fascinating analysis of how Berg, in a step-by-step process extending over years, implemented a regime of deviant sexual conduct within his group. The Children of God is perhaps most famous for two controversial practices: the recruitment tactic of "flirty fishing" (using sex to recruit) and incestuous behavior within the group. What Kent describes is

an extensive series of behavioral and cognitive reorientations regarding sex that had the veneer of divine justification rather than psychological compulsion.

. . . The initial step affected Berg's interpretation of his own sexual urges. Subsequent steps affected members of Berg's immediate family, especially his wife, daughters, and granddaughters. Berg's tenets next affected the women with whom he closely worked, then the families of these women. Finally, Berg's religiously cloaked sexual tenets affected all members of his organization, and even extended out into the community through his insistence that COG members practice recruitment and resource acquisition through sexual activities. (1994:156)

The Wrong Way Home (1994) by the psychiatrist Arthur Deikman has a chapter entitled "Hugh and Clara: A Case History" in which he describes the participation of "Hugh" and "Clara" in a psychotherapy group that evolved into a cult. In the last year of his participation, "Hugh" described the leader and group as paranoid, preoccupied with defending themselves against various "devils."

Katherine E. Betz (1997) provides an account of her twenty-one years within a group headed by a guru. She describes the evolution of sexual relations between the leader and persons in the inner circle, first unmarried members and then married members; the practice developed in strict secrecy, as a "yogic secret." This was in strong contrast to the public avowal of celibacy for the leader and unmarried members. When news of this sexual behavior finally spread to the larger community, those involved denied it, and most believed the denials of the leader and the inner-circle members. The leader later re-created the same system of secret sexual relations within a new branch of the old community, located in South Australia. When Betz left and finally made the secret public, the group collapsed.

And last, Richard Ofshe's article "The Rabbi and the Sex Cult" (1986) describes the expansion of rabbinical authority within a fundamentalist Jewish group; here, the rabbi increased his power to include the right to demand sexual services from a small group of female members.

As organizations evolve, leaders discover the ease with which people can be manipulated as they attempt to subordinate others to an extreme goal. Leaders discover that they can get away with certain things—after all, only they have the ability to be creative. They can manipulate the justifying ideology to introduce innovation in accord with their own desires. Simply put, the "solutions" to the question of how to control people (whatever the ideology) all tend to be the same, because they result from the fundamentals of social influence, for example, deference to authority and conformity to peers.

Just as the group has often evolved, so have persons' commitments to it. Initial motivations to join or stay with an organization may be diverse; often a wide range of initial interests are transformed into the precise interests of the group. Also, dependence on the group has often been cultivated, step by step. Therefore, it is not that "dependent" persons seek a group in which they can practice dependency as a way of life, but rather that the leader generates and maintains extreme dependence in members.

How are these diverse interests transformed into a few interests or a single interest? I think the research literature shows that a process of social influence occurs, continually reshaping members' behaviors, attitudes, and feelings. This process depends on both the leader(s) and the group. A potent part of the group environment may be an ideology of individuality (in the United States or other countries emphasizing individuality); although this may, to an outside observer, be contradicted by members' routine behavior, it is important in motivating persons to remain in the group.

What are the elements that might enable an authority and group to establish such extreme social influence? First, leaders must create a system of very strong control over all aspects of group life (as implied by Lifton's concept of "milieu control" or Goffman's concept of the "total institution"). Isolation and communal living make establishing milieu control more effective; these two elements are also often defining aspects of a "total institution." Isolation prevents the outside world from influencing members; communal living allows members to see if others are doing what they should be doing, so group norms can be enforced. We can see the nomadic lifestyle of the Heaven's Gate group as resulting in both isolation and communal living— members were pretty much only in touch with other members.

Once milieu control is in place,[9] two additional elements come to the fore: a charismatic leader and a group that seems to be in total agreement.[10] If the charismatic leader is seen as legitimate, authority will be deferred to routinely. If the group appears unanimous, doubt has no place in the group, and conformity is enhanced. Members, in addition to obeying authority, will follow their peers' example. Also, once a part of a group, a person often wants to belong, to fit in, to conform to other members.[11] In an organization characterized by the appearance of unanimous agreement (an element that often results in a deviant group being labeled a cult), "pluralistic ignorance" develops, so that individuals think "only I doubt." The group actively enforces adherence to its norms; members, because of close physical proximity, can easily check each other's behavior for compliance. The group, however, needs some way to examine purely internal "behavior" like thinking, in order to determine if public compliance is matched by true private conformity. This gives rise to a group norm wherein the "personal becomes public."

And what to do with people who don't conform? A system of punishments and rewards evolves, both of which are visible to all. These also need to be a part of group dynamics (e.g., everyone's shunning a recalcitrant rather than something that only a leader and a specialized group of members employ. That is, the routine social control in which we all engage in everyday life assumes a more important role in cults and this control is often directed by a leader or leaders.

New members may be welcomed by "confrontative encounter," an identity stripping à la the mental hospitals of Goffman (1961), or an unfreezing (Schein with Schneier and Barker, 1961). This process can be called by many names, among them deindividuation and, in a rough paraphrase of Frank, "removing from an assumptive world." But whatever its name, it quickly forces the individual to make a sharp break with previous identity, relationships, and social world. She or he is thus shaken from the web of existing attachments.

Synanon is a good example of how radical self-transformation undertaken in a group can go beyond the bounds of acceptable behavior. The organization's activities came to include mass vasectomies, forced sexual relationships, violence against members, former members, and nonmembers, and attempted murder, all referred to as the "Synanon Horrors" by one journalist (Anson, 1978). How did Synanon, so often lauded for its success in rehabilitating alcoholics and drug addicts where so many other institutions had failed, reach such a dire end? "Confrontative encounter" was a large part of the process.

This shaking from existing attachments makes persons susceptible to group influence. Once members, individuals often must engage in confrontative encounter themselves to remain in good standing. This makes them complicit: they act brutally, as well as being acted against.

Feeling Therapy and Other Influence Settings

The Center for Feeling Therapy represents an extreme instance of social influence. As such it points out clearly how men and women can be acted upon by authority and by groups.

This process of influence is apparent in many other contexts. There is, for example, Jonestown, the contemporary paradigm of the "worst case" cult scenario, where 912 people died. Milieu control was extremely strong in Jonestown: the settlement was located in the midst of a jungle, not easily accessible to other settlements even on foot; the Reverend Jim Jones kept his followers' passports so they could not easily leave Guyana even if they left the settlement; he regularly terrorized people with stories of the snakes and tigers to be found in the jungle; and he restricted access by outsiders (Richardson, 1982:27). In this tightly controlled setting, Jones was more easily able to persuade his followers that they risked loss of life if they tried to leave the community. He was able to present a perspective on reality that was not challenged by the outside world, at least not until Congressman Leo Ryan's fact-finding mission arrived in Jonestown in November 1978.

The People's Temple was set up to encourage strong ties (e.g., sexual ones) between Jones and its members. Relations between couples were attenuated as a result (Coser and Coser, 1979). Harsh penalties for disobeying norms were in place in Jonestown, such as confining children in water wells (Richardson, 1982:27). Monitoring, in which all members watched each other for infractions of norms, meant close surveillance of everyone in all situations (Coser and Coser, 1979). This also made it nearly impossible for men and women to seek support in developing an independent questioning perspective on Jonestown.

The social psychologist Robert Cialdini (1984:152–55) gives us a slightly different slant on the conditions within the group that were generated by the move to Guyana. In offering his analysis he uses the concept of "social proof"—persons look to others' behavior when in situations of uncertainty to determine what is appropriate. As he sees it,

> the single act in the history of the People's Temple that most contributed to the members' mindless compliance that day occurred a year earlier with the relocation of the Temple to a jungled country of unfamiliar customs and strange people. . . . In a country like Guyana, there were no similar others for a Jonestown resident but the people of Jonestown itself. (152–53)

In speaking of the calm, orderly way the people took the poison, he says:

> They hadn't been hypnotized by Jones; they had been convinced—partly by him but, more important, by the principle of social proof—that suicide was correct conduct. The uncertainty they surely felt upon first hearing the death command must have caused them to look to those around them for a definition of the appropriate response. It is worth particular note that they found two impressive pieces of social evidence, each pointing in the same direction. . . . The first was the initial set of their compatriots, who quickly and willingly took the poison drafts. . . . The second source of social evidence came from the reactions of the crowd itself. Given the conditions, I suspect that what occurred was a large-scale instance of the pluralistic ignorance phenomenon that frequently infects onlookers at emergencies. (153)

With reference to others' analyses of the Jonestown tragedy, Cialdini states his belief that most focus too much on Jim Jones as an individual and too little on the social context.

The men and women who wound up in Jonestown also constituted a selected group. Jones's earlier moves, from Indiana to California (first Ukiah, then San Francisco), tested the loyalty of members. Those who would not rearrange their lives to follow him left the organization. Jones thus wound up with his most committed followers in Jonestown.[12]

Rajneeshpuram, the Bhagwan Rajneesh's Oregon settlement, also evidenced great milieu control and thus great social influence over its members. Individuals seeking access were processed in a way that allowed most of them only a public relations view. Attempting to get beyond all these filters tried the ingenuity of those seeking to assess the town, as FitzGerald (1986) and Carter (1990) note. The great conflict between Rajneeshees and native Oregonians meant the Rajneeshees were essentially in close contact only with themselves. After the group's collapse, it was discovered that members' quarters were bugged. It looked as though the intent was to monitor closely members in both public and private.

Janja Lalich describes her ten years in a feminist Marxist-Leninist organization in her article "A Little Carrot and a Lot of Stick" (Langone, 1993:51–84). The group existed from 1974 to 1985, and her description shows that it had much in common with the Center for Feeling Therapy. Most of the members lived communally, in houses of from three to eight members, with no privacy possible. This communal living is one of the ways I would argue "milieu control" was put in place; group work in a public location was another aspect as was the organization's strong emphasis on secrecy, supposedly to ward off state infiltration and control. The kinds of contact members could have with outsiders and among themselves were limited.

"Total Institutions" and Tough Cases

Social influence also appears in less markedly deviant groups. The sociologist Erving Goffman (1961) describes mental hospitals as "total institutions," in which those entering are subject to "identity stripping." All obvious signs of their previous identity are taken away, and a patient identity is imposed. The process generates feelings of powerlessness and depersonalization even in nonpatients, as Rosenhan (1973) points out. The eight healthy persons in his now famous study who sought hospitalization were mentally prepared for the treatment they would receive. Even so, they felt so depersonalized and powerless that they wanted to leave the hospital almost as soon as they had entered.

Stannard-Friel's *Harassment Therapy* (1981) presents a case (in a mental health ward of a Roman Catholic hospital) in which the good intentions of members brought about bad actions. Staff adopted an aggressive, harassing form of therapy with a selective group of patients. Stannard-Friel feels the "totalist" environment that developed (another instance of strong milieu control) led to the extreme abuse of patients. The hospital was already set up to allow for legitimate milieu control; this program extended the control of patients. Moreover, not just anyone was selected as a good candidate for this therapy—streetwise kids were turned down in favor of middle-class children and nuns. These persons were judged to be more accepting of authority than those not selected for therapy. In implementing the hospital's new program for behavior change, the "architects" selected those who would be more obedient, so that they could rely on their socialized deference to authority.

Those applying the therapy believed in the importance of acting in concert, presenting a unified front to patients. Those who disagreed either were persuaded to remain quiet or were shamed into going along as well. Since their less dramatic methods brought about less dramatic changes, they could be accused of loafing, of not caring for patients. The appearance of unanimity thus acted as a pressure on patients and therapists to obey and to conform.

A later example, also set in a hospital, is that of a psychiatrist treating adopted children who have severe adjustment problems (Kadaba, 1992).[13] Dr. Michael McGuire employs a "toughlove" approach, which looks just like Synanon's in being strongly confrontative. Kids who resist may be medicated, restrained, or isolated. The rationale for treatment sounds like Synanon's as well: these are kids who have not been helped in any other way, and this way works! That is, the end justifies the means.

The intensification of the therapy program that I discussed in Chapter Three, involving more aggressive attack on patients (confrontative encounter) and the creation of a therapeutic community, is a response to the difficulty of women and men changing even in self-identified directions. It was precisely this belief—that ordinary therapy did not generate significant change in people—that motivated much of the encounter-group movement's techniques. The confrontative encounter frightens individuals and generates compliance, and then the therapeutic community implements and monitors desirable change.

It would seem that such "ruthlessly compassionate" (as one parent termed McGuire's technique) approaches to treatment—what I am calling confrontative encounter—are a recurrent solution to dealing with "tough" cases. Other examples might include the schizophrenic patients treated by Dr. Rosen's "direct psychoanalysis" (Masson, 1994:165–94), and Bruno Bettelheim's treatment of his supposedly seriously disturbed child patients (300–306). These are tough cases because the major mental illnesses, such as schizophrenia, have largely been resistant to less aggressive approaches like individualized, outpatient therapy.

Another instance of a tough case, as illustrated by Synanon and its myriad imitators, is dealing with drug addictions. When Chuck Dederich founded Synanon little was being done about drug addiction; that little was not having much success. Synanon initially claimed superior results, and this manufactured reputation spawned lots of emulators.

Geoffrey Skoll's *Walk the Walk and Talk the Talk* (1992) describes his ethnographic research on a drug-rehabilitation program that treated criminal offenders. The plan was modeled after Synanon, and although it had changed and become more professional, it still retained much of that group's atmosphere. The chief similarity lay in the form of therapy, "confrontative encounter," this involved placing individuals on the "hot seat" during group sessions and attacking them verbally. All patients were forced to adopt the "dope friend" identity in order to survive in the therapeutic community, just as all were forced to accept the judgment of the self as "insane" in Feeling Therapy. What this meant for the drug addicts was that they, too, had to at least pretend to agree with the community's judgment and norms of behavior—public display was an important part of how they showed progress toward rehabilitation. Unlike Feeling Therapy participants, who sought out the Center and entered voluntarily, and prepaid a fee for the initial therapy, members of this drug treatment program were between a rock and a hard place at entry. Most chose the program as an alternative to incarceration, in spite of its tough reputation. The difficulty of living in this therapeutic community with its extensive milieu control, is reflected in the high failure rate—few participants ever "graduated."

Another area in which "confrontative" encounter might produce "better" results than the usual nondirective individual therapy (e.g., Carl Rogers's approach) is in dealing with "quiet" persons, those who do not easily articulate a reflective analysis of their problem, who do not fit the YAVIS (young, articulate, verbal, intelligent, and social) profile. It is easier to frighten men and women into complying with group norms than to get them to see their problem in a reflective way.

The difficulty with group-based therapy or change situations (e.g., large group awareness programs) is that there is insufficient recognition of how groups themselves can psychologically coerce change. Assuming that real personal growth is taking place because of techniques that generate individual insight, the proponents of this approach assume that these changes will persist outside the group. Those controlling the Center for Feeling Therapy inadvertently recognized how difficult it is for change to endure outside a group and how much more likely it is to apparently persist within a group. They did not recognize, however, that this outcome is based on deference to authority and group pressure for conformity, not on their particular therapeutic approach.

The confrontative technique may appear to work (Bettelheim claimed a 95 percent success rate), but the question remains as to why. Is it because of what Stannard-Friel calls "intimidated respect," where patients fear the punishing effects of not presenting the therapeutically correct behavior? This is at least a plausible alternative explanation. The examples I have presented demonstrate that there are probably dozens of controversial programs that try to make use of radical methods of personal change. Such programs contribute to what is likely to be a continuing social problem: how do we decide what is a "good" therapy program?

Are there other groups like the Center for Feeling Therapy? I believe there are probably many of them. They do not become widely known until or unless they engage in some particularly egregious practice or collapse suddenly. The *Cult Observer*, published by the American Family Foundation, reports often on groups that sound similar, at least from newspaper clippings gathered nationwide. Temerlin and Temerlin (1982) reported their research on psychotherapy cults; Singer and Lalich (1995:172–81) described research on twenty-two psychotherapy cults by Singer and two of her colleagues; and *Crazy Therapies* (Singer and Lalich, 1996) provides still more examples.

Psychotherapy as Social Influence

Feeling Therapy meets head-on the central challenge facing any psychotherapist: bringing about change in women and men who seek therapy. This gets at the central and still unresolved issue in psychotherapy: what brings about change? Is psychotherapy in general any better than doing nothing? Is professional psychotherapy more effective than the myriad of alternative therapies or self-help groups? Is the more usual result, as Wheelis (1973) and Zilbergeld (1983) argue, no change?

The case of the Center for Feeling Therapy clearly demonstrates how important authority is in the therapy relationship—that therapy is a relationship of influence and that authority is a big part of influence. Although this analysis is now being accepted more widely it is also still being resisted.

The debate over recovered-memory therapy emphasizes how significant influence can be. Are remarkable stories discovered in therapy (e.g. satanic ritual abuse) the result of recovering of actual memories, or are they the result of unintended influence by the therapist? Richard Ofshe is one who argues for the latter, pointing to such factors as a strongly determined authority, a close-knit group, and hypnosis. The degree of conviction in these hypnotically recalled memories is no guarantee of their authenticity, since those knowledgeable about hypnosis say it can increase belief. As described by Ofshe and Watters (1994), some of these therapeutic practices sound like the cultic practices I have discussed. Moreover, like Feeling Therapy patients, the clients seem not move beyond a state of victimhood.

In the third edition of his influential *Persuasion and Healing* (1991), Jerome Frank, a longtime psychotherapy researcher describes psychotherapy as more akin to rhetoric than to science. In the earlier editions, he pointed to the American cultural values of individualism and belief in science as preventing us from recognizing how much a process of influence psychotherapy is. He described "healing cults" and "thought reform" as the situations of greatest influences with therapeutic community as perhaps their nearest approximation.

The psychiatrist E. Fuller Torrey offers a similar description in his *Witchdoctors and Psychiatrists* (1986). In seeking to compare "witchdoctors" to psychiatrists, Torrey discounts explanations describing the one as practicing "magic" and the other as practicing "science."

> The truth is not even close; it is a quantum jump away. The techniques used by Western psychiatrists are, with few exceptions, on exactly the same scientific plane as the techniques used by witchdoctors. If one is magic, then so is the other. If one is prescientific, then so is the other. The only exceptions are some of the physical therapies, in particular drugs and shock therapy, which have been shown in controlled studies to be effective in producing psychiatric change. (Torrey, 1986:11)

Using cross-cultural research on psychotherapy, Torrey sums up what he sees as the four common elements in psychotherapy:

> To reduce psychotherapy to a shorthand, one can say that it consists of a magnificent mensch (therapist with therapeutic personal qualities) utilizing an edifice complex (client's expectations and emotional arousal) and invoking the principle of Rumpelstiltskin (naming process arising from a shared worldview) to bring about a Superman syndrome (sense of mastery in the client). (231)

Torrey sees the psychotherapeutic process as involving these four features, and thus as having a universal structure, but the content of the processes differs cross-culturally, reflecting therapy's culture-bound status. Many others have also emphasized cultural influences on therapy. For example, early feminist analyses emphasized how therapy was rooted in nineteenth-century ideas of gender. And the psychologist Perry London, in *The Modes and Morals of Psychotherapy* (1985), described "morals" (or what are now called "values") as influencing the therapeutic process.

Frank and Torrey both believe a universal process is at work in effective therapy, among both professional and nonprofessional therapists. The great majority of persons who work with most therapists, in the United States or in other countries, are not seriously mentally ill. Given such a population, anything can cause change. The serious mental illnesses, however, are more resistant to psychotherapeutic schemes.

In recognizing the importance of the relationship between therapist and client, and the personal qualities of each that contribute to effective therapy, psychotherapeutic research is slowly coming around to an influence analysis of therapy.

If psychotherapy is a social influence process, then who are the most successful influencers? Social psychological research helps provide some answers to this question. Several things can lead to a person's being a successful persuader: the most knowledgeable are seen as the most influential, the more confident are seen as the more persuasive, and those who are perceived as more like us are more effective persuaders (Zimbardo and Leippe, 1991:358–67).

Thus, class differences would seem to impede treatment of lower-class clients, given that therapists in the United States are overwhelmingly drawn from the middle and upper classes. And cross-cultural differences, too, would seem to impede therapy. Torrey believes both to be true, and he believes that at the root of the difficulties is the lack of a shared worldview—clients and therapists "share ideas about neither causation nor classification" (Torrey, 1986:32).[14]

The Explosion of Psychotherapy and Public Acceptance

The 1960s and 1970s, the time of the Center for Feeling Therapy's inspiration and origin, witnessed a proliferation of innovations in the theory and practice of psychotherapy. Groups intended to allow "normal" individuals to "develop" their full "human potential," as well as other movements of social change and personal transformation (which also influenced psychological practitioners) seemed to spring up everywhere. Radical psychiatry and the women's movement, for example, questioned the goal of therapy, and thus the methods used and the process of interaction that occurs. Glenn and Kunnes's *Repression or Revolution?* (1973) and Chesler's *Women and Madness* (1972) illustrate these two perspectives. What this enormous change seemed to suggest is that anything and everything worked. This, then, makes it more difficult to define abuse.

Psychotherapy moved from a primary emphasis on psychodynamic, Freudian-influenced individual therapy to an emphasis on a variety of approaches, including various group formats. Psychological services appeared in more and more settings. Along with the increase in the importance and pervasiveness of psychological services came questions about the effectiveness and purpose of therapy, as well as about the characteristics that qualified one to offer therapy, particularly in private practice. The private practice of therapy offered greater professional autonomy and greater financial rewards. And such practice involves working with the less mentally ill.[15]

Compared to persons in other societies, Americans have always been very favorably disposed toward psychiatry and psychology, toward psychological analyses of life and social problems. And in the last thirty years, the American public has sought therapy in ever larger numbers (Hunt, 1987).[16] Since the 1960s, popular interest and belief in psychotherapy and counseling as effective means of changing oneself have grown tremendously (Goode and Wagner, 1993; Thompson, 1993).[17] Practitioners affect the lives of more persons, in a variety of ways, than ever before. As the sociologist David Mechanic points out in his preface to Mental Health and Social Policy (1989:ix):

> The mental health sector has been transformed in the past 30 years. The quantity and the diversity of mental health services available have expanded, the numbers and types of practitioners have proliferated, and the population not only finds mental health services more acceptable than in the past but they use them more commonly.

The psychologist Bernie Zilbergeld (1983) has termed this influence the "shrinking of America." As he sees it, a "therapeutic sensibility," or way of understanding the world, is now the dominant cultural ideology in the United States. He agrees here with the sociologist Philip Rieff's earlier analysis in The Triumph of the Therapeutic (1968) that this is the age of therapy. Zilbergeld argues that therapeutic ideology supplants religious or political belief systems, in a way that generates continual feelings of inferiority. By implying that women and men are not "okay" as they are, that they need therapeutic assistance with every aspect of their lives, this ideology promotes feelings of continual dissatisfaction with oneself, which in turn creates a continuing demand for psychotherapy. Psychotherapy is thus a "growth" industry. To fill the demand, a horde of practitioners of every conceivable stripe have rushed in to offer therapy. T. Byram Karasu, a prominent researcher on psychotherapy's effectiveness, has said he had given up counting therapies at four hundred (Goode and Wagner, 1993).[18] And those seeking personal change do not seek just psychotherapists; rather, they turn to a wide array of practitioners and groups.

As an alternative to individual or group therapy, self-help organizations are a very popular source of aid for persons with a variety of problems. It has been estimated that more than six million Americans a year participate, and that as many men and women will join self-help groups as will undergo psychotherapy. The number of self-help groups has, accordingly, skyrocketed. The Directory of Self Help and Mutual Aid Groups, first published in 1978, then listed two hundred groups; in 1993, it listed more than three thousand (Wolinsky, 1993).

In place of traditional psychotherapy or self-help groups, troubled individuals can also choose to consult Christian mental-health professionals; their numbers, too, have grown rapidly since the late 1960s. The "recovery move-ment," which grew out of Alcoholics Anonymous, has been called a "powerful engine in the rise of Christian psychotherapy" (Stafford, 1993). According to Stafford, "A 1991 *Christianity Today* reader survey suggests that evangelicals are far more likely to take problems to a counselor than to a pastor."[19]

And still another potential source of assistance are "alternative" thera-pies (many are probably listed among the more than four hundred to which Karasu refers). Jack Raso (1994) gives some sense of the diversity of these groups and observes that "their collective effect is widespread and formida-ble." He lists fifty-five methods, among which are the seven keys meditation program, acu-point therapy, BioEssence therapy, Crystal therapeutics, Divine will healing, Heartwood massage, neural therapy, pranic psychotherapy, song channeling (adjunct to rebirthing), and Whole health shiatsu.

A second commentator, Bill Thomson (*East West Natural Health*, May 1992), gives a fuller description of seven alternative therapies and diagnostic procedures: applied kinesiology, aromatherapy, hypnotherapy, iridology, past-life therapy, reflexology, and touch therapy. He also observes that the amount of money spent on alternative therapies is considerable:

> In place of drugs and surgery, the public is turning to (and spending
> upwards of $30 billion a year on) everything from over-the-counter
> homeopathic remedies to past-life therapy. Some treatments, like
> acupuncture, have earned wide respect. Others, such as drinking your own
> urine, seem bizarre to most people. (Thomson, 1992)

And Esalen (founded in 1962), the grand old lady of encounter groups and the human-potential movement, continues strong. According to a *Chicago Tribune* article (Condor, 1994), "Roughly 400 workshops and seminars each year accommodate about 10,000 'seminarians.'" Centers similarly interested in offering personal-growth programs are profiled in Caren Goldman's article "Enrich Yourself: A Guide to 19 Leading Centers for Personal Growth" (Gold-man, 1993).

All this demonstrates the increased popular interest in self- fulfillment, which has created a powerful demand for diverse forms of psychotherapy and for various group experiences,[20] in addition to the obvious concern with alleviating emotional pain.

What Is an Abuse of Therapy?

The cultural diversity of the United States has produced a variety of schools of psychotherapy, with no one of them being deemed clearly supe-rior. This wealth of practices and practitioners in American culture also means that it is not easy to define what constitutes an abuse in therapy. Slowly following in the wake of greater public interest in and consumption of psychological services has been attention by professionals to abuses of psychotherapy. Out of an initial belief that psychotherapy can only help has come an awareness of the harm that it can cause. The abuse most widely investigated so far has been sexual contact with clients (Gonsiorek, 1995; Pope and Bouhoutsos, 1986; Rutter, 1989; and Schoener et al., 1989).

Why Are We Vulnerable?

The amount of information on cults appearing in the media does not adequately reflect their significance as a social problem in real life. The sociological term "moral panic" might accurately be used to describe worry in the United States about cults, particularly Satanic cults. The sociologist Erich Goode (1990:89), analyzing recent concern in the United States about drug use, terms that concern a "moral panic," which he defines as

> a widespread, explosively upsurging feeling on the part of the public that something is terribly wrong in their society because of a moral failure of a specific group of individuals, a subpopulation defined as the enemy. In short, a category of people has been deviantized (Schur, 1980).

Moral panics, however, do not emerge because of public awareness of an objective threat. That is, the size of the panic is not necessarily equivalent to the size of the threat or danger. The people have a very hazy idea of how threatening or damaging certain conditions are.

This analysis can be applied to cults. In the 1970s and 1980s, concern about them was so high that it could be labeled a "moral panic." Chief among the fears was that cults embodied a new way of creating a "Manchurian candidate," an individual completely controlled by the organization. On the contrary, however, one can explain what happens in these groups as resulting from the use of systems of extreme social influence, in which individuals are resocialized to play roles within the organization (Ofshe, 1992). The reality seems to be that cults in general have not been as dangerous to society as popularly feared (i.e., they have not created "Manchurian candidates"); on the other hand, the dangers they do pose have been insufficiently recognized (Singer with Lalich, 1995:83–102, 213–43).

The public's fear over cults appears again in commentaries on the use of the internet as a recruiting tool by Heaven's Gate members—see, for example, chapter 10, "Cyberspace: Culprit or Accomplice?" of Hoffmann and Burke's *Heaven's Gate* (1997). This concern intersects with unease about the internet's dangerousness in general. For example, Ann Landers's column repeatedly features readers who claim that internet romances ruined their marriages and families. In both instances, we see the fear of the internet destroying intimate relationships.

It is no surprise that as social commentators lament the decline of the family, the bureaucratization of most social institutions, and the increase in impersonal relationships, there is also a rise in the number of religious and other cults, as well as public awareness of them, and a rise in the demand for a range of psychotherapeutic (very broadly defined) services, as earlier described. These all have the advantages of providing face-to-face interaction in a small group where the individual is valued for self, not role. Again, one can see the internet as providing for both great intimacy and impersonality in the on-line relationships that develop. In a period of perceived alienation from major social institutions, and from a sense of self, cults and therapeutic services may be viewed as an attempt to return to what sociologists refer to as "gemeinschaft" society.[21] As processes of economic concentration and centralization continue, one may assume this interest will at least remain high, if not grow.

What makes us prone to the influence of cults? Social change associated with moving from the "traditional" to the "modern" world makes us more vulnerable, as it undercuts the possibility and importance of a single "answer" or way of living. The modern world offers instead a variety of options, of identities. Berger and Berger, in *The Homeless Mind* (1974), emphasize how these increased options can lead to "homelessness" of mind. Lifton (Singer with Lalich, 1995:xi) sees a similar sense of dislocation arising from social change, resulting in "widespread feelings that we are losing our psychological moorings." One response is a "contemporary worldwide epidemic of fundamentalism," of which cults are an important expression.

The ideology of individualism, so important in American society, also makes us vulnerable, leading as it does, among other things, to isolation of individuals. This ideology tends to obscure how much ordinary behavior is the result of influence—and it leads to what Singer (with Lalich 1995:15) calls the "not me" myth of who joins cults. Nor is the degree of scientific and technological advancement of a society a measure of its people's invulnerability to influence. In reading news accounts of the Heaven's Gate group, I was struck by how people seemed to think a person who was sophisticated about computers and the internet could not be open to influence by "crazy" ideas and groups—from my perspective, everyone is vulnerable to influence.

Popular acceptance of therapeutic ideology, of the view that persons are in need of change, and that self-fulfillment is a value to be sought, further contributes to our vulnerability.

Finally, Singer (with Lalich, 1995:20) highlights two situations as making men and women prone to cult recruiting: "being depressed and being in between important affiliations." Transitional times in an individual's life make the person more suggestible and manipulable.

What I think the Center for Feeling Therapy says specifically about psychotherapy is that it is a process of influence, in which two or more people form a relationship. Psychotherapy is not, in this view, a set of neutral "techniques" which can be "scientifically" applied to "any" material with beneficial results. A plethora of options await anyone looking for personal change, whether for therapeutic or "self-fulfillment" reasons, and "consumer beware" should certainly be one's motto. Singer and Lalich's *Crazy Therapies* (1996) points out what to beware of, as well as how to select a therapist or evaluate one's present therapist. In emphasizing the need for consumer education, Singer and Lalich mention the misuse of power as one of the central factors in what goes wrong in "crazy therapies."[22] They emphasize the various dangers of psychotherapy, of groups, of leaders with "one answer" for all. As a society we do not appear to have gone very far in regulating psychotherapy. As a result, I think we will continue to face questions about what is "good" and "bad" therapy.

How to Prevent Abuse

How can the kind of maltreatment illustrated by the story of the Center for Feeling Therapy be forestalled? Marie Fortune (1989a), in discussing mainstream churches, and Ronald Enroth (1992), in discussing marginal churches, come to the same conclusion: the cultivation of a critical attitude is essential. Fortune says that

> [j]ust as any relationship or attraction to another should be tested at regular intervals in terms of the health and well-being it promotes, *so must the church maintain a critical edge in relation to its charismatic leaders*. Blind, unthinking, unconditional loyalty to anyone is the basis of tyranny and injustice. It is no less so in the church than in secular society. (1989a:132; emphasis added)

Social psychologists also suggest developing a critical attitude, based on a knowledge of social influence and how it works in general. Cialdini (1984), in describing the six key psychological processes that underlie social influence, offers "how to say no" sections. These give examples of what he means by cultivating a critical attitude such that one is less vulnerable to unwanted social influence. Zimbardo and Andersen (1993), who also stress critical awareness of influence, prescribe moving from being saturated or totally absorbed by activity to moving back and being critical of one's absorption.

For social psychology, a critical attitude is a defense, a prophylactic against undue influence (Aron and Aron, 1989). In many instances, such an attitude can be cultivated by education. For example, various groups have sprung up to combat what they see as destructive cults, and others have arisen to combat what they see as therapeutic abuse. Key to both is consumer education. A good example of an organization dealing with therapeutic abuse (particularly therapist-client sexual abuse) is the Walk-In Counseling Center in Minneapolis. Their massive reference volume, *Psychotherapists' Sexual Involvement with Clients* (Schoener et al., 1989), includes some examples of how going public with instances of abuse alerts consumers to the dangers of therapy; it also suggests that informed consumers are less vulnerable to such dangers.[23]Another organization formed to deal with therapist abuse is STOP ABUSE BY COUNSELORS, founded in February 1980 by Shirley Siegel (Siegel, 1991).

The American Family Foundation has been at the forefront of educating consumers on the harms of cults. It publishes the *Cultic Studies Journal*, the *Cult Observer* (a newsletter), and *Young People and Cults* (the newsletter of its International Cult Education Program). In addition, the group has published a series of books and several videotapes (e.g., *Cults: Saying "No" under Pressure*, narrated by Charlton Heston). The foundation has also taken to the internet to educate the public about cults, developing an excellent website (http://www.csj.org). It provides extensive information on various groups, as well as pages of links to other websites dealing with this topic.

In addition to these advocacy groups, consumers themselves have often been responsible for having therapeutic abuse recognized as harmful and the perpetrators punished.[24] Professional therapists have been prodded to reform by patients taking their grievances to disciplinary boards and to the courts. The result seems to be one of making therapists more accountable for their treatments.

The Center for Feeling Therapy's conflicting perspectives on its value were resolved largely through the efforts of concerned former patients. They were determined to rectify what they saw as the wrongs done by therapists. Key to their continued resolve in the course of the "stigma contests" they encountered was the support they offered to each other. Such mutual assistance seems characteristic of other battles to get a therapist or a therapy termed "wrong" (thus implying deviance).

For example, Jeffrey Masson (1994:165–94) discusses the case of John Rosen, a psychiatrist who surrendered his license to practice on March 29, 1983, in Harrisburg, Pennsylvania. He was about to be accused of sixty-seven violations of the Pennsylvania Medical Practices Act and thirty-five violations of the rules and regulations of the state's medical board. His path to this point began in 1977. A former patient hired a private detective to investigate whether her terrible experience with Dr. Rosen was exceptional. (This was four years after she had last seen him.) The private detective found other, similarly questionable instances of treatment. The Pennsylvania Board of Medical Education and Licensure, on the basis of her complaint and the detective's findings, then began a five-year investigation of the matter. Key to the investigation was the testimony of six former patients about the abusive treatment they had received from Dr. Rosen.

A second example is the case of Linda Hatch. She accused Melvin Wise, a prominent Miami psychiatrist, of developing a sexual relationship with her while he was treating her for panic attacks, the consequence of sexual molestation as a small child. When her complaint was reported in the *Miami Herald*, four other women came forward to make similar accusations against Dr. Wise. Why did the women suddenly come forward? According to the journalist Carol Gentry, "they didn't know there was an agency that cared, or they had been too intimidated to risk going it alone." (Gentry, 1993b). Even with this number of women making the same complaint, the road to revocation was long and difficult. The process began in October 1985 with a letter from Linda Hatch to the South Florida Psychiatric Society. It ended with the Florida Board of Medicine voting unanimously on August 7, 1992, to revoke Dr.Wise's license. After the vote, for the first time in the board's history, two laypersons, Linda Hatch and another former patient, were allowed to address it. Hatch's comments centered on the lengthiness of the process and the disrespect she (and the other complainants) experienced:

> We, the victims, cannot be expected to remain involved with a system that takes years to complete. . . . Our wounds stay open throughout this process, just when we are badly needing them to close and to heal. We need to move on with our lives. Throughout history, those of us who report sexual abuse have been treated as psychotic, labeled hysteric, portrayed as promiscuous and dismissed as expendable. . . . This must stop.[25](Gentry, 1993c)

The successful prosecution of Dr. Wise's case seemed to hinge largely on Hatch's efforts and determination to bring the psychiatrist to justice. Part of what Hatch told the Florida Board of Medicine was that "it took seven years, eight trips to Florida from her home in St. Louis and almost $30,000 of her own money to resolve her complaint against an influential Miami psychiatrist. Often her construction business and three children suffered while she carried on the struggle" (Gentry, 1993a). In response to this case, the Florida legislature made it a crime for psychiatrists, psychologists, and other therapists to have sex with their patients. Three years after this bill became law, however, Gentry reported that sex offenses by therapists were still handled by the Florida Department of Professional Regulation, and state's attorneys in two counties said they knew of no arrests (Gentry, 1993c).

Since the Center for Feeling Therapy was founded in the early 1970s, professional codes regulating therapists have been changed so that sex with clients is prohibited. Indeed, as of 1995, thirteen states have made therapist-patient sex a felony (Kane, 1995).[26]

The number of malpractice suits against therapists has risen greatly. The leading controversy in therapy circles at the moment concerns "recovered memory" therapy, with one side claiming this is abuse, not treatment of patients (Ofshe and Watters, 1994; Loftus, 1994). Sexual abuse by clergy, as another form of abuse of authority, has also generated significant public concern (Fortune, 1989a and 1989b, 1995; Schoener et al., 1989). According to an article quoted in the *Cult Observer* ("Cultic Processes Top Stories of '93," 1994), the stand off and the Branch Davidians' deaths at Waco and clergy abuse were the two hottest topics in religion covered by the news media in 1993. One might assume that public concern about various abuses of authority will remain high for some time to come.

The Future

One consequence of the United States religious pluralism, guaranteed by the First Amendment, is that the country

> has always been a haven for new and marginal religious groups. Cults, sects, and religious revivals have been a continuing feature of American life. The general attitude toward these groups has been one of resigned acceptance, so long as their practices did not violate social norms. Indeed, alternate belief groups have not encountered antagonism for their beliefs so much as for their habits and customs. (Appel, 1983:173)

The United States has a long history of such religious (and other) experiments in group living, many of which were widely condemned at the time (Kanter, 1972).[27] What these experiments point out is the continuing deviance-defining that is an essential part of social life.[28] Groups pushed the limits of conventional ways of living and disputed what should be termed "deviant." The law intervened in a variety of ways. A historical view shows how the boundary between deviant and nondeviant behavior has changed over time. For example, child abuse, sexual abuse, battering of women, sexual harassment, wifebeating and childbeating, and marital rape were once accepted as normal in some sense, and only over time have they been redefined as deviant, as social problems to be solved. Many recent controversies have concerned behaviors within particular groups that do not recognize the changed social boundaries (e.g., what is considered appropriate discipline for children, with Stonegate and Ecclesia being two examples).

Based on our long history, we should expect these varied "cult" groups to continue to crop up. With the year 2000 fast approaching, we might expect to see more millenarian groups, such as the one led by David Koresh.

"Cults" are thus a resurgent phenomenon, responding to modern life. Part of their appeal is their small size, close face-to-face relations, strong authority figure, the "answer" the group provides, and the belief that individuals can make a difference. As sociologists would say, cults provide a "gemeinschaft" world, which contrasts to the increasingly "gesellschaft" world of modernity. Large, bureaucratic organizations dominate much of social life, with the individual feeling increasingly powerless. Paradoxically, women and men have more latitude than ever before to choose identities and lifestyles. Social isolation is high, with an unprecedented number of individuals living alone. There is an increase in secular authority, which is more delimited than sacred authority. The question of who is a believable and responsible authority is problematic. There is much existential uncertainty. And finally, there is a change in attitude resulting from widespread acceptance of the therapeutic ideology and of the legitimacy of "self-fulfillment" as a value to be pursued: if unhappy with your present life, why not try something different? All of this increases the need for individuals to search for identity, intimacy, meaning, and community. People are thus vulnerable to the lure of cult recruiters.

American cultural individualism hinders us from seeing limits on our lives, and what "cult" groups reveal is precisely how much of behavior is socially constructed. Our individualism also accounts for explanations that emphasize leaders and what they do—for example, the emphasis on Jim Jones, the person, in accounting for the deaths at Jonestown—and that place less emphasis on the situation or context as shaping behavior.

Many former cultists seem to come away from their experience with what I would call a sociological view. That is, they focus on how the group shaped their choices and decisions while they were members. What they have gone through seems to have shocked them out of their strong belief in individualism. As a society, judging from media accounts, we have not come too far in analyzing what occurs: "brainwashing" still seems the term of choice, and it refers to what still seems a mysterious, all-powerful process.

Often we do not term a group a "cult" until it is suddenly exposed to our scrutiny through media coverage. We become aware of its deviantness, and the questions begin. Who could do this? Why would someone normal stay in such a group? Experts who have studied such organizations greatly differ in their answers. To sociologists of religion, a new religion is in the process of development; to social psychologists, a process of social influence is unfolding. Cults are thus a study in "deviantizing," in deviance-defining, and they thus reveal to us deeply held notions of the normal. In the end, our fascination with "cults" underscores our strong cultural belief in individualism. Fascinated by what appears to be the destruction of individuality, we are curious about what social relationships and what methods can bring it about.

Notes

Chapter One

1. This turned out to be Barbara Underwood, who later left and wrote (with her mother, Betty Underwood) *Hostage to Heaven* (1979).

2. At no point during this time did I become a Moonie. I left at the end of the three-week period that I had free, before joining my parents in San Francisco for their visit.

3. I maintained at the time that

"Brainwashing" in these accounts is a one-time phenomenon, with effects on the individual monolithic and all-binding. One is programmed to a particular, deviant belief system as if one were a robot. The "programming" involved most often seems to be a very simplistic, stimulus-response notion of how learning occurs, a repetitive process of providing information, rewarding appropriate behavior and belief, again and again and again. To reverse the process, one "deprograms" the individual, and provides alternative information in the same repetitious manner. (Ayella, 1981:2)

4. Both John Lofland's (1977) and David Taylor's (1982) articles emphasize the importance of "love bombing."

5. The figure given for the the the number of therapists who founded the Center for Feeling Therapy varies in their accounts from nine to seven.

6. In addition to these interviews with onetime patients, I spoke formally with a lawyer who handled several suits against the Center, a psychiatrist who interviewed six past members and wrote an article based on this material (Hochman, 1984), and the deputy attorney general of California who handled the license revocation hearings involving the therapists who headed the Center.

I read an assortment of legal documents, among them the pleadings; these latter set forth charges against the therapists, and I cite examples from them. The pleadings are based on the sworn affidavits of ninety-one former patients and on the opinion of four persons expert in the different fields of practice involved. The affidavits themselves are not a matter of public record.

In addition, interviewees provided me with a wealth of written materials on the Center. I read the four books published by Feeling Therapists (as well as *Life Zones*, coauthored by Corriere in 1986, after the Center had collapsed), along with published articles. I also studied newspaper articles that appeared before and after the Center went out of existence.

Given how much the authors relied on their own experience, these books and articles provide a fair amount of information on the therapists, their relationships with each other, and their treatment of patients, as well as on changes in therapy and the development of the therapeutic community. The authors refer to therapists by name, and this affords more information on how individuals felt about various matters. To take one example, the appendix of *Going Sane* (1975) provides a transcript of a complete therapy session; the authors remark that "we are willing to stand by this session and say, 'This is the best we can do'" (1975:423). One may assume that this is a session between Riggs Corriere and Joe Hart (probably the two most important leaders), since the one identified as therapist refers to the patient as "Riggs" and the one identified as patient speaks the name "Joe." In this transcript, we hear Riggs describe (among other things) his loneliness as a child and less than loving interactions with his mother and one of his sisters.

Two other sources of information were very helpful in shaping my understanding of the Center for Feeling Therapy. "Longterm Effects of Participation in a Psychological 'Cult' Utilizing Directive Therapy Techniques" (1986), a master's thesis by Kathy Knight, provided an analysis of a survey of fifty-eight erstwhile patients. Finally, *Therapy Gone Mad* (1994), by the journalist Carol Lynn Mithers, vividly describes the Center's rise and fall. Her account is based on interviews with forty-eight former patients, along with a variety of written and other materials. (She, too, was unable to interview any of the therapists.) Her description corroborates the analysis I developed from my research. Mithers provides additional details on the founding and on events leading up to the collapse that flesh out the accounts my interviewees provided, and I rely on her work here.

7. As my publisher put it in describing what he thought was the central question of my book: Why do people voluntarily subject themselves to such behavior?

Chapter Two

1. I rely heavily here on the details Mithers (1994) provides in the first two sections of her book, "Beginnings" and "Joe's Kids."

2. This "discovery" seems to date from the inception of the Center; in a 1971 article, one of the founders, Hart describes the use of dreams in his class "The Psychology of Awareness." Corriere subsequently seems to have established himself as the expert on dreams, for his 1974 dissertation was entitled "The Transformation of Dreams."

3. My understanding of this is based on the interviews I did with former patients.

4. Conferring certificates after training programs offered by the Center for Feeling Therapy were completed is reminiscent of Scientology's early conferral of "degrees." Hubbard advertised by his writing of *Dianetics*, and he suggested people try his approach. They did, independently. Hubbard wanted, however, to get full credit for his discoveries and to limit the number of their practitioners. As Wallis (1977b: 118) describes the process,

> Training in Scientology usually begins with the HAS (Hubbard Apprentice Scientologist) Course. With this, as with most other levels of training, successful completion of the course is signified by an impressive certificate, and members often affect the initials of the successfully completed courses as honorific appellations to their names—John Smith HPA, for example. It is not unknown for individuals who have been awarded a Book Auditor's certificate, after reading and successfully applying the principles and practices indicated in Hubbard's texts, to employ the style B.A. after their names. At one time

"degrees" were issued permitting the individual to employ the styles B.Scn., D.Scn., D.D., and even "Freudian Analyst" after their names.

5. I calculated this from a 1978 handout, "The Center Foundation," which listed twenty-five individuals as "staff."

6. See the sets of pleadings prepared by the California Attorney General's Office in 1983 and 1984 for examples of relationships that were broken up, parents who gave up their children, and women who had abortions.

Chapter Three

1. See Kovel (1976:138–46) and Rosen (1979:154–217) for good descriptions and analyses of Primal Therapy. This section is based primarily upon my reading of *The Primal Scream*.

2. Contrast this conception of neurotic suffering with the definition by Allen Wheelis (1973). In his view, the cause of the pain, the source of conflict, is not to be seen as lying in direct contrast to something else, as in "real" versus "unreal" selves. The conflict, rather, is woven into the fiber of one's self. R. D. Rosen (1979) makes the same point.

3. This metaphor of the self sounds like that of much of repressed-memory therapy, the hottest therapy controversy at the moment.

4. Kovel (1976) strongly criticizes the Primal Scream for mandating the concept of transference out of existence while producing a situation likely to generate a very intense form of transference. The situation is that of a therapist individually and intensely interacting with a patient for a sustained period, during which he actively elicits the patient's deepest feelings toward his parents. From this perspective, the therapist is not "there," there is no room for the individual to reflect in any way on what he might feel at the time toward the therapist, for he is not to feel for the therapist. Kovel views Primal Scream as a most fertile ground for charlatanism because of this lack.

5. And yet, there are other therapists who do the same thing; see Masson's *Against Therapy* (1994:268–79) for a description of Milton Erickson's attempts to change people quickly. In Masson's view, "The Ericksonian technique epitomizes, in a seemingly nonviolent way, what Rosen epitomizes in a violent way—the therapist-as-boss" (1994:278).

6. See any introductory sociology or social psychology textbook for discussion of the "natural" properties of groups to influence members. Primary groups (of which the small group is one) characterized by intimate, face-to-face interaction of members, have greater influence than do secondary groups, which are usually large and involve more-impersonal interaction. Asch is the social psychologist whose research convincingly demonstrated the small group's ability to generate conformity.

7. Frank (1974:322) sees democratic and scientific ideas as causing many therapists to underestimate the "extent to which psychotherapy is a process of persuasion." Janov's theory shares in this bias to an extreme degree, asserting that there is no relationship, let alone one of persuasion, even between therapists and patients.

8. Appel (1983:23–24) cites Lévi-Strauss's account of a shaman treating a woman who is unable to deliver a child naturally to show how "social myths not only make experience understandable" but "help to shape it." Appel says of the shaman's approach that

> his cure consists of a long narrative. The shaman never actually touches his patient; rather, the narrative itself provides a bridge to her physical experience. . . . As Lévi-Strauss notes, the shaman's itinerary is a true mythical anatomy, which

corresponds to a kind of emotional geography within the patient. During the course of the narration, physical sensation and fiction merge, and the patient begins to identify her experience with the story being told her. This identification in turn creates in her a physiological susceptibility—myth begins to shape experience. . . . The purpose of these details is to elicit an organic reaction, but as Lévi-Strauss points out, "The sick woman could not integrate it as experience if it were not associated with a true increase in dilation." The cure, in short, occurs in the process of translating inchoate experience into a form accessible to the conscious mind and amenable to action.

The social psychologists Aron and Aron, in *The Heart of Social Psychology* (1989), briefly summarize their discipline's main themes. Paramount among these is influence: "most social psychologists strive to make people see that social influences determine their thoughts, attitudes, perceptions, emotions, and even their very selves" (1989:22).

In discussing how other people affect the way we see and feel, they point to the classic investigations by Solomon Asch and by Stanley Schacter and Jerry Singer. Asch's studies of conformity asked students "to determine which among three comparison lines shown on a large card was equal to a standard line shown on a similar card" (ibid.:28). Unbeknownst to the student subject, the other "students" were all confederates of Asch. When these impostors all gave the same wrong answers, the real student was placed in a quandary. What happened? "[T]hree-quarters gave, at least once, the same answer as the majority—the 'objectively wrong' answer. A third did so more than half the time" (ibid.). Whether students went along or disagreed with the majority, decision making was uncomfortable. Why did people follow the majority? Aron and Aron report that

> [m]ost explanations boiled down to these three: (a) The largest number said that although they did not see the lines the same as the majority, they assumed the majority was correct and their own perceptions must somehow be wrong; (b) a small number said that although they felt they were completely correct, they did not want to say so because they didn't want to look different to the others; and (c) a few said they actually came to see the line lengths as did the majority. (29)

Though Asch used only college students in his experiments, his findings were confirmed by later work with many other types of people.

Whereas Asch's studies dealt with conformity in perception, Schacter and Singer's investigations dealt with conformity in feeling. Their 1962 study recruited healthy students to test (supposedly) the effects on vision of a new vitamin, "suproxin." All participants were given injections: 70 percent were injected with adrenalin, which is associated with "palpitation, tremor, and sometimes a feeling of flushing and accelerated breathing" (1962:382), and 30 percent (the control group) were injected with saline solution, which has no physiological effects. Four groups were created, with each receiving different information: one was told the truth about the side effects of adrenalin; another was given inaccurate information; the third was told there would be no side effects; and the fourth, the control group receiving saline solution, was told there would be no side effects. According to Aron and Aron, "The idea was that those who had a proper explanation for their arousal would be unaffected by anything that subsequently happened to them, whereas those who had no good explanation for an onset of arousal would look to their circumstances for an explanation and manifest an emotion appropriate to those circumstances" (1989:35–36).

And that is precisely what happened. Placed in either an "anger" or a "euphoric" context, those who got adrenalin and had been told to expect the adrenalin effects as "side effects" showed very little emotion. They did not join in much with the confederates. . . . Similarly, those who got the saline solution and were not physiologically aroused also showed little emotion. . . . But those who were aroused and either had no explanation for their symptoms or had been given the wrong explanation strongly showed the emotion of the condition they were in. (38)

9. While Feeling Therapists repeatedly claim that community is essential in generating a "sane" identity and lifestyle for individuals, they recognize only certain aspects of community in shaping identity. They do not see any influence or group pressure to conform in their community.

10. This is my own depiction of the implicit metaphor they use.

11. In Lifton's analysis the process of thought reform involves a set of eight psychological themes: milieu control, mystical manipulation, the demand for purity, the cult of confession, the "sacred science," loading the language, putting doctrine over person, and the dispensing of existence.

The most basic feature of this environment is "milieu control," by which Lifton means control of human communication, whether with the world outside or with oneself. The remaining seven themes of "ideological totalism" are predicated on successful establishment of "milieu control."

12. See Hinkle and Wolff (1956) and Brown (1963), particularly chapter 11, "Confessions and Indoctrination."

13. Ofshe further explains that the

combination of psychological assault on the self, interpersonal pressure, and the social organization of the environment creates a situation that can only be coped with by adapting and acting so as to present oneself to others in terms of the ideology supported in the environment. . . . Eliciting the desired verbal and interactive behavior sets up conditions likely to stimulate the development of attitudes consistent with and that function to rationalize new behavior in which the individual is engaging. Models of attitude change, such as the theory of Cognitive Dissonance (Festinger 1957) or Self-Perception theory (Bem 1972), explain the tendency for consistent attitudes to develop as a consequence of behavior. (1992:213–14)

Chapter Four

1. This is also true of the sample who talked to a former member I interviewed, who himself hopes to write a book about the Center.

2. This pattern of entry is in keeping with the research of William Bainbridge and Rodney Stark on how persons are recruited into cults and sects. See Stark and Bainbridge (1980).

3. I am interested in examining the therapist's role and not the individual therapist. Accordingly, in the quotes that follow here and in Chapter 5 I have substituted "my therapist" or "the therapist" for individual therapists' names. All interviewees' names have also been changed to protect their privacy.

4. This also illustrates what Singer (with Lalich, 1995:128) calls "proof through reframing," by which individuals' responses are interpreted in ways favorable to the group, as part of the persuasion process.

5. The two internal quotations here are from Horowitz's (1981) article about the crash of the Center. See also Morain (1981), considering the abortion in the context of Center policy on children.

Cristina discussed how this very humiliating experience was recast for the group as an example demonstrating her conviction. A passage from 60 Hours That Transform Your Life: est (Bry, 1976:64) also illustrates how ordinarily humiliating experiences can be recast to reflect the group's ideology:

> All eyes were focused on the handsome young man standing at the back of the room. His face contorted, his eyes red, he pleaded to be allowed to go to the bathroom. The trainer simply stared at him until after a while, the young man shut up and sat down. No one had physically barred his way. Nor had anyone told him that he couldn't leave. It was his choice to remain in the room.
>
> About ten minutes later he raised his hand for a microphone. "I want you to know," he announced, "that I just peed in my pants." In a crisp, staccato voice, he added: "And it really doesn't matter." Two hundred and forty-nine people cheered and applauded.

6. The quotation is from Horowitz (1981).

7. This was a new feature, included in The Dream Makers (1977) and Psychological Fitness (1978), both by Corriere and Hart.

8. Cialdini (1984:95–96) discusses Elliot Aronson and Judson Mills's research on female college students' initiation into groups.

> They found that college women who had to endure a severely embarrassing initiation ceremony in order to gain access to a sex discussion group convinced themselves that their new group and its discussions were extremely valuable, even though Aronson and Mills had previously rehearsed the other group members to be as "worthless and uninteresting" as possible. Different coeds, who went through a much milder initiation ceremony or went through no initiation at all, were decidedly less positive about the "worthless" new group they had joined. Additional research showed the same results when coeds were required to endure pain rather than embarrassment to get into a group. The more electric shock a woman received as part of the initiation ceremony, the more she later persuaded herself that her new group and its activities were interesting, intelligent, and desirable.

9. Just as in the Moonies (Ayella, 1981). It seems this may also be true of recovered-memory therapy: all problems lead back to childhood sexual abuse. See Ofshe and Watters (1994), chapter 3.

10. The definition of who could be helped (anyone, because all were insane) and the standard against which patients measured themselves (limitless human potential) were always impossibly broad.

11. The social psychologist Robert Cialdini, in his book Influence (1984), argues that "you can use small commitments to manipulate a person's self-image" (81); commitment is the key because it generates pressure to be consistent with the commitment (75); "the severity of an initiation ceremony significantly heightens the newcomer's commitment to the group" (96); "commitments are most effective in changing a person's self-image and future behavior when they are active, public, and effortful" (96); and even more important than these last three combined is taking responsibility for behavior—thinking "we have chosen to perform it in the absence of strong outside pressures" (97).

Finally, Cialdini says that

> compliance professionals love commitments that produce inner change. First, that change is not just specific to the situation where it first occurred; it covers a whole range of related situations, too. Second, the effects of the change are lasting. . . . There is yet another attraction in commitments that lead to inner change—they grow their own legs. There is no need for the compliance professional to undertake a costly and continuing effort to reinforce the change; the pressure for consistency will take care of all that. . . . In general, because of the need to be consistent within his system of beliefs, [a committed person] will assure himself that his choice to take public-spirited action was right. What is important about this process of generating additional reasons to justify the commitment is that the reasons are *new*. Thus, even if the original reason for the civic-minded behavior was taken away, these newly discovered reasons might be enough by themselves to support his perception that he had behaved correctly.
>
> The advantage to an unscrupulous compliance professional is tremendous. Because we build new struts to undergird choices we have committed ourselves to, an exploitative individual can offer us an inducement for making such a choice, and after the decision has been made, can remove that inducement, knowing that our decision will probably stand on its own newly created legs. (Cialdini, 1984:101–2)

Chapter Five

1. This certainly seems to be true in many cases involving recovered-memory therapy.

2. See Gerlach and Hine (1970) for a discussion of "burning one's bridges" to demonstrate commitment.

3. The only two children who lived in the community were Joe Hart's daughter and Konni Corriere's daughter from her first marriage. And this daughter had earlier been sent to live with her father for a year while Konni attended to her therapy (Mithers, 1994:129)

4. See David Gerstel's *Paradise Incorporated* (1982:208–11) for a discussion of Synanon's adoption of a policy prohibiting children, and the coercing of women into having abortions. Chuck Dederich soon pushed vasectomies for men in the group as the way to realize this policy of childlessness. See also Ofshe (1980).

5. In a survey of fifty-eight former patients, Knight (1986) reported that nine of the twenty-eight female respondents (32%) reported that they had stopped menstruating while at the Center.

6. Many theorized that all patients were to be shaped in Richard Corriere's image, which was described as that of a hyperactive child.

7. For an analysis of the ways in which mothers are controlled in cults and the impact on the mother-child bond, see Stein (1997:40–57). For a look at how gender influences aspects of the cult experience, see Lalich (1997).

8. In developing this critique, feminists' research has analyzed how the notion of femininity appears in advertising, film, literature, and social interaction, among other areas. See, for example, Kilbourne (1987 and 1995), Coward (1985), Freedman (1986), Goffman (1979), Henley (1977), Mellen (1975), and Millett (1970).

In addition to investingating the depiction of women as sex objects, the study of femininity as social control of women has included analysis of psychiatric judgments of mental health as being androcentric (Broverman et al., 1970; Chesler, 1972). Since the early critique of psychological notions of female mental health, feminist psychotherapists have sought to define appropriate treatments to eliminate the androcentric character of psychotherapy (Brodsky and Hare-Mustin, 1980; Greenspan, 1983; Lerner, 1988).

9. See Mithers (1994:305–33) for a vivid picture of the collapse.

Chapter Six

1. Willner suggests that we must look at the response of followers, not the leader, to know whether charismatic leadership exists. Following Max Weber's insight that "[i]t is recognition on the part of those subject to authority which is decisive for the validity of charisma" (quoted in Willner, 1984:19), she points to three "categories of indicators of charismatically oriented recognition." The first of these,

> referring to what I have called the "leader-image" dimension, consists of beliefs that identify the leader with realms beyond the human. . . . The second category of indicator denotes unconditional acceptance of the personal authority of the leader. . . . The third category includes all those indicators denoting complete emotional commitment to the leader and, by extension, to his vision or to the order he has created. (19)

2. Of eyes, Willner remarks:

> Finally, I should like to note one physical feature that can convey the suggestion of supernatural power in the possessor—eyes of a certain quality. Of all the facial features, none tends to be more perceived than eyes as external indicators of the personal qualities of an individual. . . . Only eyes are associated with the capability of exerting force outward. . . . However varied the leaders discussed here may have been in most aspects of their physical appearance—and they were—most of them seem to have shared the attribute of extraordinary eyes. (1984:149)

3. See Stannard-Friel's *Harassment Therapy* (1981:67), an analysis of intimidation that occurred in a Roman Catholic hospital. He says of staff members who refused to harass patients: "In one way, the good guys *did* lend support to harassment. By comforting the patients and validating the cruelty of the treatment, they absorbed some of the revolutionary energy that built up among the patients. As with Zimbardo's (1971:16) guards, they felt helpless to do anything to stop harassment. They, in fact, rarely did anything to interfere with the harassment of patients. As a consequence, the inaction and sympathy helped maintain the system."

4. This episode illustrates Lifton's concept "dispensing of existence."

5. This exemplifies Lifton's concept of "doctrine over person."

6. Such a realization of "universality" is not always obtained in group therapy. In Yalom's perspective, it is a potential realization, more likely to be obtained in group rather than individual therapy.

7. I am using a magnetic metaphor to describe the ties among people as having the ability to attract or repel. With Center people, it was as though a physical barrier prevented the passage of this "energy." They remained well insulated from contact with persons not connected with the Center.

8. Thus, there was both internal and external pressure to express conviction by a visible sign. This happens in other cultlike groups. For example, one "Primals" with all one's might, to show one is making progress. Participants at *est* trainings shared insights from the start, to the point of absurdity, to demonstrate how well they were "getting it."

Yet intensity of conviction, as expressed in "testifying" to insiders or proselytizing outsiders, need not represent completeness of conviction. Lifton (1961) describes such intensity as a way of trying to still one's own doubts by persuading others. Balch (1980) analyzes such intensity as part of a performance arising from desires for achievement within the group—the individual is striving to be the best, the most esteemed member, or even an "acceptable" one. In other words, the degree of conviction expressed is partly the result of a conscious choice set in the context of a struggle for social status within the group.

9. See Erik H. Erikson's *Young Man Luther* (1958:52–53, 102) for his discussion of the concept of "negative identity." He observes:

> In Martin's upbringing, then, the image of a peasant may have become what we call a negative identity fragment, i.e., an identity a family wishes to live down—even though it may sentimentalize it at moments—and the mere hint of which it tries to suppress in its children. . . .
>
> We will call all self-images, even those of a highly idealistic nature, which are diametrically opposed to the dominant values of an individual's upbringing, parts of a negative identity—meaning an identity which he has been warned not to become, which he can become only with a divided heart, but which he nevertheless finds himself compelled to become, protesting his wholeheartedness.

Robert Lifton relies on Erikson's use of "negative identity" in *Thought Reform and the Psychology of Totalism* (1961). Lifton illustrates his usage, which I adopt in my analysis of why people stayed with the Center, as follows.

> The antithesis of which the priest speaks is his negative identity— that part of him which he has been constantly warned never to become. A priest's negative identity is likely to include such elements as the selfish man, the sinner, the proud man, the insincere man, and the unvigilant man. As the reformers encourage a prisoner's negative identity to enlarge and luxuriate, the prisoner becomes ready to doubt the more affirmative self-image (diligent priest, considerate healer, tolerant teacher) which he had previously looked upon as his true identity. He finds an ever-expanding part of himself falling into disfavor in his own eyes.
>
> At this point the prisoner faces the most dangerous part of thought reform. He experiences guilt and shame much more profound and much more threatening to his inner integrity than any experienced in relation to previous psychological steps. He is confronted with his human limitations, with the contrast between what he is and what he would be. His emotion may be called true or genuine guilt, or true shame—or existential guilt—to distinguish it from the less profound and more synthetic forms of inner experience. He undergoes a self-exposure which is on the border of guilt and shame. Under attack is the deepest meaning of his entire life, the morality of his relationship to mankind. The one-sided exploitation of existential guilt is thought reform's trump card, and perhaps its most important source of emotional influence over its participants.

Revolving around it are issues most decisive to thought reform's outcome. (77–78)

The whole of Lifton's chapter 5, "Psychological Steps," is relevant to my analysis.

10. See Jean Kilbourne's 1995 video, *Slim Hopes*, illustrating advertising's role in promoting cultural norms of thinness for women.

11. Frank and Frank (1991:161–62) point out that "psychoanalysis resembles many other theories of healing in providing explanations for lack of progress that protect its core beliefs from disproof and its practitioners from despair. Patients who do not improve may be showing 'resistance,' and their criticism of the therapist may be dismissed as 'negative transference.'"

12. Jerome Frank (1974:314) goes on to say, "Having lost confidence in his ability to defend himself against a threatening world, the demoralized person is prey to anxiety and depression (the two most common complaints of persons seeking psychotherapy) as well as to resentment, anger, and other dysphoric emotions."

13. Frank and Frank (1991:152) remark, "Being all-inclusive, psychoanalysis, like many other therapeutic rationales, has great persuasive power."

14. Frank and Frank (1991:162; emphasis added) point out: "Rationalizing therapeutic failures in order to preserve a theory. . . may lead therapists to blame patients for their failure to improve. Especially when this is done covertly, by ignoring or disconfirming the patient's point of view, such behavior may increase the person's *confusion, sense of failure, and demoralization*."

Chapter 7

1. Both videotapes are available from the American Family Foundation (Bonita Springs, Florida). Examine the AFF's webpage (http://www.csj.org) for more information on exit counseling and recovery, among other issues.

Also see chapters 7 and 10 of Steven Hassan's *Combatting Cult Mind Control* (1990) for discussion of exit counseling and recovery. Hassan, a former member of the Unification Church, is now an exit counselor. His webpage (http://www.shassan.com/index.html) provides information on his background, qualifications, and activities as an exit counselor.

2. The psychologist Margaret Singer (1979) originally estimated that it takes an individual approximately six to eighteen months to move from being a cultist to feeling comfortable as a noncultist. Yet, the cult experience still significantly affected my interviewees' self-assessments years later. See chapter 12, "Recovery: Coming Out of the Pseudopersonality," in Singer with Lalich (1995) for her more recent thinking on this process.

3. See Betz (1997), who describes the collapse of a group headed by a guru when she revealed to all members the secret sexual relations between the guru and members of his inner circle.

4. My description of the two-month interruption in therapist control is partly based on Mithers (1994).

5. Ebaugh (1988:145) also defines the experience as "one in which taken-for-granted anchors of social and self-identity are suspended for the individual, leaving him or her feeling rootless and anxious. . . . The resolution of these feelings of worthlessness and anxiety were [sic] closely tied to successful efforts to begin to create and adapt to a new role in society."

This also seems to be what Balch (1985:45) describes as "floating." It is the "experience of being trapped between two symbolic worlds. Defectors had cut themselves off from the cult, often with no choice of returning, but they usually looked on the outside world with a mixture of ambivalence and dread."

6. Jon Atack (1990:41) seems to have felt the same need to understand his experience with Scientology: "By the summer of 1984, I had drifted away from the 'Tech,' but was still caught up in the quest for the truth about Hubbard and his organization. What follows is the fruit of that quest."

7. I have earlier applied Schur's concepts of "deviantizing" and "stigma contests" to cults (Ayella, 1990). Schur's *Politics of Deviance* (1980:8) uses the concept of "stigma contests" to refer to "continuing struggles over competing social definitions" of deviance.

8. See Beckford (1985:94–134) for a good discussion of the main themes of what he calls "anti-cult" sentiment, the negative connotations of "cult."

9. It is precisely this response by experts in dealing with onetime cultists that has prompted the emphasis on providing information about influence techniques as part of the "exit counseling" that has developed as a response to the early "deprogramming" of cult members. See Langone (1993), Giambalvo (1995), and Tobias and Lalich (1994).

10. According to Levine (1984:151), "More than 50% of former members of radical groups show signs of emotional upheaval severe enough to warrant treatment during the first few months after their return. Of these, about a quarter are seen by a psychiatrist, psychologist, counselor, or social workers upon their return."

Ebaugh (1988:209) notes: "Frequently, therapists first encounter role exiters who are going through the vacuum stage of the process. . . . Since this period is one of extreme anxiety and creates a sense of normlessness, it is quite common for people to seek therapeutic help at this stage of the process. If the therapist is aware that most role exiters go through a similar experience, he or she can create a context and definition of the situation for the individual such that feelings and anxieties are seen as 'normal' and to be expected rather than indicative of deeper psychological problems."

11. Compare this with SanGiovanni's (1978:ch.9) description of former nuns as adopting selective disclosure as a strategy for negotiating their "emergent role passage."

12. See Beckford (1982) for his discussion of popular opinion.

Also see Singer's (with Lalich 1995:306–7) discussion of how past members explained time spent in the cult. As one man said, "It's difficult to explain just what I did as a Governor of Enlightenment. . . . Another man said he could only put 'office manager' on an application form to describe what he did in his old cult, where in actuality he had worked as a spy for the group."

13. Even the deputy attorney general who handled the case against the therapists had this feeling at first. He told me that although he wondered what to expect before he interviewed former patients, he found them to be perfectly "normal." He compared what happened to them with what happened to him in the army—resocialization. Thus, he was able to come to understand why onetime patients stayed.

14. Richard Corriere, the head therapist, has not responded to my request to interview him. How he describes his interpretation of and response to the Center's collapse is worthy of note. In the first chapter of *Life Zones*, a book he coauthored in 1986, he recalls:

> In November 1980 . . . I lived through a major professional crisis.
>
> For a decade I had worked closely with a group of psychologists. We had established clinics in Los Angeles, Boston, Munich, Hawaii, San Francisco, and Montreal. We enjoyed a string of professional successes. We earned a good living. We seemed to be the fondest of friends as well as a close-knit team of therapists.

But when our mettle was tested by stress, we broke. Our friendship turned into the bitterest enmity. We had failed to work on our attitudes toward each other and our work. In falling out among ourselves, we demolished what we so painstakingly constructed.

The most painful part for me was the realization that our friendships had been so thin. Virtually overnight, men and women to whom I would have entrusted my life were gone from my life.

I felt utterly abandoned and lost. I did not know where to turn. I became depressed. I was so distraught that almost anything from an old ballad to the TV nightly news would make me cry. When I was at my most depressed, I saw no way out of my plight. Nothing I had done or achieved before mattered. My spirit was crushed. (Corriere and McGrady, 1986:35–36)

He goes on to say that he recovered when he realized that "I had given up the *attitude* of play. My colleagues and I had created our own crisis because we had become too serious, too important, too focused on work, and we weren't paying enough attention to the other arenas of our lives"(37).

The book then attempts to impart this "player attitude" to readers so that they can change their lives for the better.

The dissatisfactions of Mr. Corriere's erstwhile patients do not figure in this explanation, and he does not mention that there are both civil suits and license-revocation hearings going on against him and his former colleagues.

15. Cialdini (1984:97–98) states the social psychological finding that "we accept inner responsibility for a behavior when we think we have chosen to perform it in the absence of strong outside pressures."

16. I do not mean to imply that individuals did not assume some responsibility for being at the Center. Rather, although recognizing ways in which they did participate, they came to believe that the therapists, as professionals, were more responsible for what occurred at the Center than were the patients.

17. In reviewing the book *You Must Be Dreaming*, by Barbara Noel with Kathryn Watterson, Judith Herman says of Noel's accusation and lawsuit against the world-renowned psychiatrist Dr. Jules H. Masserman that "[r]ape survivors who recover best are those who discover a larger meaning in their personal ordeal and who join with others to seek justice" (Herman, 1993:7).

This resolve to help others and prevent future abuse seems a common response among onetime cultists from a variety of groups, as well as among those abused by therapists (see Gonsiorek's *Breach of Trust*, 1995).

18. See Cheryl Downey-Laskowitz (1986) and Lois Timnick (1986a, b). All three articles discuss the two perspectives on the case. For example, Timnick reports on September 21 that

[t]he defense,. . . in hearings that are now nearing an end, has painted a very different picture of an innovative "therapeutic community" that troubled young adults seeking a fuller life freely chose to join.

Corriere testified that the idea of forming such a community had grown out of "how lonely [therapy clients] were" and that it had evolved as "a group of people who had access to each other, gave each other support and help, who were dependable —[it was] probably more akin to a small town mentality of the 1950s. . . . "

... In some instances, the defense contends, the recollection of a complaining witness may have been colored by a personality that tends to exaggerate and over-dramatize. In others, the person may be simply unable to face painful problems from the past. Sometimes, there may be very little disagreement over what was said or what happened but a great difference in each side's interpretation. And in some cases, the alleged events just didn't occur, Watts [their attorney] said. (1986a)

Timnick's article also offers some of Corriere's specific interpretations of onetime patients' testimony against him.

19. In his opinion in the hearing against the five psychologists, Judge Neher mentioned that "[n]one of the respondents displays any remorse for, or indeed any understanding of, the damage or potential for damage of any of their actions. There is no question that if the opportunity arose they would repeat the acts or similar acts"(Neher, 1987:18).

20. Various materials produced by professionals working with former cultists and by the former cultists themselves all emphasize the need for social support (in addition to information on the dynamics of influence) as key to recovery.

Chapter Eight

1. As soon as I say the Center for Feeling Therapy was a cult, difficulties arise. Trying to define "cult" has occupied researchers since the first wave of these groups appeared in the late 1960s. There is no consensus, except perhaps among sociology of religion analysts, who have traditionally differentiated between "cult" and "sect," with the word "sect" probably being closer to what members of the general public think of when they hear the word "cult." (See Wallis, 1975.)
Also see James Beckford's (1987:390–91) discussion of the various concepts used to analyze these controversial groups, and see Robbins, Shepherd, and McBride (1985) and Robbins (1988) for fuller understanding of the sociology of religion's perspective on "new religious movements."

2. See the discussions by Lifton (quoted in Singer with Lalich, 1995:xii), Singer and Addis (1992:169–70), Singer with Lalich (1995:7–10), Ofshe (1992:212–24), and Zablocki (1991) of the defining features of cults. The elements they emphasize (among others) include the importance of the leader, a social psychological process of persuasion, the organized use of a peer group, and manipulation. Singer (with Lalich, 1995:64) also emphasizes the necessity to "[k]eep the person unaware of what is going on and how she or he is being changed a step at a time." Examples of onetime cult members who use Lifton's eight themes of "ideological totalism" to characterize the groups they were in are Hassan (1990) and Tobias and Lalich (1994).

3. These people spoke of Bettelheim as being authoritarian, arbitrary, confrontational, having a "legendary temper"; they described his school as being insular and characterized by a climate of fear, with no privacy allowed to patients (or to staff in some instances). All feelings were to be shared, and these were differentiated into "orthogenic" and "unorthogenic," the latter feelings being bad. See Pekow (1990) and Masson (1994:301–306).

4. As I have noted in earlier chapters, the model posits "unfreezing," inducing change, and "re-freezing." The first step involves an assault on individual identity, the second involves specifying the new identity to be taken, and the third involves stabilizing the new identity by using the environment.

5. In Milgram's eyes, what conditions move a person from an autonomous to an agentic state? Perception of a legitimate authority and entry into the authority system. Since the entry is voluntary, it "creates a sense of commitment and obligation" and constitutes an internalized basis for obedience (Milgram, 1975:140–1). There must be some link between the authority's function and the nature of the commands—what he or she is must relate to what he or she asks one to do. The authority must justify what he or she is doing through reference to some ideology to obtain willing obedience—"Science" justified what Milgram's experimenters asked subjects to do.

What are the consequences for the individual of being in the agentic state? All activity becomes pervaded by the relationship to the experimenter. This entails paying strict attention to the authority and very little attention to oneself. Subjects become prone "to accept definitions of action provided by legitimate authority," marking a redefinition of the situation. "Because the subject accepts authority's definition of the situation, action follows willingly" (145). The subject feels a loss of responsibility—she or he feels responsible to authority, but not responsible for the content of the actions. And finally, the self-image changes. The actions that occurred are not seen as stemming from motives of one's own, and hence do not reflect on self-image—they are "virtually guiltless" actions (147).

6. Initially, Milgram's experiments were carried out with men aged twenty to fifty, drawn from a variety of occupations. Later he used women in his experiments; he found that although their obedience level was virtually the same as that of men, they experienced a higher level of conflict (Milgram, 1975:63). When the experiments were conducted in a less prestigious setting than Yale University, 48 percent of his subjects (compared to the earlier 65 percent) delivered the maximum shock (69).

7. Philip Zimbardo's prisoner-guard experiment at Stanford University illustrates the power of a situation to influence behavior. Subjects were randomly assigned either the prisoner or the guard role and were put into the prison the experimenters had constructed. The experiment had to be stopped after only four days because participants had become too deeply involved in their respective roles. In the 1988 videotape illustrating the experiment, *The Stanford Prison Experiment*, Zimbardo describes even himself, an experienced researcher, as having gotten much too involved personally in his role of administrator of the prison.

8. These seven steps (in their words) are

1. Create your own reality
2. Create a granfalloon, which "requires the creation of an in-group of followers and an out-group of the unredeemed"
3. Create commitment through dissonance reduction
4. Establish the leader's credibility and attractiveness
5. Send members out to proselytize the unredeemed
6. Distract members from thinking "undesirable" thoughts
7. Fixate members' vision on a phantom

9. I use the term "milieu control" rather than "total institution" because I think "milieu control" can be put in place in short-term, noninstitutional settings, such as the *est* or Lifespring trainings. To refer to such settings as "total institutions" does not make as much sense to me.

10. Singer (with Lalich, 1995:xx) believes "charisma is less important than skills of persuasion and the ability to manipulate" and that "[c]ults come to reflect the ideas, style, and whims of the leader and become extensions of the leader."

11. Lifton's analysis in *The Nazi Doctors* (1986) shows that a desire to fit in motivated

novice Nazi physicians assigned to the prisoner-selection process at concentration camps to conform and carry out the selections. Lifton shows how a process of socialization helped these doctors become killers—I would of course say a social influence process.

12. See Reiterman and Jacobs's *Raven* (1982) for the single best description of Jim Jones and the People's Temple. The authors successfully attempt to humanize Jones, showing the complexities of the man and the organization he created.

13. Michael McGuire, a psychiatrist developed, the McGuire Program for Adopted Adolescents, now based in Eugenia Hospital, Lafayette Hill, Pennsylvania.

14. Clients in the "culture of poverty" are seen as "less likely to seek therapy, are less likely to be accepted for therapy, are more likely to be assigned to inexperienced therapists, will terminate and be terminated sooner, and are more likely to be treated by short-term and somatic therapists. In short, they are not considered to be 'good' clients by most psychotherapists" (Torrey, 1986:31–32).

15. The sociologist David Mechanic (1989:xi) says that few psychiatrists or other mental health professionals want to work with the chronically mentally ill. E. Fuller Torrey makes the same point about the psychiatric industry in Washington D.C.: therapists prefer private practice with the "worried well" (Harden, 1981).

16. Hunt (1987) says that "*one American in three* has been in psychotherapy, and in 1987, 15 million of us will make roughly 120 million visits to mental health professionals—*nearly twice as many visits as to internists*" (emphasis added).

17. According to a *U.S. News and World Report* poll, "81 percent of Americans think that therapy for personal problems would be helpful 'sometimes' or 'all the time.'" (Goode and Wagner, 1993). The same article reports that "more than 16 million Americans seek mental health treatment each year, but the majority of people who could benefit from therapy never seek help."

18. Two newer forms of therapy are counseling by phone—for example, "Shrink Link," "TLC" (Telephone Link Counseling) (described in Heyes, 1985), and "Summit Solutions Network" of San Francisco (Parker, 1994)—and by computer (*Chicago Tribune*, 1990).

19. Stafford continues: "Thirty-three percent sought 'professional' help, versus 10 percent who looked to a pastor" (Stafford, 1993).

20. See Hogan (1979) for analysis of this demand. The sociologist Ian Robertson (1989:35) discusses how "self-fulfillment, the commitment to achieving the development of one's individual personality, talents, and potential," has become an important new value, particularly for young members of the middle class. This analysis is based on surveys showing young people becoming more concerned with material success and on the burgeoning market for self-help books.

21. The German sociologist Ferdinand Tönnies used the word "gemeinschaft" to refer to relations in pre-industrial, communal societies, characterized by "commitment to others, a feeling of unity, and strong emotional ties." Modern society, in contrast, is characterized by "gesellschaft," in which relations are "based on the rational pursuit of each party's own interests" (Smelser, 1981:167; the descriptions are his).

22. See Singer and Lalich's (1996) chapter 9, "How Did This Happen? And What Can You Do?" for excellent suggestions to consumers. Also see Siegel (1991).

23. See Zimbardo and Andersen (1993) for one of the best articles explaining social influence in general. The authors present a section entitled "Checklist of Twenty Ways to Resist Unwanted Social Influence."

24. See Bates and Brodsky (1989), Plasil (1985), and Walker and Young (1986) for accounts of individual therapy abuse and attempts to call the abusers to account.

25. See Gentry (1993a, 1993b, 1993c).

26. See Kane (1995) and Roberts-Henry (1995) for their analyses of the effect of criminalization in, respectively, Wisconsin and Colorado

27. Roy Wallis (1988:355–71), in comparing the regulation of "new religious movements" (nrms) in the United States and the United Kingdom, sees government in the United States as being unable to "exercise effective low level control over nrms." This allows greater freedom for new religious movements to deviate from conventional society. "This freedom creates a level of self-confidence (enhanced by the political influence which wealth or numbers can provide), a sense of their own power, and a sense of their right to freedom from all interference. That in turn encourages them to indulge their whims, sexuality, sadism, or hostility toward the wider society and their enemies" (Wallis, 1988:359)

28. The sociologist Edwin Schur (1980) has coined the term "deviantizing" to describe deviance-defining, which he sees as essential to social organization.

A Canadian sociologist, Stephen Kent (1990:397), in discussing the "new religions/ countercult" debate, says that "antagonistic parties attempt to define or label themselves as normative or tolerable at the same time that they present their opponents as being unfavourable and intolerable. These attempts are strategies or tactics that both sides utilize when trying to acquire resources for themselves, often while simultaneously trying to achieve the denial of resources to their competitors and detractors." Kent argues that in pluralistic societies "groups still can receive resources if they are defined merely as deviant in a tolerable way. If groups must settle for deviant designations, then *the most desirable label is tolerable legitimacy,* meaning that their right to non-normativeness remains guaranteed under Canadian law" (401).

References

After the Cult: Recovering Together. 1994. Bonita Springs, Fla.: Videotape. American Family Foundation.

Andersen, Susan, and Philip G. Zimbardo. 1984. "On Resisting Social Influence." *Cultic Studies Journal* 1 (2): 196–216.

Anson, Robert Sam. 1978. "The Synanon Horrors." *New Times,* January 27, 29–50.

Appel, Willa. 1983. *Cults in America: Programmed for Paradise.* New York: Holt, Rinehart, and Winston.

Aron, Arthur, and Elain N. Aron. 1989. *The Heart of Social Psychology.* Lexington, Mass.: Lexington Books.

Atack, Jon. 1990. *A Piece of Blue Sky: Scientology, Dianetics, and L. Ron Hubbard Exposed.* New York: Carol Publishing Group.

Ayella, Marybeth F. 1990. " 'They Must Be Crazy': Some of the Difficulties in Researching 'Cults.' " *American Behavioral Scientist* 5 (33) : 562–77.

———. 1985. "Insane Therapy: Case Study of the Social Organization of a Psychotherapy Cult." Ph.D. diss., University of California at Berkeley.

———. 1981. "An Analysis of Current Conversion Practices of Followers of Reverend Sun Myung Moon." Unpublished manuscript.

Bainbridge, William Sims. 1978. *Satan's Power: A Deviant Psychotherapy Cult.* Berkeley, California: University of California Press.

Bainbridge, William Sims, and Rodney Stark. 1980. "Scientology: To Be Perfectly Clear." *Sociological Analysis* 41(2): 128–36.

Balch, Robert W. 1985. " 'When the Light Goes Out Darkness Comes: A Study of Defection from a Totalistic Cult." Pp. 11–63 in *Religious Movements: Genesis, Exodus, and Numbers,* ed. Rodney Stark. New York: Paragon House Publishers.

———. 1982. "Bo and Peep: A Case Study of the Origins of Messianic Leadership." Pp. 13–72 in *Millennialism and Charisma,* ed. Roy Wallis. Belfast, U.K.: Queen's University.

———. 1980. "Looking Behind the Scenes in a Religious Cult: Implications for the Study of Conversion." *Sociological Analysis* 41(2): 137–143.

Balch, Robert W., and David Taylor. 1977. "Seekers and Saucers: The Role of the Cultic Milieu in Joining a UFO Cult." *American Behavioral Scientist* 20:839–60.

Barker, Eileen. 1988. "Defection from the Unification Church: Some Statistics and Distinctions." Pp. 166–84 in *Falling from the Faith,* ed. David G. Bromley. Beverly Hills, Calif.: Sage Publications.

———.1984. *The Making of a Moonie.* New York: Basil Blackwell.

Bates, Carolyn M., and Annette M. Brodsky. 1989. *Sex in the Therapy Hour.* New York: Guilford Press.

Beck, Melinda, Karen Springen, and Donna Foote. 1992. "Sex and Psychotherapy." *Newsweek*, April 13.

Beckford, James. 1987. "Cults and New Religious Movements: An Overview." Pp. 390–94, vol. 19, in *The Encyclopedia of Religion*, ed. M. Eliade et al. New York: Macmillan.

———. 1985. *Cult Controversies: The Societal Response to the New Religious Movements*. New York: Tavistock.

———. 1982. "Beyond the Pale: Cults, Culture, and Conflict." Pp. 284–301 in *New Religious Movements*, ed. Eileen Barker. New York: Edwin Mellen Press.

Behar, Richard. 1991. "The Thriving Cult of Greed and Power." *Time*, May 6.

Bell, Colin, and Howard Newby, eds. 1977. *Doing Sociological Research*. New York: Free Press.

Berger, Peter L., and Brigitte Berger. 1974. *The Homeless Mind: Modernization and Consciousness*. New York: Vintage Books.

Berger, Peter L., and Thomas Luckmann. 1967. *The Social Construction of Reality*. Garden City, N.Y.: Anchor Books.

Betz, Katherine E. 1997. "No Place to Go: Life in a Prison without Bars." *Cultic Studies Journal*, 14 (1): 85–105. (Special issue, "Women under the Influence: A Study of Women's Lives in Totalist Groups," ed. Janja Lalich.)

Black, David. 1975. "Totalitarian Therapy on the Upper West Side." *New York*, December 15.

Brodsky, Annette M., and Rachel Hare-Mustin, eds. 1980. *Women and Psychotherapy*. New York: The Guilford Press.

Bromley, David G., ed. 1988. *Falling from the Faith: Causes and Consequences of Religious Apostasy*. Beverly Hills, Calif.: Sage Publications.

Bromley, David G., and Ansom D. Shupe. 1981. *Strange Gods: The Great American Cult Scare*. Boston: Beacon Press.

Broverman, I. K., D. M. Broverman, F. E. Clarkson, P. Rosenkrantz, and S. R. Vogel, 1970. "Sex-role Stereotypes and Clinical Judgments of Mental Health." *Journal of Consulting Psychology* 34: 1–7.

Brown, J.A.C. 1963. *Techniques of Persuasion*. Baltimore: Penguin Books.

Bry, Adelaide. 1976. *60 Hours That Transform Your Life*: est. New York: Avon Books.

California Attorney General's Office. 1984. *Pleadings, Filed before the California Board of Medical Quality Assurance in the Matter of Woldenberg et al*. Los Angeles, October 4.

———. 1983. *Pleadings, Filed before the California Board of Medical Quality Assurance in the Matter of Woldenberg et al*. Los Angeles, September 14.

Carter, Lewis. 1990. *Charisma and Control in Rajneeshpuram: The Role of Shared Values in the Creation of a Community*. Cambridge: Cambridge University Press.

Chesler, Phyllis. 1972. *Women and Madness*. Garden City, N.Y.: Doubleday.

Chicago Tribune. 1990. "Computers May Help Aid Depression," January 30.

Cialdini, Robert B. 1984. *Influence: The New Psychology of Modern Persuasion*. New York: Quill.

Conason, Joe, with Ellen McGarrahan. 1986. "Escape from Utopia." *Village Voice*, April 22.

Condor, Bob. 1994. "Coastal Karma; At Esalen, a Weekend of Mind-Body Conditioning Leaves All the Baggage Behind." *Chicago Tribune*, October 23.

Conway, Flo, and Jim Siegelman. 1978. *Snapping*. Philadelphia: J. B. Lippincott.

Cooper, Paulette. 1972. *The Scandal of Scientology*. New York: Tower Publications.

Corriere, Richard, and Joseph Hart. 1979. *Psychological Fitness: 21 Days to Feeling Good*. New York: Harcourt Brace Jovanovich.

———. 1977. *The Dream Makers: Discovering Your Breakthrough Dreams*. New York: Funk and Wagnalls.

Corriere, Richard, Werner Karle, Lee Woldenberg, and Joseph Hart. 1980. *Dreaming and Waking.* Culver City, Calif.: Peace Press.

Corriere, Richard B., and Patrick McGrady. 1986. *Life Zones.* New York: William Morrow.

Corsini, Raymond J., ed. 1981. *Handbook of Innovative Psychotherapies.* New York: John Wiley & Sons.

Corydon, Bent. 1992. *L. Ron Hubbard, Messiah or Madman?* Fort Lee, N.J.: Barricade Books.

Coser, Lewis A. 1974. *Greedy Institutions: Patterns of Undivided Commitment.* New York: Free Press.

Coser, Rose Laub, and Lewis Coser. 1979. "Jonestown as a Perverse Utopia." *Dissent,* spring, 158–63.

Coward, Rosalind. 1985. *Female Desires.* New York: Grove Press.

CQ Researcher. 1993. "Cults in America," May 7.

"Cultic Processes Top Stories of '93." 1994. *Cult Observer.* 11 (4): 6.

"Cult of Cruelty." 1981. Los Angeles: CBS affiliate. Five-part television series. May.

Deikman, Arthur J., M.D. 1994. *The Wrong Way Home.* Boston: Beacon Press.

Downey-Laskowitz, Cheryl. 1987. "State Revokes Licenses of 3 Psychologists Tied to Now Defunct Therapy Cult." *Orange County Register,* September 30.

————. 1986. "Therapists of Defunct LA Center under Fire: They Had Control—24 Hours a Day." *Orange County Register,* March 30.

Ebaugh, Helen R. F. 1988. *Becoming an Ex: The Process of Role Exit.* Chicago: University of Chicago Press.

Enroth, Ronald M. 1992. *Churches That Abuse.* Grand Rapids, Mich.: Zondervan Publishing House.

Erikson, Erik. 1958. *Young Man Luther.* New York: W. W. Norton.

FitzGerald, Frances. 1986. *Cities on a Hill: A Journey through Contemporary American Cultures.* New York: Simon and Schuster.

Ford, Wendy. 1993. *Recovery from Abusive Groups.* Bonita Springs, Fla.: American Family Foundation.

Fortune, Marie M. 1995. "Is Nothing Sacred? When Sex Invades the Pastoral Relationship." Pp. 29–40 in *Breach of Trust,* ed. John C. Gonsiorek. Thousand Oaks, Calif.: Sage Publications.

————. 1989a. *Is Nothing Sacred? When Sex Invades the Pastoral Relationship.* San Francisco: Harper and Row.

————. 1989b. "Betrayal of the Pastoral Relationship: Sexual Contact by Pastors and Pastoral Counselors." Pp. 81–91 in *Psychotherapists' Sexual Involvement with Clients: Intervention and Prevention,* ed. Gary Richard Schoener, Jeanette Hofstee Milgrom, John C. Gonsiorek, Ellen T. Luepker, and Ray M. Conroe. Minneapolis: Walk-In Counseling Center.

Frank, Jerome. 1974. *Persuasion and Healing.* New York: Schocken Books.

Frank, Jerome, and Julia B. Frank. 1991. *Persuasion and Healing.* 3d. ed. Baltimore: Johns Hopkins University Press.

Freedman, Rita J. 1986. *Beauty Bound.* Lexington, Massachusetts: D.C. Heath.

Friedan, Betty. 1963. *The Feminine Mystique.* New York: Dell Publishing.

Gentry, Carol. 1993a. "Abused by the System." *St. Petersburg Times,* April 25.

————. 1993b. "One Doctor, Five Women, Five Sex Allegations: Whom to Believe?" *St. Petersburg Times,* April 25.

————. 1993c. "'We Need to Move on with Our Lives.'" *St. Petersburg Times,* April 26.

Gerlach, Luther P., and Virginia H. Hine. 1970. *People, Power, and Change: Movements of Social Transformation.* New York: Bobbs-Merrill.

Gerstel, David U. 1982. *Paradise Incorporated: Synanon.* Novato, Calif.: Presidio Press.

Giambalvo, Carol. 1995. *Exit Counseling.* Bonita Springs, Fla.: American Family Foundation.

Glenn, Michael, and Richard Kunnes. 1973. *Repression or Revolution? Therapy in the United States Today*. New York: Harper and Row.

Glock, Charles Y., and Robert N. Bellah, eds. 1976. *The New Religious Consciousness*. Berkeley and Los Angeles: University of California Press.

Goffman, Erving. 1976. *Gender Advertisements*. New York: Harper and Row.

————. 1961. *Asylums*. Garden City, N.Y.: Doubleday, Anchor Books.

Goldman, Caren. 1993. "Enrich Yourself: A Guide to Nineteen Leading Centers for Personal Growth." *Natural Health*, May.

Gonsiorek, John C., ed. 1995. *Breach of Trust*. Thousand Oaks, Calif: Sage Publications.

Goode, Erica, and Betsy Wagner. 1993. "Does Psychotherapy Work?" *U.S. News and World Report*, May 24.

Goode, Erich. 1990. *Deviant Behavior*. Englewood Cliffs, N.J.: Prentice-Hall.

Greenspan, Miriam. 1983. *A New Approach to Women and Therapy*. New York: McGraw-Hill.

Hall, John R. 1982. "Apocalypse at Jonestown." Pp. 35–54 in *Violence and Religious Commitment*, ed. Ken Levi. University Park: Pennsylvania State University Press.

Harden, Blaine. 1981. "The City Shrinks Dream About." *Washington Post*, November 22.

Hart, Joseph. 1980. "Feeling Therapy: A Functional Approach to Psychotherapy." Pp. 222–24 in *The Psychotherapy Handbook: The A to Z Guide to More than 250 Different Therapies*, ed. Richie Herink. New York: New American Library.

Hart, Joseph, Richard Corriere, and Jerry Binder. 1975. *Going Sane: An Introduction to Feeling Therapy*. New York: Jason Aronson.

Hart, Joseph, Richard J. Corriere, and Werner Karle. 1981. "Functional Psychotherapy." Pp. 362–77 in *Handbook of Innovative Psychotherapies*, ed. Raymond J. Corsini. New York: John Wiley and Sons.

Hassan, Steven. 1990. *Combatting Cult Mind Control*. Rochester, Vt.: Park Street Press.

Henley, Nancy M. 1977. *Body Politics: Power, Sex, and Nonverbal Communication*. Englewood Cliffs, N.J.: Prentice-Hall.

Heyes, Eileen. 1985. "Got Hang-Ups? Counseling by Phone May Be an Answer." *Los Angeles Times*, June 7.

Herink, Richie, ed. 1980. *The Psychotherapy Handbook: The A to Z Guide to More than 250 Different Therapies*. New York: New American Library.

Herman, Judith Lewis. 1993. Review of *You Must Be Dreaming*, by Barbara Noel with Kathryn Watterson. *New York Times Book Review*, January 10.

Hinkle, Lawrence E., and Harold G. Wolff. 1956. "Communist Interrogation and Indoctrination of Enemies of the State." *Archives of Neurology and Psychiatry* 76:115–74.

Hoban, Phoebe. 1989. "Psycho Drama: The Chilling Story of How the Sullivanian Cult Turned a Utopian Dream into a Nightmare." *New York*, June 19.

Hochman, John. 1984. "Iatrogenic Symptoms Associated with a Therapy Cult: Examination of an Extinct 'New Psychotherapy' with Respect to Psychiatric Deterioration and 'Brainwashing.'" *Psychiatry* 47 (4): 366–77.

Hochschild, Arlie Russell. 1979. "Emotion Work, Feeling Rules, and Social Structure." *American Journal of Sociology* 85(3): 551–75.

————. 1975. "The Sociology of Feeling and Emotion: Selected Possibilities." Pp. 280–307 in *Another Voice*, ed. Marcia Millman and Rosabeth Moss Kanter. New York: Anchor.

Hoffmann, Bill, and Cathy Burke. 1997. *Heaven's Gate: Cult Suicide in San Diego*. New York: Harper Collins Publishers.

Hogan, Daniel B. 1979. *The Regulation of Psychotherapists*. 4 vols. Cambridge, Mass.: Ballinger Publishing.

Horowitz, Joy. 1981. "Feeling Therapy Dream Goes Sour." *Los Angeles Times*, July 16.

Hubner, John, and Lindsey Gruson. 1988. *Monkey on a Stick: Murder, Madness, and the Hare Krishnas*. New York: Penguin Books USA.

Hunt, Morton. 1987. "Navigating the Therapy Maze: A Consumer's Guide to Mental Health Treatment." *New York Times*, August 30.

Janov, Arthur. 1970. *The Primal Scream*. New York: Dell Publishing.

Johnson, Catherine. 1988. *When to Say Goodbye to Your Therapist*. New York: Simon and Schuster.

Johnson, Doyle Paul. 1979. "Dilemmas of Charismatic Leadership: the Case of the People's Temple." *Sociological Analysis* 40(4): 315–23.

Kadaba, Lini S. 1992. "For Adopted Children Who Are in Trouble." *Philadelphia Inquirer*, July 26.

Kane, Andrew W. 1995. "The Effects of Criminalization of Sexual Misconduct by Therapists: Report of a Survey in Wisconsin." Pp. 317–33 in *Breach of Trust*, ed. John C. Gonsiorek. Thousand Oaks, Calif.: Sage Publications.

Kanter, Rosabeth. 1987. "How the Top Is Different." Pp. 86–93 in *The Social World*, ed. Ian Robertson. New York: Worth Publishers.

Kanter, Rosabeth Moss. 1972. *Commitment and Community*. Cambridge: Harvard University Press.

Kelman, Herbert C., and V. Lee Hamilton. 1989. *Crimes of Obedience: Toward a Social Psychology of Authority and Responsibility*. New Haven: Yale University Press.

Kent, Stephen. 1994. "Lustful Prophet: A Psychosexual Historical Study of the Children of God's Leader, David Berg." *Cultic Studies Journal* 11 (2): 135–88.

———. 1990. "Deviance Labelling and Normative Strategies in the Canadian 'New Religions/Countercult' Debate." *Canadian Journal of Sociology* 15 (4): 393–416.

Kilbourne, Jean. 1995. *Slim Hopes: Advertising and the Obsession with Thinness*. Northampton, Mass.: Media Education Foundation. Videotape.

———. 1987. *Still Killing Us Softly: Advertising's Image of Women*. Cambridge, Mass.: Cambridge Documentary Films, Inc. Videotape.

King, Dennis. 1989. *Lyndon LaRouche and the New American Fascism*. New York: Doubleday.

Knight, Kathy. 1986. "Longterm Effects of Participation in a Psychological 'Cult': Utilizing Directive Therapy Techniques." Master's thesis, University of California at Los Angeles.

Kovel, Joel. 1976. *A Complete Guide to Therapy*. New York: Pantheon Books.

Lalich, Janja, ed. 1997. Special issue, "Women under the Influence: A Study of Women's Lives in Totalist Groups." *Cultic Studies Journal*, 14 (1).

———. 1993. "A Little Carrot and a Lot of Stick: A Case Example." Pp. 51–84 in *Recovery from Cults*, ed. Michael D. Langone. New York: W. W. Norton.

Lambert, M. J., A. E. Bergin, and J. L. Collins. 1977. "Therapist-Induced Deterioration in Psychotherapy." Pp. 452–81 in *Effective Psychotherapy: A Handbook of Research*, ed. A. S. Gurman and A. M. Razin. New York: Pergamon Press.

Langone, Michael D., ed. 1993. *Recovery from Cults*. New York: W. W. Norton.

Lerner, Harriet Goldhor. 1989. *Women in Therapy*. New York: Harper and Row.

Levine, Saul. 1984. *Radical Departures: Desperate Detours to Growing Up*. New York: Harcourt Brace Jovanovich.

Liddick, Betty. 1976. "Going Sane Around the Clock." *Los Angeles Times*, June 13.

Lieberman, Miles A., Irvin D. Yalom, and Matthew B. Miles. 1973. *Encounter Groups: First Facts*. New York: Basic Books.

Lifton, Robert Jay. 1986. *The Nazi Doctors: Medical Killing and the Psychology of Genocide*. New York: Basic Books.

———. 1985. "Cult Processes, Religious Totalism, and Civil Liberties." Pp. 59–70, *Cults, Culture, and the Law*, ed. Thomas Robbins, William C. Shepherd, and James McBride. Chico, Calif.: Scholars Press.

———. 1961. *Thought Reform and the Psychology of Totalism: A Study of Brainwashing in China*. New York: W. W. Norton.

Lofland, John. 1977. "'Becoming a World Saver' Revisited." *American Behavioral Scientist* 20 (6): 862–75.

Loftus, Elizabeth, and Katherine Ketcham. 1994. *The Myth of Repressed Memory*. New York: St. Martin's Press.

London, Perry. 1985. *The Modes and Morals of Psychotherapy*, 2nd ed. Washington, DC: Hemisphere Publishing.

———. 1971. *Behavior Control*. New York: Harper and Row.

Maliver, Bruce L. 1973. *The Encounter Game*. New York: Stein and Day.

Masson, Jeffrey Moussaieff. 1994. *Against Therapy*. Monroe, Maine: Common Courage Press.

McCullough, Marie. 1997. "'Cults' Influence Is Growing, Say Two Researchers." *Philadelphia Inquirer*, May 30.

Mechanic, David. 1989. *Mental Health and Social Policy*. Englewood Cliffs, N.J.: Prentice-Hall.

Mellen, Joan. 1975. *Woman and Their Sexuality in the New Film*. New York: Dell.

Milgram, Stanley. 1975. *Obedience to Authority*. New York: Harper Colophon Books.

Millett, Kate. 1970. *Sexual Politics*. New York: Ballantine.

Mitchell, Dave, Cathy Mitchell, and Richard Ofshe. 1980. *The Light on Synanon*. New York: Seaview Books.

Mithers, Carol Lynn. 1994. *Therapy Gone Mad*. Reading, Mass.: Addison-Wesley Publishing.

Morain, Dan. 1981. "They Wanted to Change Psychology." *Los Angeles Herald Examiner*, January 11.

Neher, Robert A. 1987. *Opinion in the Matter of the Accusation Against: Richard J. Corriere, Stephen David Gold, Joseph T. Hart, Michael Roy Hopper, and Werner Karle. Before the Psychology Examining Committee, Division of Allied Health Professions. Board of Medical Quality Assurance, State of California*. Los Angeles.

Ofshe, Richard. 1992. "Coercive Persuasion and Attitude Change." Pp. 212–24, vol. 1, in *Encyclopedia of Sociology*, ed. Edgar F. Borgatta and Marie L. Borgatta. New York: Macmillan.

———. 1986. "The Rabbi and the Sex Cult: Power Expansion in the Formation of a Cult." *Cultic Studies Journal* 3(2): 173–89.

———. 1981. "Synanon: The Failure That Founded Tradition." Unpublished manuscript. Berkeley, Calif.

———. 1980. "The Social Development of the Synanon Cult: The Managerial Strategy of Organizational Transformation." *Sociological Analysis* 41(2): 109–27.

———. 1976. "Synanon: The People Business." Pp. 116–37 in *The New Religious Consciousness*, ed. Charles Y. Glock and Robert N. Bellah. Berkeley and Los Angeles: University of California Press.

Ofshe, Richard, Nancy Berg, Richard Coughlin, Gregory Dolinajec, Kathleen Gerson, and Avery Johnson. 1974. "Social Structure and Social Control in Synanon." *Journal of Voluntary Action Research* 3(3–4): 67–76.

Ofshe, Richard, and Margaret Singer. 1986. "Attacks on Peripheral versus Central Elements of Self and the Impact of Thought Reforming Techniques." *Cultic Studies Journal* 3 (1): 3–24.

Ofshe, Richard, and Ethan Watters. 1994. *Making Monsters*. New York: Charles Scribner's Sons.

Olin, William. 1980. *Escape from Utopia: My Ten Years in Synanon*. Santa Cruz, Calif.: Unity Press.

Oliver, Myrna. 1981. "Man Sues, Asserts He Was Enslaved by Therapy Group." *Los Angeles Times*, October 8.

Parker, Penny. 1994. "Phone Therapy: Does Calling for Help Work Better than Office Visit with Counselor?" *Denver Post*, April 19.

Pekow, Charles. 1990. "The Other Dr. Bettelheim." *Washington Post*, August 26.

Personal Growth. 1974. "Feeling Therapy." 22:3–12.

Philipson, Ilene J. 1993. *On the Shoulders of Women: The Feminization of Psychotherapy*. New York: Guilford Press.

Plasil, Ellen. 1985. *Therapist*. New York: St. Martin's.

Pope, Kenneth S., and Jacqueline C. Bouhoutsos. 1986. *Sexual Intimacy between Therapists and Patients*. New York: Praeger.

Pratkanis, Anthony, and Elliot Aronson. 1991. *Age of Propaganda: The Everyday Use and Abuse of Persuasion*. New York: W. H. Freeman.

Raso, Jack. 1994. "The Three Faces of Medical Unreason: Overview of Alternative Medicine Techniques." *Nutrition Forum*, September.

Reiterman, Tim, and John Jacobs. 1982. *Raven*. New York: E. P. Dutton.

Richardson, James T. 1982. "A Comparison between Jonestown and Other Cults." Pp. 21–34 in *Violence and Religious Commitment*, ed. Ken Levi. University Park: Pennsylvania State University Press.

Rieff, Philip. 1968. *The Triumph of the Therapeutic*. New York: Harper Torchbooks.

Robbins, Thomas. 1988. *Cults, Converts, and Charisma*. Beverly Hills, Calif.: Sage Publications.

Robbins, Thomas, William C. Shepherd and James McBride, eds. 1985. *Cults, Culture, and the Law*. Chico, Calif.: Scholars Press.

Roberts-Henry, Melissa. 1995. "Criminalization of Therapist Sexual Misconduct in Colorado: An Overview and Opinion." Pp. 338–47 in *Breach of Trust*, ed. John C. Gonsiorek. Thousand Oaks, Calif.: Sage Publications.

Robertson, Ian. 1989. *Society*. New York: Worth Publishers.

Rosen, Robert D. 1979. *Psychobabble*. New York: Avon Books.

Rosenhan, D. L. 1973. "On Being Sane in Insane Places." *Science* 179 (Jan.): 250–58.

Rothbaum, Susan. 1988. "Between Two Worlds: Issues of Separation and Identity After Leaving a Religious Community." In *Falling from the Faith: Causes and Consequences of Religious Apostasy*, ed. David G. Bromley. Beverly Hills, Calif.: Sage Publications.

Ruitenbeek, Hendrik. 1970. *The New Group Therapies*. New York: Avon Books.

Rutan, Scott J., and Cecil A. Rice. 1981. "The Charismatic Leader: Asset or Liability?" *Psychotherapy: Theory, Research, and Practice* 18(4): 487–92.

Rutter, Peter, M.D. 1989. *Sex in the Forbidden Zone*. Los Angeles: Jeremy P. Tarcher.

SanGiovanni, L. F. 1978. *Ex-Nuns: A Study of Emergent Role Passage*. Norwood, N.J.: Ablex Press.

Schacter, Stanley, and Jerry Singer. 1962. "Cognitive, Social, and Physiological Determinants of Emotional State." *Psychological Review* 69: 379–99.

Schafer, Roy. 1976. *A New Language for Psychoanalysis*. New Haven: Yale University Press.

Schein, Edgar H. with Inge Schneier and Curtis H. Barker. 1961. *Coercive Persuasion*. New York: W. W. Norton.

Schoener, Gary Richard, Jeanette Hofstee Milgrom, John C. Gonsiorek, Ellen T. Luepker, and Ray M. Conroe, eds. 1989. *Psychotherapists' Sexual Involvement with Clients: Intervention and Prevention*. Minneapolis: Walk-In Counseling Center.

Schur, Edwin M. 1980. *The Politics of Deviance: Stigma Contests and the Uses of Power*. Englewood Cliffs, N.J.: Prentice-Hall.

Siegel, Lee. 1993. "The Power of the Placebo Effect Is Bolstered by a Survey." *Philadelphia Inquirer*, July 2.

Siegel, Shirley J. 1991. *What to Do When Psychotherapy Goes Wrong*. Seattle: Stop Abuse by Counselors Publishing.

Singer, Margaret. 1995. "Leaving a Cult: Exiting and Recovery Information for Ex-Members, Families, and Friends." Bonita Springs, Fl.: American Family Foundation. Videotape.

————. 1979. "Coming Out of Cults." *Psychology Today*, January, 72–82.

Singer, Margaret, and Marsha Emmer Addis. 1992. "Cults, Coercion, and Contumely." *Cultic Studies Journal* 9 (2): 163–89.

Singer, Margaret, and Janja Lalich. 1996. *Crazy Therapies*. San Francisco: Jossey-Bass Publishers.

Singer, Margaret, with Janja Lalich. 1995. *Cults in Our Midst*. San Francisco: Jossey-Bass Publishers.

Singer, Margaret, and Richard Ofshe. 1981. "Issues in the Study of Totalistic Groups: Relevant Literature—Theoretical Problems— Methodological Concerns." Paper prepared for the Staff College of the National Institute of Mental Health.

Siskind, Amy. 1990. "Two Utopian Communities in the United States: The Oneida Community and the Sullivan Institute/Fourth Wall Community." Paper presented at the 1991 annual American Sociological Association meetings, Cincinnati, August.

Skoll, Geoffrey R. 1992. *Walk the Walk and Talk the Talk*. Philadelphia: Temple University Press.

Smelser, Neil. 1981. *Sociology*. Englewood Cliffs, N.J.: Prentice-Hall.

Stafford, Tim. 1993. "The Therapeutic Revolution: Christian Counselors." *Christianity Today*, May 17.

Stannard-Friel, Don. 1981. *Harassment Therapy: A Case Study of Psychiatric Violence*. Cambridge, Mass.: Schenkman Publishing.

Stark, Rodney, and William Sims Bainbridge. 1980. "Networks of Faith: Interpersonal Bonds and Recruitment to Cults and Sects." *American Journal of Sociology* 85(6): 1377–95.

Stein, Alexandra. 1977. "Mothers in Cults: The Influence of Cults on the Relationship of Mothers to Their Children." *Cultic Studies Journal*. 14 (1): 40–57. (Special issue, "Women Under the Influence: A Study of Women's Lives in Totalist Groups," ed. J. Lalich.)

Taylor, David. 1982. "Becoming New People: The Recruitment of Young Americans into the Unification Church." Pp. 177–230 in *Millennialism and Charisma*, ed. Roy Wallis. Belfast, U.K.: Queen's University.

Temerlin, M. K., and J. W. Temerlin. 1982. "Psychotherapy Cults: An Iatrogenic Perversion." *Psychotherapy Theory, Research, and Practice* 19(2): 131–41.

Tennov, Dorothy. 1976. *Psychotherapy: The Hazardous Cure*. Garden City, N. Y.: Anchor Books.

Thompson, Tracy. 1993. "What if You Need Medical Care?" *Washington Post*, November 2.

Thomson, Bill. 1992. "Alternative Therapies." *East West Natural Health*, May.

Timnick, Lois. 1987. "Psychologists in 'Feeling Therapy' Lose Licenses." *Los Angeles Times*, September 30.

————. 1986a. "Inquiry Targets Disputed Psychotherapy Methods." *Los Angeles Times*, September 21.

————. 1986b. "Licenses of Mental Health Therapists Targeted in Major Malpractice Case." *Los Angeles Times*, April 21.

————. 1981. "Nineteen File Suit against Their Ex-Therapists," *Los Angeles Times*, June 30.

Tobias, Madeleine Landau, and Janja Lalich. 1994. *Captive Hearts, Captive Minds: Freedom and Recovery from Cults and Abusive Relationships.* Alameda, Calif.: Hunter House Inc., Publishers.

Torrey, E. Fuller, M.D. 1986. *Witchdoctors and Psychiatrists: The Common Roots of Psychotherapy and Its Future.* Rev. ed. of *The Mind Game.* Northvale, N.J.: Jason Aronson.

———. 1972. *The Mind Game: Witchdoctors and Psychiatrists.* New York: Emerson Hall Publishers.

Underwood, Barbara, and Betty Underwood. 1979. *Hostage to Heaven.* New York: Potter.

Vaughan, Diane. 1986. *Uncoupling: How Relationships Come Apart.* New York: Random House.

Walker, Evelyn, and Perry Deane Young. 1986. *A Killing Cure.* New York: Henry Holt.

Wallis, Roy. 1988. "Paradoxes of Freedom and Regulation: the Case of New Religious Movements in Britain and America." *Sociological Analysis* 48(4): 355–71.

———. 1982a. "Charisma, Commitment, and Control in a New Religious Movement." Pp. 73–140 in *Millennialism and Charisma*, ed. Roy Wallis. Belfast, U.K.: Queen's University.

Wallis, Roy, ed. 1982b. *Millennialism and Charisma*, ed. Roy Wallis. Belfast, U.K.: Queen's University.

———. 1977a. "The Moral Career of a Research Project." Pp. 149–69 in *Doing Social Research*, ed. Colin Bell and Howard Newby. New York: Free Press.

———. 1977b. *The Road to Total Freedom: A Sociological Analysis of Scientology.* New York: Columbia University Press.

———. 1975. "Scientology: Therapeutic Cult to Religious Sect." *Sociology* 9: 89–99.

———. 1974. "Ideology, Authority, and the Development of Cultic Movements." *Social Research* 41(2): 299–327.

Watkins, Paul. 1979. *My Life with Charles Manson.* New York: Bantam.

Weber, Max. 1970a. "Bureaucracy." Pp. 196–244 in *From Max Weber: Essays in Sociology*, ed. Hans Gerth and C. Wright Mills. London: Routledge and Kegan Paul.

———. 1970b. "The Sociology of Charismatic Authority" Pp. 245–64 in *From Max Weber: Essays in Sociology*, ed. Hans Gerth and C. Wright Mills. London: Routledge and Kegan Paul.

Weinberg, George. 1984. *The Heart of Psychotherapy.* New York: St. Martin's Press.

Weisbrod, Carol. 1980. *The Boundaries of Utopia.* New York: Pantheon Books.

West, L. J. 1984. "Psychiatry, Brainwashing, and the American Character." *American Journal of Psychiatry* 120(9): 842–50.

West, L. J., and Margaret T. Singer. 1980. "Cults, Quacks, and Nonprofessional Psychotherapies." Pp. 3245–58 in *Comprehensive Textbook of Psychiatry*, ed. H. I. Kaplan, A. M. Freedman, et al. Baltimore: Williams and Wilkins.

Wheelis, Allen. 1973. *How People Change.* New York: Harper Colophon Books.

Willner, Ann Ruth. 1984. *The Spellbinders: Charismatic Political Leadership.* New Haven: Yale University Press.

Woldenberg, Lee, Werner Karle, Stephen Gold, Richard Corriere, Joseph Hart, and M. Hopper. 1976. "Psychophysiological Changes in Feeling Therapy." *Psychological Reports* 39:1059–62.

Wolinsky, Howard. 1993. "When Talk Is Therapeutic: Support Groups Provide Forums for the Ailing." *Chicago Sun-Times*, May 31.

Wright, Stuart. 1987. *Leaving Cults: The Dynamics of Defection.* Vol. 7. Washington, D.C.: Society for the Scientific Study of Religion.

Yablonski, Lewis. 1965. *Synanon: The Tunnel Back.* New York: Macmillan.

Yalom, Irvin D. 1975. *The Theory and Practice of Group Psychotherapy.* New York: Basic Books.

Yapko, Michael. 1994. *Suggestions of Abuse.* New York: Simon and Schuster.

Zablocki, Benjamin. 1991. "The Scientific Investigation of the Brainwashing Conjecture." Paper presented at the annual meeting of the American Association for the Advancement of Science, Washington, D.C., February 17.

———. 1980. *Alienation and Charisma*. New York: Free Press.

———. 1971. *The Joyful Community*. Baltimore: Penguin Books.

Zilbergeld, Bernie. 1983. *The Shrinking of America: Myths of Psychological Change*. Boston: Little, Brown.

Zimbardo, Phillip G. 1988. *The Stanford Prison Experiment*. Stanford, Calif.: Stanford University. Videotape.

Zimbardo, Philip G., and Susan Andersen. 1993. "Understanding Mind Control: Exotic and Mundane Mental Manipulations." Pp. 104–25 in *Recovery from Cults*, ed. Michael D. Langone. New York: W. W. Norton.

Zimbardo, Philip G., and Michael R. Leippe. 1991. *Attitude Change and Social Influence*. Philadelphia: Temple University Press.

Index